ANATOMY
OF A
SCANDAL

ANATOMY

OF A

SCANDAL

A STUDY OF THE PROFUMO AFFAIR

CLIVE IRVING

RON HALL   JEREMY WALLINGTON

M. S. MILL CO. AND
WILLIAM MORROW AND COMPANY
NEW YORK   1963

Contents

'With expediency rather than morality as a guide, it could often be thought "right" to tell a lie (indeed, this has sometimes been sanctioned even by religion). But the demands of truth are absolute both in religion and morality. The law, therefore, ought to uphold this principle.'

LORD DENNING

Prologue

IF, SOME WHILE ago, a malevolent force had sat down before a computer and pressed buttons marked 'Scandal, 1963' it would almost be a believable explanation for what followed. Certainly nobody could have fed into a computer a programme more skilfully designed for such a cataclysmic result.

The Profumo affair of 1963, and all its odious proliferations, sprang from seeds planted years before. The worlds of politics, the law, Society, property manipulation and the Press were all enmeshed, and the resulting chain reaction was supplemented by the notoriety of crime and the polemics of outraged morality. In the end, it transcended sanity and threatened to bring down a Prime Minister and his Government, tarred the reputation of the country, aggravated the frictions of an evolving society, and left a path of shattered reputations and ruined careers.

It transformed nonentities into celebrities; exposed rogues and racketeers; and it converted apathy into a mood of self-questioning which would last for a long time. Ultimately, it might even have done some good. It was, though, an expensive path to reform.

Why did it all happen? Before the crisis broke the surface, much was wrong underneath. Only a nation harbouring a latent neurosis could have been thrown into such a spasm: Britain became so preoccupied by the Profumo affair that the world itself seemed lop-sided, and values were confused and vision dangerously localised.

Here is the story of what happened, why it happened and the people caught up in it.

The Age of Christine

A POLITICIAN CAN, with one phrase, put a character to an age by which he, and it, will always be judged. On July 20, 1957, at an open-air rally at Bedford, Mr Macmillan, in his first year as Prime Minister, was reviewing the country's economy. He said: 'Let's be frank about it. Most of our people have never had it so good. . . .'

This phrase was spontaneous, but it exhibited a genius for conveying an idea which had so far been without such succinct expression. Indeed, from any other mouth, it might have acquired the arrogance of a baron distributing alms in a moment of repentance. But in this case it had the ring of credibility; it caught the national imagination and even, perhaps, its lust.

It was, though, out of context. The purpose of the speech was not to ignite a bonanza, but to warn of the dangers of complacency. Later in it Mr Macmillan had said: 'But amidst all this prosperity there is one problem that has troubled us in one way or another ever since the war. It is the problem of rising prices.'

As it happened, this was diagnosis but not prognosis.

The Conservative Central Office later became embarrassed by the phrase – which had fallen into popular use as 'You've never had it so good.' It never became an official election slogan. The Conservatives claimed that it was popularised by Labour politicians. It was certainly inconstant to both parties: in 1959 it helped the Tories to win another five years of office. In the winter of 1962–63 it rebounded with a hollow irony.

Its trouble was that it could be blamed for inducing not only indulgence, but two greater sins: euphoria and apathy. It was no accident that a film called *I'm All Right, Jack* became a mirror of the same age.

But in 1957 Britain was thickening its waistline for the first time for fifteen years. 'Go round the country,' said Mr Macmillan at Bedford, 'go to the industrial towns, go to the farms and you will see a state of prosperity such as we have never had in my lifetime, nor indeed ever in the history of this country.' It was true. The advance of materialism, which came much earlier in the United States, was inevitably beginning to emerge in Europe. By then it had American manifestations, and had already been dubbed by an American, Professor Galbraith, 'The Affluent Society'. These three words, combined with Mr Macmillan's version, were later to become the target of reproach. Mr Macmillan's caution at Bedford revealed that he then saw how easily abundance might get out of control: but the cornucopia was in his hands, and its future was his responsibility.

A month after Mr Macmillan's Bedford speech, another of the growing pains of post-war Britain was emerging. In September the Wolfenden Report on Homosexuality and Prostitution was published. The Wolfenden Committee had been sitting since 1954. It embraced, of course, one of the most sensitive social issues in the country. When Lord Hailsham was asked why there was such a delay in producing the report, he said: 'I should have thought it was an inexhaustible subject for discussion.'

The committee had two tasks: to consider the law and practice relating to homosexual offences and the treatment of convicted homosexuals; and to examine prostitution and report what changes in the law and its operation were desirable.

Crystallised, the committee's recommendations in 1957 were: (1) that homosexual acts between consenting adults in private should be no longer a criminal offence; (2) penalties for street offences should be increased; (3) landlords letting premises at exorbitant rent for prostitution should be deemed in law to be living off immoral earnings; (4) that an increase in small advertisements in shops offering the services of 'masseuses', 'models', etc. would be 'less injurious' than the presence of prostitutes in the streets.

The committee foresaw a possible extension of the call-girl system and the danger that new classes of 'middle-men' might arise. But their general feeling was that prostitution was a private sin which should not be allowed to affront the eyes of society.

Both the Church of England and the Catholics were basically in favour of the recommendations. It was, in fact, a realistic piece of social pragmatism, although it was attacked for being fundamentally a 'brushing under the carpet' approach. For years some streets in London had been crawling with overt prostitution, ranging, according to social strata, from Park Lane and Curzon Street in Mayfair, for the top end of the trade, to Soho for the mass market, and down to Stepney in its oldest and least sophisticated form. Americans, whose Embassy was near the heart of the Mayfair province, were particularly appalled by the openness of the business – though it would only be fair to say that the same Americans who found London such a disgrace thought the same situation 200 miles away in Paris to have a native charm and character. In New York, prostitution had long since gone underground, or, more precisely, well above it, on the call-girl system.

Following publication of the report, there was, in 1957, no sign of any legislation. In the words of Sir John Wolfenden himself, there was 'a conspiracy of silence'. It was not until November 1958 that the Street Offences Bill, resulting from the report, was debated in Parliament.

The Bill took no action on homosexuality, but on prostitution it accepted most of the report's recommendations, and substantial fines and jail sentences were introduced for street soliciting (previously the fine had been an automatic £2, regarded by the girls as a 'licence fee'). Indeed on one point the Bill went farther than the committee – by acting on a reservation made by the three women members (Mrs Mary Cohen, Mrs Kathleen Lovibond and Lady Stopford) that the maximum penalty for a man convicted of living on immoral earnings should be increased. The report had said two years was adequate. The Bill increased it to a maximum of *five* years for pimps and procurers.

Of the psychology of pimping, a witness before the committee had said: 'This man (the pimp) may be literally the "bully", which is another of his titles . . . but he is frequently

5

the only person in the world towards whom she feels affection and sense of possession . . . he may be the one humanising element in the life of the woman on whom he lives.'

In the debate on the Bill, Mr David Renton, the Under-Secretary at the Home Office, said: 'The most important question is how we can prevent the needless flow of young and sometimes beautiful girls, many from good homes, reaching this terrible market . . .'

In 1957 a girl of fifteen with long legs and a tendency to pout threw up a job in Slough and decided to move to London. Her name was Christine Keeler. Until then her home had been a converted railway carriage at Wraysbury. When the railway carriage had been built at the turn of the century Wraysbury was a quiet stretch of Thames-side Buckinghamshire, a small village sprawled out along a main road. But in the years since then, the land between the village itself and the river had gradually become littered with the improvised homes of poor families without roots and the weekend retreats of the middle-class. The development was unplanned and chaotic: shacks, bungalows, houses, caravans and even a night-club.

Christine Keeler's parents – her mother had remarried, and was now called Huish – had moved there from Hayes soon after she had been born. The river was only a few feet away from the home, at the bottom of the garden. The wheels were still on the coach, leaving a two-foot gap from the ground which kept out the damp.

In this prosaic colony the young girl grew up. She was three when the war ended. In her early years at school she became something of a tomboy, physically adventurous, lithe and daring. Wraysbury was dotted with gravel pits, and Christine Keeler came to reign over them as a nymph in a home-made knitted bikini. The eyes of boys fell upon her, and she revelled in it. At fifteen she left the small Victorian school and was rest-less. The jobs at Slough were dull, and the magnetism of London, only fourteen miles to the east, was irresistible. And so, in 1957, she took a job in a Soho gown shop, and went to live in a flatlet in St John's Wood.

It was only a few weeks later that she made her first essay

6

into modelling. Wearing a bikini, she was pictured in typical starlet pose by a magazine photographer. She was long-legged, small-bosomed, but for a girl of fifteen surprisingly mature-looking. The picture appeared in the magazine *Tit-Bits* on March 22, 1958 – precisely five years to the day before Mr Profumo was making his notorious denial to the Commons that he had had an improper relationship with her.

As often with young models, the long, disingenuous caption that appeared with the picture represented her as just the sweet-little-girl-next-door. It began: 'Though she's only fifteen, Christine Keeler is pretty enough to be a professional model. But the idea doesn't appeal to her because, quite frankly, she rather prefers animals to people, and her hobby is dog-, cat- or even bird-sitting.' There followed a detailed description of all her doggy and budgie friendships. The caption ended: 'It's not surprising that pretty Christine's ambition is to have a large house full of animals or that her pet hates include cruelty to animals. Like any other young girl, or older girl for that matter, she loves dancing, the theatre and gay parties.'

The opportunities for gay parties began rapidly to increase.

The London into which Christine Keeler had cast her fortune was undergoing dramatic changes. Outwardly, the skyline was being transformed as the empty scars of the blitz were at last being developed with towering blocks. The city acquired more hard, neon-lit brassiness, and Americanisation manifested itself in the worst sense: the odour of hamburger bars oozed out to the pavements and the place began even to *smell* like New York. Inwardly, the moral climate was continuing its tortured readjustments.

The Street Offences Bill became the Street Offences Act and went into operation in August 1959. There was still no new legislation on homosexuality. That issue, it seemed, was politically too hot to handle. But on June 29, 1960, a motion in the Commons calling for early implementation of the Wolfenden recommendations on homosexuality, although heavily defeated, revealed some interesting alignments. Among the Conservatives who supported the motion were Mr Enoch

7

Powell and Lord Lambton. Among the Conservatives who took the opposite view were the Attorney General, Sir Reginald Manningham-Buller (now Lord Dilhorne), Peter Rawlinson, the Solicitor-General, and Mr Martin Redmayne, the Chief Whip.

Meanwhile, the Street Offences Act was beginning to produce results. In 1960 the number of convictions in England and Wales for living on immoral earnings was 160 (in 1954 it had been 114). A year later it had jumped to 219. It seemed that since the prostitutes had been driven off the streets their dependence on more organisation and protection had increased significantly.

Statistics apart, some obvious effects of the new laws could be seen with one walk round Soho. The prediction of an increase in the thinly-veiled euphemisms of 'masseuse' and 'model' in small advertisements in newsagents' shops was something of an underestimate. Innuendoes to suit the most complex perversions were devised, and in some cases the prosaic postcard was superseded by illuminated signs. And if the girls had left the streets it was, often, only to go as far as a first-floor window. The business had come to require more resources and capital. Girls whose flats had all the emulated vulgarity of Hollywood film sets could earn up to £100 a day with regular clientele. But for men who wanted to avoid the total commitment, another growth industry was springing up: the strip club. These raised titillation to an intricate and exotic art form.

On April 14, 1961, Paul Quinn, or Paul Raymond, a pioneer of the strip-club business, was fined £5,000 and ordered to pay 500 guineas costs at the London Sessions on a charge of keeping a disorderly house at the Raymond Revuebar, Walker's Court, Soho. The Chairman of the Sessions, Mr R. E. Seaton, told Quinn: 'Your establishment and others have been vying with each other to see what degree of disgustingness they can introduce to attract members from all classes who are only too ready, out of curiosity or lust, to see the filth portrayed in this establishment. This, I think, is the fourth or fifth case I have had, and this is by far and away the worst.'

In his evidence, Quinn had said the list of membership for

8

his club included many well-known names. 'There are very few well-known names who have not been there,' he boasted. The list included, he claimed, at least thirty 'practising solicitors'. There was a whipping scene in the Revuebar show. There was also a girl called Julie Mendez, who was a snake-charming stripper. She performed with the aid of three boa-constrictors and a python, and earned £85 a week.

The prosecution did not stifle the strip-club industry: on the contrary, it proliferated. But like all apparent goldmines, the rush diluted the nature of the product – it had, anyway, been inhibited in scope by the threat of police action. The clubs ranged from the sumptuous to the seedy. Almost any vacant cellar-space in Soho, however primitive, could apparently be filled by offering women in various forms of dress and frenzy to the accompaniment of canned music.

About the clients something of a cliché grew up: the archetypal member was imagined as a furtive businessman from Birmingham, down for a conference or trade exhibition. Wherever the clients came from – and they varied from club to club – Quinn's claim appeared to be true: many looked reasonably placed in the Jaguar belt. A stripper made perhaps the most accurate remark about the men who sat staring up at her through the cigarette and cigar smoke: 'They don't look very happy,' she said.

In 1959 Christine Keeler became a waitress in a Baker Street restaurant. One of the customers was a girl, Maureen O'Connor, who worked at Murray's Cabaret Club. Here was a creature from the world she really sought; an introduction was made, her potential realised, and the ambition fulfilled. On August 26, 1959, Christine Keeler passed from the dream to the dreamland, and crossed from day into night, where social frontiers were blurred.

Murray's Club was of a different generation and a different style to those that were to follow. It was run by the doyen of West End cabaret clubs, Percival Murray, and run with an iron hand. For the forty-five girls working there as singers, soubrettes, dancers and showgirls the discipline was of a

9

severity essential with such a concentration of the desirable. The dancers and showgirls earned a minimum £8. 10s. a week but more was available from the customers. They were not obliged to answer requests to sit at tables, though most of them did. Customers usually tipped for this company, from £2 to £5, but the girls were not allowed to ask for money; if they were discovered doing so they were instantly sacked.

Christine Keeler was a showgirl, and though the costumes were ornate they stopped short of her breasts. Discipline, which she found difficult to accommodate, was in the hands of the two 'matrons'. They were assisted by two 'head girls' who, to complete the Roedean hierarchy, were helped by 'prefects'. Each prefect was in charge of one of the eight dressing-rooms, which contained four to six girls.

The main offences were being late, missing a cue, or taking time off without permission. [Miss Keeler was frequently penalised for taking weekends off.] Lesser offences were forgetting to wear nail varnish, missing the free weekly visit to the hairdresser, and failing to cover light patches left by swimsuit straps after sunbathing.

The showgirls were drawn from all over the country, and usually started between sixteen and nineteen. New showgirls were carefully watched, and parents who wanted to check up on them were invited to have dinner there. In spite of the fact that their daughters' breasts were bare, they usually left happy and even proud.

Clients, who paid a guinea membership fee, and a 25s. entrance fee for each night, were mixed – Northerners, Americans and a customary flow of Arabs. One night, when Christine Keeler was being entertained by an Arab, she was introduced to an osteopath named Stephen Ward.

The British moral climate was painfully evolving in another way, too: in the world of publishing. This time the effort was towards a more permissive attitude, though in fact it was a reaction to a Draconian attempt to restrict. This, like the Wolfenden Committee, began in 1954 and had a long breeding period, and a very bitterly fought one.

The first tremor was from a seat of reaction: the West

Country. Boccaccio's *Decameron*, a classic by any definition, was among sixty-five titles on sale in a local bookshop which the magistrates of Swindon ordered to be destroyed, on the grounds of obscenity. No amount of pleading on the grounds of the book's acknowledged quality could deter the magistrates: the ritual destruction was performed. The act was seen, though, as something more important than a piece of backwoods intransigence: a law that permitted it was equally out of date. (The *Decameron* was subsequently removed from the Home Office list of obscene books.)

More alarming were the consequences of another case in 1954, involving a publisher named Reiter being prosecuted over some pornographic books. Reiter's defence sought to enter as evidence some books from more established publishing houses which they claimed were equally pornographic, not ostensibly to raise the status of their client's work but to demonstrate that public taste was more liberal. They were not allowed as evidence, but in the Court of Criminal Appeal the Lord Chief Justice suggested that the other books 'might be looked at'. They were, and the Director of Public Prosecutions decided to act. Some of the books were *The Image and the Search* (Heinemann); *The Philanderer* (Secker and Warburg) and *The Man in Control* (Arthur Barker). Heinemann were acquitted by the Judge after two juries had disagreed on a verdict; Secker and Warburg were acquitted, as were Arthur Barker.

In spite of the ineffectiveness of the prosecutions, publishers were worried by what appeared to be a repressive, and even fatuous, attitude towards modern novels.

As a result, publishing interests set up a committee, under Sir Alan Herbert, to devise a Bill which would reform the law. It met considerable resistance, but the energy of some politicians, notably Mr Roy Jenkins, succeeded in getting the Bill referred to a Select Committee of the House of Commons. On March 20, 1958, they reported in favour of it. Although the Government had to yield to the pressure for reform, it wrote an entirely new Bill of its own, retaining only the title of Sir Alan Herbert's Bill: The Obscene Publications Bill. In fact, through persistent haggling, most of the Herbert Committee's desires were written into the final version, which became the Obscene Publications Act of 1959.

There remained the question of which book would be used as a test case under the new Act. In August 1960 the target was selected: D. H. Lawrence's *Lady Chatterley's Lover*. It had first been published thirty-two years before, but had been banned in Britain ever since, although by 1960 there must have been a good few thousand copies of it which had been smuggled in over the years, mainly the edition published on the Continent. Penguin Books had decided to end its rarity value and to publish it as a paperback in unexpurgated form.

Two of the most important changes brought about by the Obscene Publications Act had been to require the Court to consider a book as a whole, and that there could be no conviction if 'publication . . . is justified as being for the public good . . . in the interests of science, literature, art, or learning, or other objects of general concern'. To establish this quality it was possible for the first time to admit the evidence of experts. On this ground Penguin produced thirty-five witnesses. And, with the help of this impressive authority, they won.

Such ground is not gained without hardening the resolution of those committed to the opposite view. In Scotland, particularly, there was moral outrage. Booksellers refused to sell *Lady Chatterley*, and in Edinburgh Miss Agnes Cooper, a 62-year-old former Belgian Congo Missionary, adopted some African techniques of symbolism. She burned a copy of *Lady Chatterley* in front of a large crowd. In Nottingham, where Lawrence had been educated, the book was banned in the city's libraries.

On this tide of reaction, a parliamentary association was formed in February 1961, with the declared aim of 'defending moral principles in public life'. Its management committee included, for the Tories, Mr Ray Mawby and Sir Charles Taylor, and for Labour Mr Robert Mellish and Mr Leslie Lever. And public burnings were catching on. Barbara Cartland, the romantic novelist, showed a lewd magazine to a startled audience of Conservatives at Lemsford, and then set light to it. 'I hope our small fire at Lemsford will start a big fire all over the country,' she said.

But for the most part, the publication of *Lady Chatterley* was seen as an important milestone in the changing attitudes to sexual morality. Some, at least, of the pretences were gone. In London W.1. it would be an unsophisticated person indeed who would raise his eyebrows in surprise at a 48-year-old society man sharing his home with a 19-year-old model. By June 1, 1961, the two millionth copy of *Lady Chatterley* was sold.

On June 1, 1961, Stephen Ward moved into a flat at 17 Wimpole Mews, Marylebone. Christine Keeler went there with him. By then the girl from Wraysbury had already had an eventful life.

2

Profumo, the Liaison Man

JOHN DENNIS PROFUMO gave his name to a scandal in which his own identity was lost. The consequences of the affair transcended his own contribution to it, but to understand what happened it is essential to see him more clearly. It was an unusual name to label a British political crisis. The story behind it is testimony to the way in which exotic blood is swiftly assimilated into the English mainstream. Britain has taken in and embraced many families of Italian origin. The Profumos were one of them.

In 1843, when Italy was littered with operatic kingdoms, the King of Sardinia accorded to a merchant called Antonio Profumo the title of Baron of Sardinia. Antonio worked hard for the title. He had a considerable appetite for public life: he was President of the Court of Commerce at Genoa, three times Mayor of the city, and became not only a baron but a Senator. This instinct for political life was a family characteristic; Pietro, the second Baron, became Principal Private Secretary to Cavour, the Prime Minister to King Victor Emmanuel II. He organised the Italian Consular Service, and in 1851 came to Britain as Sardinia's Ambassador Extraordinary at the Great Exhibition. At this time Pietro had a son called Giuseppe, aged two. It was Giuseppe who, twenty-six years later, spread the Profumo family tree to Britain. There were already powerful links between the British and Italian aristocracy – moulded under the Prime-Ministership of Lord John Russell – and he found himself readily accepted in society. In 1875 he married a London girl called Annie Mills, anglicised his name to Joseph, and in September 1885 became a British citizen.

Two sons were born to Joseph and Annie; and the elder was given the fashionable Victorian names of Albert Peter Anthony Profumo. In August 1903 Albert was, like his father, given confirmation of his right to the family title by King Humbert I, and he continued to use the style of an Italian baron throughout his life. But already the Profumos were becoming absorbed into the fabric of British society. Albert mixed the family blood further by marrying a Scots girl, Martha Kennedy Walker of Edinburgh. In 1912 they had a son, but he died after only a few months. On January 30, 1915, John Dennis Profumo was born.

By now the assimilation of the British branch of the Profumos was almost complete. They bought Avon Carrow, a squirish mansion near a hamlet called Avon Dassett, 12 miles east of Stratford-on-Avon. Socially, this was as deep into the British squirearchy as you could go: south Warwickshire had been by-passed by the railways and preserved from the Industrial Revolution which had devoured the acres not much farther to the north. John Profumo's father, suave, accomplished and rich, had built up a highly successful practice as a barrister in the Middle Temple, and had become a K.C. in 1919. The family fortunes, securely invested in an insurance company, swelled his considerable income from the Bar. Although the aftermath of the Great War was changing for ever the old social order, the Profumos had the wealth and the breeding to make their position inviolate. At their country seat, the family, only second-generation British, melted into the landscape. By 1937, their estate and pedigree were duly chronicled in *Burke's Landed Gentry*.

It was in this silver-spoon atmosphere that the young John grew up. There was another son, Philip, and two sisters, Elizabeth and Mary. Inevitably, the family's politics were Conservative, and Baron (Albert) Profumo contested two elections as a Tory, in 1906 and 1909, but unsuccessfully. John was sent to Harrow. He was not a particularly distinguished scholar, but he was popular and good at sports; he spent two years in the Rugby XV. This physical impact continued when he went up to Brasenose College, Oxford. He represented the University at steeplechasing and won the handicap event at pole-vaulting. The lines of his future were already being laid down. At the University he had decided to take up politics, and he took a degree in Agriculture and Political Economy.

In those days young men of dash took to the air. Flying was

a fashionable sport, and still enough in its infancy to have a swashbuckling, informal flavour. John Profumo joined the University Air Squadron, and felt the tang of wind in the wires. These part-time pilots were later to find their skill in great demand, but war then seemed remote, and most of the planes being flown were still biplanes. The young men in goggles and flying suits were social cavaliers, and John Profumo went to one of the great weekend arenas for the breed: the parties at the home of Sir Lindsay Everard, the well-heeled Tory M.P. for Melton who lived in grand style at Ratcliffe Hall in Leicestershire. Here the grandees of the Midlands had colossal splashes: the young Profumo would turn up for the day to find that the whole party had been equipped with suitcases and arrangements made for them to fly off from Everard's private aerodrome to the Continent for a jamboree. A guest at one of these parties was Hermann Göring, an ace exhibit in the aristocracy of aviation. Politically the place was thick with influential people, and it was an atmosphere in which a political aspirant like John Profumo could make valuable contacts.

The Profumos (motto: *Virtute et Labore*) made an attractive family: the father, assured and secure in the legal establishment, and the children with their wide, county interests—hunting, polo, flying, horse shows, house parties and Conservative fêtes. This was the heartland of the hunts, and the Profumos hunted with the Warwickshire, the Pytchley and the Quorn. They were always beautifully turned out. While it was still a rare sight they would turn up with an immaculate horse box towed by a pristine Rolls, with the family dressed for sport by Savile Row. A friend remembers them 'always bubbling with good form'.

John hobnobbed with the local M.P.s, although the family was probably above the typical social level of most politicians. Certainly, when he left Oxford no money or effort was spared to widen his knowledge and enable him to see things for himself: he went right round the world, stopping off in Russia, China, Japan and the United States.

His first political post was as chairman in one of the wards of the East Fulham Conservative Association, but he also became chairman of the West Midlands Federation of the

Junior Imperial League, displaying already the beginnings of a great eagerness for office. At the astonishingly young age of twenty-one he was chairman of the whole East Fulham Association. This began a fateful friendship, for the constituency's M.P. was the Hon. W. W. Astor, who later, as Lord Astor, was to figure so largely in the Affair.

By then the pacifism of the Astor family and their friends at Cliveden was plainly doomed, and the young Profumo, whose sights were now set firmly on Westminster, decided to look at Hitler's Europe for himself. In the summer of 1938, against the backdrop of the gathering storm, he flew there to 'study economic conditions'. On the flight back his propeller dropped off, but he was safely across the Channel and made a forced landing at Lympne.

All the time he was hustling: to Geneva for the International Labour Conference and the fading League of Nations; between the political fields of Warwickshire and Fulham; by the time he was twenty-four he was a governor of two London hospitals, the Westminster and the Great Northern. The pace was breathtaking, the effort tireless. He was the epitome of a young man determined to carve out political success – and quickly. Connections were cultivated all over the place. It was hard work, but he liked it. And in March, 1939, keeping pace with his ambition, he was adopted as prospective Conservative candidate for the Kettering Division, at the age of twenty-four. John Profumo was the youngest candidate in the country. The impact of this young man on the Northamptonshire town was considerable. Kettering had a smart county core, surrounded by featureless streets of red Victorian workers' terraces: the Industrial Revolution went to work in shoes made in Kettering factories. The steel works of Corby were also in the division, and here, if anywhere, a Tory candidate would find the going tough. But even here John Profumo charmed his way. His opportunity to enter Parliament came with a by-election, after the outbreak of war, in 1940. Profumo, then a young officer, took over a suite of rooms at the Royal Hotel, Kettering, and launched into the campaign with typical panache. He had a sharp, personable face and striking eyes, the hair, just beginning to recede, was

17

neat and glossed. His supporters saw in him a future Prime Minister. He was certainly the most outstanding candidate Kettering had ever had.

He was a good speaker, and had support from the sister who was particularly close to him, Mary, who later was to become Lady Balfour of Inchrye. A local Conservative official recalling him as he was then said: 'He and his family always clearly believed in the ruling class. This never showed in a nasty way, but he believed in it.' Certainly his charm was genuine, although some people found him perhaps a shade too anxious to be liked. His conviction in caste superiority did not rebound. He disarmed Kettering and was returned with a majority of 11,298 over an 'anti-War' opponent.

At twenty-five John Profumo was the youngest M.P. at Westminster. And within a few weeks of taking his seat he joined rebellion: on May 8, 1940, he was one of thirty Conservative M.P.s who voted against Chamberlain and so created the situation for Churchill to become Prime Minister. Some of the other insurrectionists were Harold Macmillan, Robert Boothby and Quintin Hogg, the future Lord Hailsham. This formed early and important allegiances. It had been a day of great political courage – and foresight.

By the time John Profumo entered Parliament, he had been a serving officer for about six months. Before the war he had joined not the R.A.F., which his enthusiasm might have suggested, but the Territorial Army, in the 1st Northants Yeomanry. The army was, in fact, to direct his energies in a way that ensured the success he sought. Both his charm and his showmanship were to be called upon. When the war began he was a second lieutenant, and in a unit which was ill-equipped and confronted by the need for improvisation. His first army assignment was to join an improvised Heath Robinson outfit called the Yeomanry Armoured Detachment which was to act as a mobile reserve if an invasion came. Part of this was created by mounting guns from destroyers on lorries, and the rest by 14-pounder guns towed by Selfridge's delivery vans. The unit had few radios and scarcely anyone who could operate them. The resourceful Second Lieutenant Profumo was put in charge of a troop of motor cyclists to maintain some kind of communications. His commanding officer at the time was Major-General Sir Evelyn Dalrymple Fanshawe, for long a friend of the family, and later Chairman of the Kettering Conservative Association.

In 1940, after the by-election, he was switched to the somewhat more orthodox 20th Armoured Brigade and the following year promoted to Captain. His rôle there was one which enabled his flair for public relations to be asserted in a striking way. He became a liaison officer between the army and the R.A.F. And in 1942 he pulled off the *coup de grâce* of interservice morale-boosting, by writing, producing and playing in a musical called *Night and Day* which was put on at the Arts Theatre in Cambridge. The leading rôle was played by Frances Day, who was supported, in addition to the impresario, by members of the W.A.A.F., the A.T.S., aircraft hands, gunners and signallers. The costumes were borrowed from Ensa. Captain Profumo demanded from the cast the same selfless dedication that he put into the show himself: rehearsals went on for ten days from 7.30 p.m. until 2 a.m. *Night and Day* was, needless to say, a hit: 2,500 servicemen and women saw it. Captain Profumo said: 'It is essential from the point of view of winning the war that the two Services should be looked upon as one.'

A year later, by then a Major, he had forsaken the footlights for the battlefield. He was in the North African campaign, and was mentioned in dispatches. All the time, of course, he was M.P. for Kettering as well. His agent did not, apparently, always appreciate his Member's preoccupations. Major Profumo, in a wireless caravan buried in two haystacks in Tunisia, told an acting war correspondent called John Strachey: 'What about this, John. I've just received a letter from my agent which got here after weeks by plane, sea convoy and fast Arab, and he says, blandly, "I assume you will have read the Beveridge Report and made up your mind about it." '

By 1944 he was a Lieutenant-Colonel and on the headquarters staff of the most aristocratic of the army commanders, Field Marshal Alexander. He was the senior air-staff liaison officer, and won the O.B.E. in the Italian campaign.

Still the youngest M.P., he flew from Italy to London to

make, on November 16, 1944, one of the most memorable speeches by a serving Member. His mission was to press for guarantees of leave for men posted from the Mediterranean to the Far East, and to raise other questions of Service welfare. He said: 'I hope no woman will be permitted to serve within possible reach of these Japanese animals,' and called the Women's Services' clothes allowance of £12 10s. 'niggardly'. An army of P.RO.s could scarcely have made a choice of subjects more likely to produce warm popular acclaim. The *Daily Mail* reported the next day: 'From the personal standpoint the success of the day was scored by Colonel Profumo. Not only was his speech a model of force and conciseness, the style was just right. Colonel Profumo, a lithe and vivid figure, whose words received the congratulations of the Minister and many other speakers, made himself with all modesty the spokesman of many overseas. He showed the House that he knew their sentiments, that they could not have a better voice. Many of the Government's statements were made directly in answer to him.' The Kettering newspaper reported: 'The speech made a deep impression on all who heard it.'

The impressive Colonel Profumo then went back to the Italian campaign. Only three generations before, his family had been transplanted from these shores. When he had first returned with the Allied forces in September, 1943, it had been on the slender foothold of the Salerno beaches. He was immensely impressed by Field Marshal Alexander's conduct of the campaign, and it had certainly been a tough and bloody fight. But the Germans were in retreat.

When, in 1945, the Germans in Italy surrendered it was Colonel Profumo who escorted the vanquished Nazi generals back through the Allied lines to end the war in the Mediterranean. He later turned war reporter to describe the experience for the Kettering newspaper. With an almost Churchillian sense of the melodramatic, he wrote: ' "If I retreat," shouted Mussolini from the balcony of his Palazzo Venezia in Rome, at the height of his power, "then kill me." Today he lies stiff and cold in a Milan mortuary. He HAD retreated, and with him the much-vaunted German Army Group "C", comprising some twenty-two Nazi and six Fascist Divisions. . . .

'May 3rd, 1945, will remain uppermost in my memory throughout my life. I had the privilege of being sent with an Allied escort through the lines to the hastily-prepared Alpine hide-out where stood the headquarters of the German Commander-in-Chief, South West, for the purpose of conducting the conquered Nazi general and high-ranking officers of his staff to the headquarters of General Mark W. Clark. The meeting took place at night by the light of torches. It was very formal and quiet, save for the clicks of Nazi boots. There was no handshaking.'

A few months later, like many Conservatives, Colonel Profumo found that despite his war record the allegiances in his constituency had changed. In the 1945 General Election he lost his seat at Kettering. But there was compensation: he was again selected for a liaison job. He was promoted to Brigadier and made Chief of Staff of the post-war British Liaison Mission to Japan. He was there for two years, and this time, instead of Lord Alexander, there was a powerful personality of different character: the autocratic, almost megalomaniacal General Douglas MacArthur, who was industriously transforming the previously feudal Japan into a Coca-Cola democracy. MacArthur impressed him as Churchill had done before and Macmillan did later. A loyalty was formed between the young British Brigadier and the seasoned American General.

In 1947 he left the Army and went back into politics: into the propitious berth of the Conservative Central Office, where R. A. Butler and his young men were tearing apart the ancient party machine and attempting to remodel it to the new egalitarianism. The Profumo flair for public relations was once again brought into play. He became the party's 'broadcasting adviser'. (The head of the B.B.C. at that time was Sir William Haley.)

While in this backroom rôle he re-emerged in 1948 on the hustings, adopted as candidate for Stratford-on-Avon, a new division created, after border revision, from part of the old Leamington Spa division. Mr Profumo had for several years been friendly with the member for Leamington Spa, Anthony Eden, who strongly supported the new candidate.

Here the new grandee of the Profumos was on home ground.

21

The young buck of pre-war days, now noticeably balding, had become an intensely ambitious politician. Although his family still followed the county sports, his own interest in hunting had waned. If he won his seat he was clearly fodder for early promotion. He fought a three-cornered contest in 1950, and won with a majority of 9,349.

For his first two years back at Westminster he spoke mainly on broadcasting and defence. When General MacArthur was under attack for his atomic ambitions in Korea he found a champion in the Member for Stratford-on-Avon.

In 1952 he took office for the first time, as Joint Parliamentary Secretary at the Ministry of Transport and Civil Aviation in Sir Winston Churchill's Government. His knowledge of flying meant that he had found a ministerial vocation, but it was not a happy time for British civil aviation. The policies drawn up by the Brabazon Committee while the war was still on, to make Britain dominant on world air routes, had produced nothing but expensive white elephants, the most conspicuous being the Brabazon itself. Demonstrating his verve, Mr Profumo flew in an air race from London to New Zealand as steward and cook.

In November 1953 Mr Profumo himself backed a loser. Speaking at a dinner about the seemingly appalling problem of the huge runways which would be required for the introduction of jet airliners, he forecast the return of the flying boat. Another of his enthusiasms was commercial television: he was one of its political backers.

By this time his bachelor days were nearly over. On January 5, 1954, he married Valerie Hobson, who was then playing the lead in *The King and I* at Drury Lane. Her previous marriage to Anthony Havelock-Allen, a film producer, had been dissolved in 1952. It was a surprisingly small and quiet wedding at St Columba's, in Pont Street. Valerie Hobson soon afterwards gave up her stage career and became a devoted supporter of her husband's career. Later, he said of their partnership: 'When I married my beautiful and talented wife I quickly found that I had become a most popular speaker. People used to invite me to open their bazaars, adding, "you'll of course bring along your charming wife." I tumbled to it all when a Socialist asked me to open his bazaar. "You'll of course bring along your charming wife," he added. When I told him that would be impossible he replied: "Don't bother then. Come along yourself – next year."'

In 1957 there was a change of office. Mr Profumo became Parliamentary Under-Secretary for the Colonies. It was a sticky wicket, and, describing one of his performances in a debate on Cyprus, *The Guardian* said: 'Mr Profumo, a brisk, capable young man, gesticulated and half-danced his way through an attempted justification for the missing policy.' From the Labour benches, Sir Frank Soskice called his performance a 'disingenuous piece of dialectic'. But Mr Profumo was showing himself quite proficient at talking his way out of tricky situations.

There was a brief interlude between November 1958 and January 1959 as Parliamentary Under-Secretary at the Foreign Office, and then he was promoted nearer to the seat of power: Minister of State for Foreign Affairs. The rise had been equal to the expectations of his admirers in Kettering in 1938.

Then in the July (a month significant in his destiny) of 1960 Mr Macmillan chose him for the political front line by making him Secretary of State for War. Once more the circumstances of the job suited the Profumo *forte* for promotion and persuasion; the War Office was in need of an advertising man as well as a Minister. The army's problem was that it had become a part of political policy to abolish conscription and create the first all-Regular Army for twenty years. The army had to be sold. The minimum target was 165,000 men by 1963, and Mr Profumo set out to get them with all his huckstering instincts. Television advertising was contemplated for the first time, and campaigns were drawn up which portrayed army life as a mixture of a Cook's tour and *Boy's Own Paper* escapades. But it worked.

Mr Profumo had a talent for finding headline-catching phrases for his speeches. Many of his contributions to defence debates were, in fact, straightforward recruiting speeches, peppered with breezy colloquialisms, aimed at showing that the army provided a 'cracking good life'. The *Daily Express* commented on one speech: 'The sprightly fellow bristled with new ideas . . .'

By June 16, 1961, *The Times* reported that the Minister of War was in his 'jauntiest and breeziest vein'. In this office Mr Profumo certainly seemed to have found his *métier*. It was fulfilment for his talents, and the force of his personality was unabated. He was popular among his colleagues, though some still felt that the earlier tendency towards ingratiation had not left him. He had, said one critic loftily, 'no reputation among the Tory brigadiers'. Certainly, intellectually he was no political heavyweight but no one could deny his intense desire to be successful. Members on both sides of the House liked him, and after a Labour M.P. who had crossed swords with him in a debate went into hospital, Mr Profumo made a point of sending him flowers.

There had really never been any doubt that John Profumo would be a popular man. He had been something of a buck but now he was happily married to a charming wife of whom he was patently proud. His political calibre was yet to be fully tested; enthusiasm and charm had helped his success. What kind of an army could he produce?

This seemed the only question in 1961. There was no hint of any other challenge to his character or integrity.

3

The Psychology of Stephen Ward

THE PICTURE THAT emerged of Dr Stephen Thomas Ward, when he was tried at the Old Bailey in July 1963, was as dark as it had to be, but it was possibly darker than the truth. Sounding chronically outraged as a good prosecuting counsel must, Mr Mervyn Griffith-Jones told the jury: 'We have come in this case to the depths of lechery and depravity.'

Depravity Dr Ward sank to. But lechery, for Ward at any rate if not some of his acquaintances, was the wrong word altogether. What motivated Stephen Ward was something deeper and more subtle than the farmyard requirements of the lecher.

The defects which controlled his actions could have been part of him at birth, flaws with no physical manifestations; or, more conventionally, they could have been founded in some traumatic event in his childhood. In families with more than one son (Ward had two brothers and a sister) it often happens that one of them rebels. It is, perhaps, even more common in a family where the father is a churchman – Ward's father was vicar of Lemsford, near Hatfield, Herts, where Stephen was born on October 19, 1912, and subsequently of Holy Trinity, Twickenham, of St Matthias, Torquay, and finally canon of Rochester Cathedral. Stephen Ward not only disliked the conformity and regulation of vicarage life but he could not believe in God.

Ward received little discipline from his mother. The fact that she was related to the aristocracy might also have disturbed him; he might have had glimpses of a life which seemed more attractive than his own, and coveted it. His mother, gentle and quiet, indulged his taste for money and fast cars; he indulged his taste for girls. When he was eighteen, he picked up a French girl on holiday, took her back to Torquay and hid her in the basement of his house for three weeks until she was discovered.

His friends knew little of his childhood for he rarely talked of it in detail and the few facts he gave revealed no traumatic experience. Whatever the reasons for his instability, his close friends were aware that under the charming and intelligent surface there were more disturbing elements.

His mother told friends she believed he was brilliant and would one day be famous. Expecting more of a man than he is capable of is a conventional way of creating a failure; while Ward's natural intelligence was undisputed his academic application seems to have been limited. He made no particular impact on any of his several schools, one of them public (Canford, Dorset), nor did he cope with his course in osteopathy in brilliant fashion. It usually takes about three years to qualify in the art (osteopaths refuse to call it a science); Stephen Ward took five to get his degree at Kirksville, Missouri, the osteopathic college founded by the man who established the art, Dr Andrew Taylor Still.

Ward had begun a dissolute existence before he went to America in 1934. His natural talent as an artist – he later made it a little more sophisticated by going to Slade classes – enabled him to flatter girls by sketching them. There was a stream of girls throughout his adolescence in Hamburg (as a translator), in London (as a floor-sweeper) and in Paris (as a student at the Sorbonne and guide to foreign tourists). 'It did not take me long,' Ward once said, 'to find out that more people were interested in real live girls than the Mona Lisa.'

It is possible that Ward saw in osteopathy the opportunity to satisfy his desire for increased social status, for osteopathy was and is fashionable among important people. But it is more likely that the war, the crossroads, particularly socially, for many a life, had more effect than anything else on his direction.

Ward had been in practice in Torquay for only a short time when war was declared. It began badly for him; the Royal Army Medical Corps did not care for osteopaths and he had to enter the Royal Armoured Corps as a private. But, half-way through, the Army decided it must not risk doctors in the front line and created a new class of 'officer, stretcher-bearer' for men with medical experience. Shortly after being commissioned as a lieutenant, Ward's instability nearly ruined the opportunity: he went absent without leave and lost a pip.

It was not until the very end of the war that Ward began to make the most of his opportunities as an officer. It happened in an odd way. In 1945, he was sent to a hospital, as a patient, in Poona, India. By then a captain, he had been relieved from active service for being 'emotionally maladjusted', that blanket Army euphemism for everybody from a near-lunatic to a minor neurotic.

There was apparently little wrong with him for he recovered quickly and became an ambulatory patient. This minor emotional crisis, caused probably by his incompatibility with Army regulation and life, was the first of several. Ward, according to his medical acquaintances in and around Harley Street, craved two things – and neither of them was directly women. He had an obsessive desire to be accepted, socially and as a man, and he wanted significance. A more ideal place than Poona could hardly have been chosen. Rich Indians and Anglo-Indians accepted English officers without question. And Captain Ward was an extremely likeable and charming one. He already had tremendous social poise, and he had a remarkable facility for convincing strangers within minutes that he was really an old friend.

Ward was much sought-after by the maharajahs. (The Barodas, in particular, would send their car to the hospital for him.) His social patter was faultless; his bridge excellent; and his success with women, though it is believed he had no affairs in India, was instantaneous. He was deeply attached to a young titled woman at home.

His life in India served as an apprenticeship for what was to come. At first he did not do well, settling for a job in an osteopathic clinic in London. But one day the American Embassy phoned to ask the clinic to recommend an osteopath to tend the United States Ambassador, Mr Averell Harriman. Ward took the call. He thought about it for a few minutes, then phoned back to recommend himself. According to Ward – Harriman has no recollection of the event – the trick charmed the ambassador and he recommended Ward to his friends.

Ward's spare-time work expanded and, in 1947, he headed for Cavendish Square, just south of Harley Street, and set himself up in a flat in a large block on the west side.

He bought a practice and, at first, was in extreme financial trouble. But his difficulties were short-lived. Both his business and his social life – and with Harley Street practitioners the two overlap considerably – began to expand and his name to spread to a widening circle. His maharajahs helped – seven prominent Indians became his patients. So did Sir Winston Churchill; it was Sir Winston, in fact, who pressed him, during one of his visits with his osteopath's table to Sir Winston's home, to take up drawing again. Mrs Duncan Sandys, six other Churchills, Danny Kaye, Elizabeth Taylor, Paul Getty and ex-King Peter of Yugoslavia were treated by him at various times.

Stephen Ward, though polite as a conversationalist, dispensed his political views determinedly; broadly, he was hostile to America and pleaded the Russians' point of view, although his support was idealistic and emotional and not founded on any wide knowledge of Marxist-Leninist theory; he was well informed and able to give an intelligent appraisal of events which made him well worth listening to. Despite his 'pink' ideas, he often said he would never act in any way to the detriment of Britain (though, during Cuba, he may have done so to a minor degree). His patients, often busy, important men, were interested and charmed by him and frequently introduced him to their social circle.

He began to build up, too, a lively and diverse ring of male friends (his titled fiancée lasted only a little longer than the war). Baron, the photographer, and Prince Philip, then a lively but rather impoverished bachelor were among his acquaintances. Ward always gave bottle parties, and seldom spent much money on providing a buffet. But his invitations were eagerly accepted—there would always be a medley of all kinds of interesting people, good conversation and the women were as attractive and intelligent as anyone could wish. Some time before Prince Philip's engagement to Princess Elizabeth was officially announced, Ward got to hear about it. He was less than discreet: the opportunity to seem *au fait* with Royal secrets was too good an opportunity to miss, and he casually dropped hints of his knowledge to many of his friends.

The exterior of Stephen Ward's life remained successful, even flourishing, throughout the 'fifties. He had many highly respectable friends; the gossip columns referred to him as the 'society osteopath'. But, underneath, another social pattern had been developing.

There are, of course, many people who combine large or even peculiar sexual appetites with successful professional lives and who, though their private activities may be well known in their professional circles, continue to promote their businesses. But there was another element in Ward's activities which must have ultimately destroyed his standing. He was, in a sense, a beatnik; smooth, charming and intelligent but none the less a scavenger of experience for all that.

At first, this characteristic manifested itself in no more harmful a form than shocking his friends. He would, perhaps, outrageously expose a friend's confided weakness to another and, his face screwing up with laughter, delight in their embarrassment. It was the same fiendish delight that a child can have when he discovers a means to disconcert his parents. (Childishness never left Stephen Ward. He revelled in thrillers and mediocre crime films and he sometimes became excited at the most ridiculous television stories. He once said that 'Children's Hour' helped him relax.)

This anarchic element in his make-up was to develop to such an extent that he forgot the rules altogether. But in the exciting days when success was coming fast, he was getting sufficient thrill from his advance into society and his enlarging circle of male and female friends to suppress its more outrageous requirements.

The Cavendish Square flat was cavernous and anybody who wanted to stay would readily be given a room. Ward's generosity with his time and accommodation was almost ridiculous; people could stay for weeks on end without ill-feeling. But when it came to money, Ward's generosity ended. He would make them pay for laundering their bed linen. When he entertained he would lay on tea and coffee or, if someone else provided the gin, he would provide the vermouth. Friends at the Cavendish Square 'hotel' might sleep there, but they would starve before he would give them a meal. One mistress, who later became a much-publicised film starlet, used to complain to her friends: 'He is a beast! He starves me.'

He delighted in helping his friends. He fancied himself as an amateur psychiatrist, understanding the failings of others and helping to put them right. He believed he was classless and saw himself as a bridge for those who wanted to climb from the working and middle classes. 'There is no class structure in my life,' he said. 'There are people I like and people I don't like.' His assistance to these people (they were male as well as female) possibly gave him a sense of power over their destinies which helped to satisfy his craving for significance.

For the most part the girls in Ward's life were merely a means for the achievement of status. But occasionally out of the endless procession – one even used to come up from Bristol for a few days' shopping and stay with him, perhaps or perhaps not sleeping with him, depending on their mood – a girl would evoke stronger feelings in him. When this happened, her inevitable departure would produce a violent emotional reaction in Ward. One of the first was almost a childhood sweetheart, Mary Glover, to whom he was verbally betrothed when he went to America. When she wrote and told him she was marrying someone else, he flew to England in a rage to try to stop the wedding. Ward was rarely angry except when people, like Christine Keeler and John Lewis, the ex-M.P., who plays a part later in the story, undermined his self-esteem. And then he could become really vicious.

The next crisis in his relationship with women came in 1947. One of his girls, Eunice Bailey, who came from Streatham, attracted more than his sense of power. Ward fell deeply in love with her. And when she left him he was shattered. He tried to commit suicide. At that time, when his skill as an osteopath was becoming known, it would have been a funeral to be proud of; many famous people would have been sorry to see him go; it is even possible he might have earned a mention in *The Times*. But the Middlesex Hospital saved him for the Profumo-Keeler-Ivanov disaster. (Eunice Bailey, incidentally, later married the rich son of a knight, who died, and is now married to a dollar millionaire like two other former girl friends of Ward.)

In 1949, Ward left Cavendish Square for a flat in Devonshire Street. He also rented a house in De Walden Street, in the same area. He had decided, at thirty-six, to get married to Patricia Baines, a twenty-one-year-old actress. She said recently: 'I was desperately unhappy with him. And he was a very unhappy man. I think basically he was in conflict with himself most of the time.'

Their divorce, three years later, provides a different picture of Ward's sexual requirements from the one shown later at the Old Bailey. No one coming away from the trial could have felt Ward was anything less than a lustful, middle-aged woman-chaser with a variety of reasons for wanting them. In fact, his sexual requirements were probably less than normal.

The marriage to Pat Baines lasted just six weeks. Its complete failure could have done nothing to make this deeply disturbed man any happier. At the root of his desire for a place in society was a desperate sense of insecurity; the one time that he had attempted to find security since he left his indulgent home in the West Country it had served only to accentuate his abnormality. The grounds of the divorce were cruelty.

Publicly, he declared: 'I suppose I have been one of the most successful men in London with girls since the war. I have never had any trouble getting the women I want. The secret is my basic interest in women as people; they fascinate me. I am not handsome. I have never been rich. Even today at fifty I can get most of the girls I want.'

Privately, he was gratified when a girl would agree to pose for him in her underwear, wearing extremely high-heeled shoes and displaying stockinged legs. Sometimes he would just look at the legs. Sometimes he might photograph them. Such fetishes usually indicate a basic feeling of disgust at normal sexual relations; the exciting pristine leg is sufficient. Ward's requirements were at the same level as the man who buys a half-crown 'Silky' book.

'I was never meant to be married,' he once declared. 'I belong to them all.' For a god, he had a large Achilles' heel.

31

Ward was thirty-seven at the time of his divorce. It is not the best age for a highly-strung man to go through an emotional crisis; any man powered by an uncontrollable desire to fulfil his image of himself would be inclined to accelerate the search, at a time when more stable men are coming to terms with themselves. And Ward's beatnik side was beginning to require stronger 'kicks'.

There was, however, in his descent one further period of comparative stability. Paul Tanfield, gossip columnist of the *Daily Mail*, felt sufficiently moved in 1958 by Ward's prolonged attachment to Margaret Brown, a twenty-two-year-old international model, to ask when they were going to get married. Ward, who was not averse to being quoted by newspapers, said they felt they were not quite ready for it. After two years they broke up and Miss Brown later married the millionaire American songwriter Jule Styne ('Three Coins in a Fountain').

But Maggi Brown was only an island in a sea of impermanence. From the time of his marriage's failure, Ward's circle of women became even wider. It was as if he were desperately trying to prove his potency. For him, the feeling that a man is judged by the quality of the woman on his arm became an obsession.

The women on Ward's arm, though always lovely, were frequently not at heart the well-bred, metropolitan creatures they appeared to be. Connoisseurs of Dr Ward's tastes could espy a potential 'Ward girl' a mile off: she would be no particular size although her shape would be good, possibly modelish. Essentially, she would be graceful with a natural, not tutored, elegance, healthy-looking and zestful. Voices, clothes, even, in one case, teeth, did not really matter.

More often than not, his protégées would be provincial or suburban born (Keeler from Wraysbury, Rice-Davies from Birmingham, Eunice Bailey from Streatham). He would know precisely how to bring the best out of them. They would respond to his charm and flattery, becoming all the things he told them they were. It is a gift which many men, probably still puffing with indignation at the dubious revelations of the trial, would envy. This is how one Ward girl described it:

'He made you feel needed. With his eyes fixed on you and his voice saying everything you ever wanted to hear, you became the only girl that mattered. Stephen flowed over with sympathy and understanding. He wasn't a bit handsome, but that didn't make any difference. You felt comfortable and happy with him and there wasn't a cloud in the sky.'

A close friend of Ward's said: 'People were always asking where the devil he got the girls. He didn't get them, he made them.'

The Ward girls would change radically within no time. No legacy of the provinces would be apparent in their accents, though the very lack of colour in their tones would sometimes make people wonder; they became classless and sophisticated.

Christine Keeler was fashioned in Ward's metropolitan mould. He once described her as a 'dear, lost girl'. Later he said about her: 'She was just an alley-cat when I took her up. She was filled with all sorts of wild ambition – she wanted to be a model, an actress, have some sort of social background. She wanted too much, too quickly and perhaps too early. She could have become a duchess. It's a shame.'

As with Christine Keeler, his relationship with his girls was nearly always of the brother-and-sister type. According to one acquaintance: 'He was their pal. He was not jealous of them, nor possessive.' His interest in them was certainly less sexual than Professor Higgins's in Eliza Doolittle. His satisfaction would come with their launching: without me, he felt, they could not have made it. And, of course, the fact that their subsequent husbands or patrons were obliged to him was an addition to his sense of self-importance.

Exactly when Stephen Ward's search took him down into the seedier side of London life is not clear but it probably began soon after the divorce. By the time he met Keeler he was swamped by depravity. He had rented a cottage on the estate of Lord Astor; it became the scene of parties where nude variations of children's games were played; he cultivated the company of prostitutes and drug addicts and tried marijuana himself; he went to whipping parties at the home of a family of sado-masochists; he was, according to Keeler, getting 'kinkier and kinkier' all the time; in West London clubs he would compare girls and experience with acquaintances like Peter Rachman and Dennis Hamilton. 'They would discuss girls,' said a friend, 'rather like erudite stamp-collectors comparing rare perforations.'

Although Ward's acquaintanceship with Hamilton was only slight, and with Rachman often uneasy, the three had a great deal in common. Besides their mutual obsession for girls, all three had tremendous charm, all took delight in flouting accepted codes of behaviour, all achieved massive notoriety, and all died extraordinarily. The connecting link between them, apart from an overlap of girl friends, was that all, at some time of their lives, occupied the same flat at Bryanston Mews, Marylebone.

Hamilton, the late husband of Diana Dors, was the man responsible for introducing a curious voyeur fetish into the milieu which Ward had entered. At his Thames-side home at Maidenhead, only a little way up the river from Cliveden, he had a two-way mirror fixed in the bedroom ceiling, so that the activities inside could be watched. It may have been he who took the idea to Bryanston Mews, where he afterwards lived for a brief period. The flat was subsequently occupied first by Rachman, then by Ward. When the flat later figured in the court proceedings against Ward, the police produced some evidence that a two-way mirror had once been fixed in the bedroom wall.

Both Hamilton and Rachman were involved in property speculation, though the extent of Rachman's operations was much greater. He was a stateless Pole – born Perec Rachman – who had arrived in Britain after the war, almost penniless. During the 1950s he built up a slum empire in West London by methods which, when they were exposed after his death, created political uproar. Essentially there were three strands to his technique. First, to buy properties occupied by statutory tenants paying controlled rents, then, by a mixture of intimidation and exploitation of racial tension, force them to leave, thus massively increasing the property's value. Then to 'sweat' the property, either by overcrowding it with immigrant West

Indians, or letting it at exorbitant rents to brothel-keepers or club-owners. And thirdly, to take advantage of weaknesses in company law and housing regulations to confuse attempts by the authorities to pin down his activities. However, in 1959, when his acquaintanceship with Stephen Ward was developing, Rachman was in process of cleaning up his business and selling off much of his slum empire. It is possible that Ward was not even aware of the dubious sources of Rachman's huge income and lavish spending, for despite his somewhat sinister appearance, Rachman, socially, was by no means an unattractive personality: courteous, intelligent, witty, and almost excessively generous.

For a while Christine Keeler, who was with Ward the day he met Rachman for the first time, went to live with him at Bryanston Mews, but left him at the end of 1959. The following year, Rachman met yet another girl friend through Ward.

Mandy Rice-Davies, like Christine Keeler, had barely left school when she arrived from Birmingham in October, 1960, to seek her fortune in London. She seems almost immediately to have met Miss Keeler, who by then – for the third time – had returned to work in Murray's Cabaret Club. Miss Rice-Davies was introduced in turn to Ward and Rachman, then decided that she, too, would like to become a showgirl. She applied for a job at Murray's, gave her age as eighteen and a half (in fact she was sixteen).

Mandy stayed at Murray's for only two months. On New Year's Eve, both she and Miss Keeler failed to turn up for work. Neither worked there again. For a while the ex-showgirls had a flat of their own, then they split up – Miss Keeler to live with a Persian boy, Miss Rice-Davies to live with Rachman. But with the certainty of homing pigeons, they each eventually returned to live with Ward.

One of the stranger aspects of Ward's tortured life is that at the same time as he was involved in his worst depravities, he was becoming more and more respected artistically and was meeting more people of real social importance than ever before. He drew the Duke of Edinburgh and no doubt exchanged reminiscences of their earlier days together. All told, nine members of the Royal Family and several Ministers sat for the series of portraits he was completing for the *Illustrated London News*. He let his practice slip in favour of his art. At the peak of his success as an osteopath he showed a friend his diary: next to every half-hour mark was a name. Yet he was content to let it go to an extent; his art, slick but essentially amateurish, was becoming a better entrée than his osteopathy.

The paradox is made all the more disturbing by the fact that, for some time before this period, lurid stories about Ward's activities had been circulating among many important people, including some Members of Parliament. The 'Ward set-up' as it was known was accepted almost as part of the social life of London. The descriptions of it, like the Old Bailey's, were probably over-simplified and consequently exaggerated; his low-life activities were being identified too closely with his collection of 'Ward girls'. As the *Daily Sketch* later overstated it so superbly: 'It was food from Fortnum and Mason, drink from Justerini and Brooks, and girls from Stephen Ward.'

The accounts of his 'set-up' seemed to have little effect on his acceptance by Society. The years of excess of the Chelsea Fringe, often the stamping-ground of the aristocracy's most highly-qualified males, had rubbed off on the higher levels of society, and the prevalent attitude among a large number of people was that total sexual indulgence was not only tolerable but healthy. Ward was being relished in satanic detail one moment – and talked to the next.

The stories about Ward had been heard by a substantial cross-section of Tory M.P.s and at least one Cabinet member, a fact which later made the widespread acceptance of Profumo's denial even more incomprehensible.

News of the set-up must never have reached Sir Colin Coote, editor of the *Daily Telegraph* and a patient of Ward's. For Sir Colin heard of Ward's wish to do drawings of leading Soviet personalities, and arranged a lunch for him with the Soviet naval attaché, Captain Eugene Ivanov, at the Garrick Club early in 1961. David Floyd, the newspaper's correspondent on Communist affairs, was also there.

Ward's relationship with Ivanov reveals two other aspects of his character: his habitual name-dropping and his complete, almost childish, disregard for money. One of their haunts together was a bridge club, then known as the Connaught, in Edgware Road. Ward had been going there for years before he first brought Ivanov along; he would pay at least two visits a week, frequently taking parties of girls and men, some well-known, with him. Once he took a famous film actress there. But if nobody famous was with him, Ward would make up for it by dropping names. He was forever working into the conversation the fact that he had drawn members of the Royal Family.

The Connaught (now the Marble Arch Club and between times the Ambrose) is a medium-stake gambling club with a clientele that reflects its middle position. There are four tables, one downstairs, the rest upstairs with a bar, set among the plush seats and gilded ironwork. Ward, with his important friends and his charm and politeness, made an impact there.

If Ward's visits to the club provide something of an insight into his character, Ivanov's show more than a little of his intelligence and mathematical ability. Unless he was employing the old bridge trick of denigrating his experience of the game – and such a trick would soon have been uncovered by the devotees at the club – Ivanov was an appalling player when he first arrived. He went there only about five times – the last, it is believed, in mid-January, two weeks before he left the country – yet he became a very competent player. In a short period, though he obviously practised between visits, his intelligence and mathematical grasp enabled him to achieve a standard of play that would have been unusual in anyone who had been playing for less than two or three years.

Ivanov, though always polite, was uncommunicative. He would never talk of himself or of politics though he allowed himself one little joke which would crop up at some time during every visit. When it came to choosing the red or the blue pack, he would always take the red, saying: 'What else do you expect?' In the end there was never any question of his taking the blue pack and the other players would automatically push the red pack over to him.

Ward's attitude to money and material possessions was probably one of the most attractive sides of his character.

Although in some respects he was ludicrously mean – probably partly because he never had enough to spare – he was almost unaware of money. His cars were, in succession, a second-hand Triumph and a Jaguar – they were both bought on H.P. and were never cleaned; his shoes and suits were ordinary; when he had no invitations, he ate cheaply, mostly in the coffee bars around Marylebone High Street; he allowed himself a monogram on his shirts but his motive for this might have been as much a safeguard against the vagaries of the laundry as flamboyance; his flat contained unexceptional modern furniture; his financial affairs were handled at one time by his nurse, later by his solicitor, and, after the Profumo storm broke, by a Fleet Street literary agent. He didn't care about money and he demonstrated this attitude graphically at the bridge club. He used it virtually as a bank. When the time came to settle up at the club he would fish out one of the cheques stuffed in his pockets. The cheques, varying from £15 to £30, were payments made out to him by clients, some famous. He would hand them to the proprietor who would put them through his own bank account; not one bounced. Ward would win or lose between £20–£30 an evening at the club. (He would sometimes not draw out the balance owing to him after his losses had been settled but leave himself in credit with the club.) When he came with Ivanov the stakes would drop to the Russian's level. They always played bridge – chemin de fer and poker are also played at the club – usually for 2s 6d a point. Ivanov's losses or winnings would be nominal, at the most £12 but usually between £6 and £8. Ivanov paid out, happily, in cash, but sometimes Ward paid for him out of his cheques.

In the end, what did Ward really amount to? Certainly the Old Bailey's assessment of him can be discarded as too crude a précis to be anywhere near the truth. Dr Ellis Stungo, the Harley Street psychiatrist who was a friend of Ward's for eighteen years, says:

'Ward was an immature psychopath. An immature psychopath is like a spoilt child who must have his way. He presses his aims with determination though he stops short of violence. He goes after an immediate objective without regard for convention, propriety or suitability; he *must* have it. He is totally selfish.

'Ward's objective was esteem; he wanted to impress his acquaintances and be accepted in Society. I don't think he was as sexually potent as was made to appear and he possibly compensated for his inadequacy by seeking to impress. This would account for his behaviour – his obsession to make the acquaintance of well-known people, his compulsive name-dropping and Walter Mitty posturings and his eagerness to introduce girls to men (not, I am certain, for pecuniary motives).

'His occasional petty meanness and disregard for money fitted into the pattern – the kind of esteem he wanted was not the sort that could be bought, and money was therefore irrelevant. His tremendous charm also fitted into the pattern. Intelligence and charm are the attributes of this type of psychopath – confidence tricksters, for example, are usually psychopathic.'

When Ward took thirty-five grains of Nembutal in the early morning of Wednesday, July 31, 1963, he must have realised there was no longer the remotest chance of reaching the objectives to which he had devoted his life. Suicide was the only way left of regaining esteem.

4

July 1961

LOOKING BACK ON July 1961, it is possible to imagine a deliberate design in its events so completely did they conspire to sow the seeds of crisis two years later. The pattern was there, spread far wider than a few acts of fornication.

It was a decisive month in the rôle of British military power, beginning an interplay, eventually destructive, between the Minister of War and his most persistent Labour critic, George Wigg.

It was a turning point in the economy, which two years later led to dissatisfaction with the Tory leadership at the same time as the Profumo affair was to explode.

It was a time of overhaul in the Security Services, with effects that sensitised the atmosphere for Ivanov's involvement in 1963.

It saw, through the most devastating damages ever awarded against newspapers for libel, a significant change, a new fear, in the attitude of the Press towards rumour which so pent up the details of the '63 scandal.

And it was the month when, at a swimming pool in Cliveden, in Buckinghamshire, the first meeting took place between Christine Keeler and John Profumo.

Towards the end of June the Government became alarmed by the new and aggressive posture of General Kassem of Iraq, who had been making belligerent noises about Kuwait, the tiny sheikhdom wedged on the western coast of the Persian Gulf. Kuwait was vital to Britain's economy for it supplied forty per cent of her crude oil. On June 30, the order, top secret, went out from the British Cabinet for 6,000 troops to go to Kuwait at top speed.

The operation was to serve two purposes: to deal with

Kassem if necessary and to demonstrate the theory of the new tactical textbooks; it was to be a model for dealing with limited 'brush-fire' wars, where the need is for a compact, versatile fighting force to be delivered anywhere in a hurry. It was the kind of thing Profumo's War Office had glamorised in their recruiting films; and it was also a demonstration designed to remove the painful memory of the Suez invasion when part of the British force took a week to sail from its Mediterranean bases to Port Said.

As much a political as a military exercise, the strain was felt in the offices of the Secretary of State for War. It seemed he too was being invaded – by the offices of the Ministry of Defence, over-anxious to prove that this was a *centrally* controlled 'battle', with the Service Ministries following the directions of a supreme command. One general became so irritated by the Defence Ministry's interruptions that he left his phone off the hook. For John Profumo, the political head of the army, sitting as he was in the middle of a tug-o'-war between the designs of his political superiors and the outraged generals, it was possibly the most trying moment of his career.

The eyes of Colonel George Wigg, M.P., suspecting that the operation was perhaps another Tory adventure with the army he was so attached to, and the more shrewd among the news-papers observers, were on every move Profumo and his fellow Ministers made. And soon the signs that the Kuwait operation was not the success it was being made out to be began to become apparent: men, unacclimatised to the tremendous heat of the Persian Gulf, were collapsing daily; machines were seizing up; the manœuvres had made holes in the Strategic Reserve which could prove disastrous if trouble was to break out elsewhere (and there were signs that Berlin was on the boil again).

Yet, on Saturday, July 8, the Minister of Defence, Mr Harold Watkinson, told his constituents at Woking in Surrey: 'I am happy to let this operation speak for itself as a model of the task which British forces are seeking to do in the modern world, to fulfil our obligations and keep the peace, and as a model of the way to go about it.'

The same day, the tired Profumo seized an invitation from

his old friend, Lord ('Bill') Astor, to come to Cliveden for the weekend and join a house-party. And in the warm evening 'Bill' took him to the swimming pool where a long-legged, pretty girl was bathing half-nude. The next day she was back there again, this time in the company of a Russian, Captain Eugene Ivanov, naval attaché at the Soviet Embassy in London.

After the weekend, there was a further week of intense strain for the War Minister. Criticisms of the Kuwait action were beginning to seep into print. The *Times*'s leader column had this to say: 'Using most of the resources of R.A.F. Transport Command and the commands overseas, and with several days' warning, it has taken a week to concentrate and deploy a reinforced brigade group. There are too obvious gaps in the composition and equipment of the force . . . nor is the air situation satisfactory . . . behind the force now deployed lies a tenuous reserve. . . .'

On Tuesday, the 11th, the same day as *The Times* leader, Mr Profumo had a public engagement, a reception at the Soviet Embassy for Russia's first Cosmonaut, Major Yuri Gagarin. The War Minister met for the second time his acquaintance of the weekend, Ivanov.

A few days later the Kuwait crisis began to subside. If the efficiency of the manœuvre could be questioned, its efficacy plainly could not. Kassem had been frightened away (if he ever intended to come) and not a shot had been fired in anger. On July 19 the withdrawal of troops began. The same day Mr Profumo announced a new bright idea to stimulate Army recruitment – bounties of £200 for regular soldiers who extended their service by three years and to National Service-men who signed on regular engagements, and better leave arrangements for men serving abroad. He told the House of Commons that he was confident that he would reach the Army's target of 165,000. Recruiting, he said, was already up 27 per cent on the previous year. His buoyancy did nothing to allay the watchfulness of the redoubtable Wigg. In fact, the Profumo system for improving the recruitment figures irritated him more than a little. Surely, he was getting his results by simply lowering the limits of physical fitness and intelligence for recruits?

Profumo's buoyancy was to be pricked a little a week later. For a political animal, the reply that he gave to a Parliamentary question from Mr Christopher Mayhew, the Labour M.P. for Woolwich, on July 26 was amazingly inept. Three men in Kuwait had lost their way and had been captured by Kassem's men. Mr Mayhew asked Mr Profumo what instructions were given men in their training for cases where, as often happened in desert conditions, a patrol lost its bearings. The War Minister's reply seemed bathetic: 'The instructions to all troops, but particularly to those on active service, whenever they get lost, especially near another country, *is to return to their unit.*' At this point, not surprisingly, laughter interrupted him. He went on: '. . . I am seeing whether the instructions need any alteration to prevent a repetition.'

A week later, Mr Wigg raised for the first time the question of the strategy behind Kuwait. Something needed explaining he said; the operation was not quite the success it had been made out to be. It was, he said bluntly, a wash-out. The Americans and the Russians knew it was a wash-out and Britain's prestige throughout the Middle East had fallen considerably. It was Mr James Ramsden, Mr Profumo's Parliamentary Under-Secretary, who replied. Mr Wigg's information, he said, was based on Press reports. *His* was based on military intelligence. He said that discharging such an important engagement as this in such good time and with such efficiency had given a tremendous fillip to Service morale; the same was true for Britain generally.

That was the last of Kuwait for the time being. Other crises diverted attention. But Mr Wigg, a little insulted by the reply, for his military sources were excellent, and still deeply disturbed by the whole affair, had not forgotten it.

Economically, July 1961 was the month in which the spree came to an end. It had started before the 1959 election, and reached its apogee towards the end of 1960. The label of the 'Affluent Society', exploited with that talent for contagion which only advertising men possess, had stuck – though it depended on which part of the country you lived in. The resentment which festered when the spree had to stop found expression in the Tory Party, combining two years later with the disastrous unemployment figures and the total failure to enter the Common Market into a swell of discontent.

Britain had emerged from a decade of austerity, and the material appetite was understandably insatiable. The yardstick by which necessity is judged has always to be modified: in 1961 Britain had entered the world in which the washing machine, refrigerator and motor-car could no longer sanely be seen as basically superfluous indulgences.

Between 1959 and 1961 the number of car licences had risen over five million for the first time: by the end of May 1961, there were 5,610,000, and it was calculated by somebody with a mind for a graphic statistic that if all the cars in Britain were placed on all the roads in Britain there would be only thirty-five yards between each of them. In the first quarter of 1961 consumer spending went up by 2 per cent. It continued to rise in April and May.

The state of mind was euphoric. This was not shared, however, by the men responsible for economic policy. The bounty had been accompanied by inflation.

The Chancellor of the Exchequer was Mr Selwyn Lloyd. He had succeeded Mr Heathcoat Amory, the provider of affluence, in July 1960. By July 1961, Mr Lloyd was wearing a censorious expression. The public had got wind of the changing mood. On Saturday, July 15, there was a rush to buy cars and other capital goods before the spree was halted. And on Tuesday, July 25, the sixth British economic crisis since the war was declared official: Mr Lloyd instituted what became known, in his own delicious phrase, as 'The Pause'.

With the economy patently sick, the Prime Minister was looking across the Channel to Europe. The Common Market was emerging as a formidable economic bloc: managing to combine galloping prosperity with stable policy and, more menacingly, intending to cut down its own internal tariff barriers and make trading tougher for those outside. Mr Macmillan had, in fact, already made up his mind to fly in the face of his party's Right Wing and make the historic decision to apply for membership of the Market. On Monday, July 31, he announced that Britain had decided to make a formal application to join.

This was a new conception of Britain's future rôle. Mr Macmillan believed in it with passion. His personal future as Prime Minister seemed to be pinned to it.

The same month that John Profumo was enmeshing himself in a dangerous triangle with Keeler and Ivanov, a naval clerk called John Vassall was working with some dedication in the Fleet Section of Military Branch 11, the secretariat of the Naval Staff in the Admiralty. The Navy was just recovering from one of its worst spy episodes: the Portland case. This involved the Portland Naval Base and the activities there of Henry Houghton and Winifred Gee, two Civil Servants. Houghton and Gee had sold nuclear submarine secrets to Gordon Lonsdale, a Soviet agent whose real, Russian, name was never disclosed. Together with a husband and wife team called the Krogers, they had been operating an extensive commerce in secrets, employing all the sophisticated apparatus of modern espionage, including microdot messages and a high-powered radio transmitter hidden in a suburban bungalow.

A committee under Sir Charles Romer investigated naval security after the Portland Case and recommended that it required an overall director. (Houghton had been reported twice as a security risk, but there had been no action.) On July 5, Lord Carrington, the First Lord of the Admiralty, announced that he was to appoint a Director of Security, 6ft. 7 in. Royal Marine, Colonel J. L. A. Macafee. There was a general feeling of satisfaction. Surely, after the appalling Lonsdale case, there might be an end to the series of security scandals that had plagued Britain since the war's end? Vassall, and the Profumo scare, were yet to come.

July 1961, was a traumatic month for the Press. On July 19, £100,000 damages were awarded against the *Daily Telegraph* in a libel action to Mr John Lewis and his company, Rubber Improvement Ltd., although a stay of execution was granted. The action was over an article in the *Telegraph* of December 23, 1958, headlined 'Inquiry on Firm by City Police'. Two days later £117,000 were awarded against the *Daily Mail* to Mr Lewis and his firm for a report in the *Mail* on the same day as the *Telegraph's* headlined 'Fraud Squad Probes Firm'.*

These awards marked a new severity in the handling of libel cases, a trend which had been worrying Fleet Street for some time. The libel laws in Britain are stiffer than in many other countries, particularly America. The balance between protecting individuals from unjust attack and providing society with an alert watchdog in its free Press is always difficult to strike, and attempts to reform the laws, which date from the eighteenth century, had succeeded in making only minor changes.

Many lawyers felt that with public opinion (perhaps under legitimate provocation) becoming hostile to the Press, juries were tending to be unrealistically severe in estimating libel damages. Certainly, even some of the judges were alarmed. This background substantially contributed to a new timidity in dealing with exposure stories: the newspapers resorted more and more to innuendo although several inquiries on which they had spent considerable money and energy were dropped altogether. Two years later the dangers both of tenuously-based innuendo, and intimidated and stifled exposure were to be well demonstrated.

* In April 1962 the Court of Appeal allowed appeals by both papers with costs and ordered a new trial. In May 1962 Rubber Improvement asked Lloyds Bank to appoint a receiver and in November 1962 the company announced it was winding up voluntarily. In March 1963 the Court of Appeal judgment was upheld, a new trial being ordered. Lord Devlin described the damages as ridiculously out of proportion.

5

The Affair

MR PROFUMO'S AFFAIR with Christine Keeler will not go down in history as one of the grand passions of the twentieth century. It was short, and its ending was as abrupt as that of the nearest parallel this century – the affair between Lord Curzon, Foreign Secretary after the First World War, and Elinor Glyn. The parallel is only approximate. In Profumo's case there was no hint of the romantic aura surrounding the liaison between a peer of the realm and a lady who was not averse to living out her own novels of high-class but torrid passions. There was no sinning with her on tiger skins in decadently luxurious hotels. The assignations were furtive, the spiritual possibilities limited, and when it was all over, the two went back to their fixed places in society apparently unmarked by either suffering or regret, and unaware that the affair itself would be a minor scene in a much bigger drama.

The setting for their first meeting was propitious. Adultery, according to Byron, is much more common where the climate is sultry. In Britain, the summer of 1961 had not begun very well. But by the second week in July there was a minor heat-wave. On Saturday, July 8, the temperature in London reached 70 degrees, and the atmosphere was close. Those who could were leaving the capital.

Miss Keeler was on her way to spend the day at Dr Ward's cottage on the Cliveden estate. Dr Ward had at this time known Lord Astor for about ten years, and had rented the cottage for a peppercorn rent of £1 a year. It was derelict when he took it over, and Dr Ward made many improvements. On her way out there, Miss Keeler called at a club and met a man who offered to drive her the thirty miles into Buckinghamshire. Taking the A4 past London Airport, they saw a girl at a bus-stop and invited her to join the party, which she did. The party at

Dr Ward's cottage that day comprised just Miss Keeler, the girl from the bus stop, the boy friend who drove them to Cliveden and Dr Ward.

While this little soirée was going on, a more formal week-end party had been assembling up at the Big House itself. Lord Astor was expecting, as his principal guest, Field Marshal Ayub Khan, the President of Pakistan, who had arrived in London for a three-day stop on his way to Washington. Mr Profumo, his wife, Lord and Lady Dalkeith and a number of Tory M.P.s were among the twenty or thirty guests.

To the house party, Cliveden afforded a welcome escape from a stifling London. From the outside a monstrous, neo-Renaissance pile (built in the 1850s), it afforded inside cool, echoing halls and dark corridors, full of heirlooms and armour. It is set in spacious, rolling grounds, and the atmosphere of leisured country relaxation is doubtless heightened at the weekends by the absence of trippers, who are only allowed into this property on Wednesdays and Thursdays during the summer.

The mere mention of Cliveden was still associated with the Cliveden set of the 'thirties, with the political establishment, moral rectitude, and the country's most powerful political figures gathered together each weekend to sort out the world. But this was only an interlude in Cliveden's history. Social lassitude seemed to be a more permanent feature, for Alexander Pope, in the third of his *Moral Essays* castigated the second Duke of Buckingham, the Restoration rake who squandered his fortune in a house on the same site:

'Gallant and gay, in Cliveden's proud alcove
The bower of wanton Shrewsbury and love.'

Mr Profumo himself must have been feeling in need of relaxation. It was the end of the first week of the Kuwait operation, and it had been a week of anxiety and hard work for the War Minister. In the relaxing atmosphere of Cliveden he could forget for a moment his worries over the effectiveness of the operation in the sweltering Persian Gulf.

After dinner the evening was still warm and sultry. Realising

48

that his hospitality might in this atmosphere prove enervating, Lord Astor took some of his guests, 'complete with tiaras and cigars', as a friend later put it, for a stroll down to the pool.

A short distance from Cliveden House itself, past the clock tower, were the stables surmounted by mews flats occupied by the Cliveden staff. Beyond the stables, and overlooked by the flats, was the swimming pool, walled so that, apart from the view from the servants' quarters, it had complete privacy.

That night Lord Astor's party opened the door to the pool and encountered Dr Ward's party, also enjoying the twilight. The temperature at that time was still about 60 degrees (it did not fall below that all night) and the Ward party, in high spirits, had walked up from his cottage, along a path parallel to the Thames, past the western side of the house, and into the pool for a cooling frolic.

Lord Astor has since said that he would never have allowed nude bathing in the pool, since it was overlooked by the servants' flats; and that spare swimsuits were provided in the changing rooms for people who happened to have come without them. But what happened next has become one of the most bizarre moments in recent political history. As Miss Keeler later described it in the *News of the World* she was naked in the pool, Dr Ward having thrown her costume into the bushes as a joke.

Dr Ward later gave a slightly different version. Nearly everyone was in the water, he said, except himself. The party had taken advantage of Lord Astor's provision of swimsuits, which, Dr Ward said, were brief. In any case, the net result was that Miss Keeler was wearing little else but a dripping towel when she was introduced to the dinner-jacketed Profumo. 'There were no introductions in the formal sort of way,' said Dr Ward in his account. He and Profumo were anyway already acquainted, as they first met in 1956. Mrs Profumo, reported Miss Keeler, 'was very charming, but seemed wary of me.' Lord Astor, however, appeared to feel no premonition that might justify wariness, and, according to Dr Ward, he invited the party at Ward's cottage to a swim on the following day.

It was likely that, give or take the odd sartorial detail at this first meeting, Christine Keeler would have made a distinct

49

impression. She was nineteen, obviously attractive, yet with the veneer of poise and sophistication that Dr Ward seemed able to produce in his protégées. Like other girls who benefited from his tuition, she could maintain her poise in almost any society. In addition, she had a naturally gay personality and a kind of coltish grace that she used to advantage. The slight awkwardness of gesture, the delicate joints and air of faint surprise would contrast with the more predictable attractions in dress and deportment of Lady Astor and Mrs Profumo in full evening finery.

This first meeting on Saturday evening was the prologue to the drama that followed. The first scene in the political upheaval that was to result from it came the next day. The man who drove Miss Keeler out to Cliveden on Sunday (she had returned to London late on Saturday) was Captain Ivanov.

On a day even warmer than the Saturday – it was 73 degrees – Ivanov met the War Minister for the first time. The swimming pool provided a suitably classless mingling of high political brass and nymphs of less exalted background. (President Ayub Khan's High Commissioner in London later informed the *News of the World* that the President had no recollection of meeting Miss Keeler at the swimming pool.) However hazy the recollections of those who were there, it seems that a swimming race was held, in which the condition was that none of the competitors should move his legs. Mr Profumo won – using his legs. And, according to Miss Keeler, told Ivanov: 'That will teach you to trust the British Government.'

Ward said later: 'To me there was a certain piquancy in introducing Capt. Ivanov, a Russian, into this scene and obviously the name Cliveden meant something to him. He had heard of the Cliveden Set, of course. And I could almost see his brain ticking over as he was introduced: What was Ayub Khan doing here with the War Minister?

'So I explained: nothing. There was no significance in the meeting, these were just the kind of guests you could expect to see house-partying at Cliveden any weekend.

'Ayub Khan took masses of pictures and Jack Profumo took

some – including one of me, Christine and two girls who had come with us.'

Miss Keeler later claimed that the man she was most interested in that day was Ivanov. They left the party early and went back to London. But before she left, Mr Profumo asked for her phone number. 'Talk with Stephen. He has my number,' she replied. It was his number too, since she was living in his flat.

It is not surprising that some of the people who were at Cliveden that weekend have difficulty in remembering the precise details of what happened. Apart from the understandable amnesia brought on by the affair's later notoriety, the two days at Cliveden would have seemed only a pleasant but unremarkable break from city life. Dr Ward went back to his practice, Miss Keeler went back to hers, and Mr Profumo returned to an arduous week of War Office duties. His next weekend was far less pleasant than his stay at Cliveden. He had an engagement at the Castlemartin Army Camp in Wales, where amid much publicity German Panzer troops were due to arrive for training. Arrangements had been made for him to sleep under canvas but the wind was gusty and he retreated to a more comfortable bed in an officer's hut.

Before Mr Profumo had time to develop his attachment to Miss Keeler, there were signs that the sudden fusion of various elements at Cliveden that weekend would in fact have disastrously fissile results for some of those present. On Wednesday, July 12, four days after the first meeting between the War Minister and the model, Dr Ward had a visit from Mr K. Woods of War Office Security. It was the second in five weeks. The first had been on June 8 – five months after Dr Ward had first met Ivanov at the Garrick Club lunch.

By June 8, the Security Services were obviously worried over the developing association between Dr Ward and the Russian. Many people in London have contact with men from the Russian Embassy, not necessarily always at arm's length. Ivanov would, of course, be regarded as a greater security risk than, say, one of the Russian journalists in London. Even so, very few people among the many who knew Ivanov in London were warned to be careful. By June 8 M.I.5 must have thought that the Ward-Ivanov link merited one of their rare personal interventions. The fact that the second discussion with Dr Ward on July 12, during which he was warned to be on his guard, came so quickly after the first, indicates the degree of concern caused by Ivanov's deliberate penetration into Society.

More important at this second meeting with M.I.5, in the light of what was to follow, was an apparently innocuous revelation casually thrown out by Dr Ward. Pursuing his usual habit of dropping the right names however wrong the circumstances, he let slip that he knew Mr Profumo. The War Minister was therefore part of the same social circle that included Ivanov. Until then the Security Services had no inkling of this fact.

While M.I.5 went away to ruminate over the implications of this startling juxtaposition, Mr Profumo was pursuing another relationship of which the Security Services were equally ignorant. His affair with Christine Keeler was constricted and clandestine, relieved by a certain virile flamboyance on his part, and on hers by an appealing madcap quality. There was a modern and altogether unromantic utility about their meetings. They had to take place in odd corners of London because Mr Profumo was anxious to see as little as possible of Dr Ward.

While this was going on during July, the security mills were grinding away slowly and surely at the grains of information dropped by Dr Ward. They were not, however, grinding particularly small; for when the secretary to the Cabinet, Sir Norman Brook (now Lord Normanbrook) called to see Mr Profumo on August 9, he did not ask about the War Minister's potentially dangerous affair. The head of the Security Services had told the Cabinet office about Mr Profumo's acquaintance with Ward and Ivanov and it was only about this that Sir Norman had been delegated to warn the Minister.

It is important to realise that at this stage, although M.I.5 had been so apprehensive about the possible dangers of Dr Ward associating with Ivanov, and had been even more concerned when they discovered (by chance) the War Minister's place in this orbit, they had nonetheless failed to come across

Miss Keeler. Even Miss Keeler's existence was apparently unknown to them, and therefore to Sir Norman Brook. From the form of the warning it would not have escaped Mr Profumo that the affair had apparently gone undetected.

There is some confusion about the way in which the affair ended. On the day he had been warned by Sir Norman Brook – only thirty-two days after his first meeting with Christine Keeler – Mr Profumo wrote to her. The letter was to crop up again and again as the scandal snowballed, and ended up gleefully reproduced on the front page of the *Sunday Mirror*.

'Darling,

In great haste and because I can get no reply from your phone –

Alas something's blown up tomorrow night and I can't therefore make it. I'm terribly sorry especially as I leave the next day for various trips and then a holiday so won't be able to see you again until some time in September. Blast it. Please take great care of yourself and don't run away.

Love, J.

P.S. I'm writing this 'cos I know you're off for the day tomorrow and I want you to know before you go if I still can't reach you by phone.'

It has been assumed from Miss Keeler's memoirs in the *News of the World* that the affair ended that night with her refusal of Mr Profumo's demand that she should stop living at Wimpole Mews with Dr Ward. In fact she gave no date for this conversation and the War Minister at this stage need not have felt unduly alarmed about the affair. The Government knew about Dr Ward and Ivanov but not, apparently, about Miss Keeler. Mr Profumo, according to Miss Keeler, objected to Ward's hold over her. For a time, at the end of 1961, she took a flat in Dolphin Square.

The exact chronology of the affair is difficult to establish from the naturally scanty evidence of those involved. It is certain, however, that by the end of 1961, the affair was dead, if not safely buried. Miss Keeler returned to Wimpole Mews and Mr Profumo was unable to compete with Dr Ward's emotional hold over the girl. As Miss Keeler described it, in words more direct than poignant: 'We were getting towards the end of the affair . . . He wanted me to leave the flat but I didn't go. Stephen was so close to me. Jack said he wouldn't see me if I didn't leave. I told him he must make the choice. I never met him again. . . .'

In this undramatic way, the affair fizzled out. The War Minister carried on with his recruiting campaign, confident that there was now no danger of the liaison leaking out (M.I.5 still did not know of it) and Miss Keeler went back to her spiritual home in Marylebone, from which she made occasional forays. One of them, unfortunately for all concerned, was to live in Brentford, Middlesex, with a West Indian called John Edgecombe.

While Miss Keeler was alternating between her twin activities of improving race relations in Brentford and keeping up morale in the frenetic atmosphere of Marylebone, Mr Profumo was leading an evenly-paced life at the War Office in 1962. Only one incident occurred that could have made Mr Profumo ponder on the ease with which the sleeping beast of British Puritanism could be awakened when stung by any suspicion of moral laxity in others.

In June 1962, there was trouble with the British Army of the Rhine. Some soldiers, particularly in Scottish units, ran wild in the garrison town of Minden. There were reports that the morale in Germany was low, and that relations between the British troops and the German population had seriously deteriorated.

There were several explanations of this: National Servicemen had had their period of conscription extended by six months because of the Berlin crisis in the previous autumn. They were now impatient to get home. Housing conditions for married men were poor, and there was resentment among newcomers who discovered local Germans to be much more affluent than themselves.

After taking a short holiday in Switzerland – the accounts of the trouble were exaggerated, Mr Profumo said – he came up with an alternative solution to the midnight curfew that had been imposed at the end of June on all bachelor soldiers in B.A.O.R. Why not, he suggested, send out more Army girls to Germany? He was immediately accused by the Opposition

54

of producing an immoral solution to the morale problem. Mr Emrys Hughes, ready as always to point out the straight and narrow path to erring wayfarers, said in the House of Commons that the idea was 'disgusting and abominable.'

Replying to the attack a few days later, Mr Profumo reaffirmed his belief in the gentling effects of female company. 'The rôle of the W.R.A.C. in B.A.O.R., as elsewhere, is to carry out responsible military tasks and thereby release soldiers for service with fighting units. At the same time our troops in Germany undoubtedly benefit from their companionship.'

Not quite the whole of Britain was shocked by the War Minister's pioneering idea. Miss Elizabeth Macfie, a former W.R.A.C. colonel, wrote to *The Times* to say she saw no reason why the life of men in Germany should be monastic. Anyway, she said, 'the benefit would be mutual as the character of young women is not usually improved when they are so thin on the ground as to be lords of all they survey'. The Minden disturbance eventually faded out, but the heat of moral rectitude had given Mr Profumo some foretaste of what was to come.

Much more disturbing, though it passed almost unnoticed at the time, was a comment published at the end of July, when Mr Profumo could well have been congratulating himself on the secrecy apparently maintained about his affair with Miss Keeler. Robin Douglas-Home, like other well-connected contributors to the glossy magazines, had his ear firmly and accurately to the ground. The July 31 issue of *Queen* carried an article by him under the heading, 'Sentences I'd like to hear the end of . . .' The fifth of Mr Douglas-Home's intriguing collection of unfinished sentences must have puzzled many readers. It read: ' . . . called in M.I.5 because every time the chauffeur-driven Zis drew up at her *front* door, out of the *back* door into a chauffeur-driven Humber slipped . . .'

This was the first allusion in print to a scandal that did not reach the stage even of limited rumour except in a small circle of London Society, until some months later. There was as yet no end to Mr Douglas-Home's sentence: but if Mr Profumo saw it, his complacency must have been shaken.

6

Diplomatic Pimping

IN THE YEAR following the start of the Profumo-Keeler affair, Stephen Ward's Walter Mitty yearnings had branched out in another direction. The brief brushes he had with the Security Services in 1961 became exaggerated in his mind and embellished in his conversation. As well as the compulsive name-dropping which peppered his coffee-bar chat, he would often make oblique references to himself as a confidant of the Security Services. He even told one close acquaintance – who had known him long enough to be highly sceptical of such claims – that he 'often advised the Foreign Office on security matters'. Ward had begun to see himself not only as a manipulator of people and social situations, but of the affairs of state.

The culmination of Ward's new rôle came during the Cuba crisis. On Monday, October 22, 1962, President Kennedy made his broadcast announcing that Russian missiles had been discovered in Cuba, and that as the first stage of retaliation the U.S. Navy was to blockade Cuba. The broadcast began at 7 p.m. Washington time. In London it was midnight. This left the British newspapers with little time for calm judgments. And the general reaction was far from calm.

Certainly, in the immediate shock, many people in Britain were prepared to believe the worst of America. There was no knowing how Kennedy himself could cope with a crisis which had brought the world to the threshold of nuclear war. There was a tendency to think that he had over-rated the Cuba threat. Some people in Britain feared that the American military-industrial tiger had got out of hand and that Kennedy could not prevent the lust for all-out war.

In this situation, the Russians sensed the hesitation in the British attitude to the crisis. On Tuesday, the Soviet Government made a statement obviously designed to exploit these doubts. It said, among other things: 'The Soviet Union calls upon all governments and peoples to raise their voice in protest against the aggressive actions of the United States with regard to Cuba, resolutely to denounce these actions and to raise an obstacle to the United States Government unleashing thermonuclear war.' This was backed up the following day by the Soviet Chargé d'Affaires, Mr V. A. Loginov, who called on Lord Home, the Foreign Secretary, to express the hope that the British Government would do all in its powers to stop the Cuba situation developing into nuclear war – apparently with the aim of persuading Britain to bring pressure to bear on the United States.

Simultaneously, other Russian Embassy officials in London began working to the same ends by more devious and subtle means. Ivanov appears to have been briefed to work through unofficial channels and sow the seeds of an idea by which, it was said, the British Government could 'solve' the Cuba crisis to the satisfaction of all sides. The exact authority given to Ivanov was, of course, unknown. He claimed to the various people he spoke to that he was acting directly on orders from Moscow; that he could vouch for Mr Khrushchev's action if the idea was accepted; and that any communication passed to him would be on Mr Khrushchev's desk within 20 minutes. Was it likely that such powers could have been entrusted to a relatively junior diplomat? *Tass*, the Soviet news agency, afterwards issued a denial that Ivanov had any secret mission at all over Cuba. But it was quite possible: for no other Soviet diplomat had both Ivanov's sophisticated command of the English language and his social entrées into the Tory establishment.

The first thing Ivanov did was to enlist the help of his friend Ward. They talked together over lunch on Wednesday. Ivanov's line was this: the Americans had created a situation in which America and Russia were on a collision course, and there was no room for either side to find a compromise without intolerable loss of face. The peace-loving Soviet Government were in a dilemma; naturally they did not want war, but they needed an excuse to allow them to save their pride if they backed out of the situation. Only Britain could provide this –

by appealing to both sides to attend an emergency Summit Conference in London. Ivanov said that if this were done he could give an undertaking that Khrushchev would immediately accept the invitation and would take steps to relieve the tension. Ships taking arms to Cuba would be turned back and the removal of the rocket bases would be discussed. Thus honour on both sides would be satisfied.

Ivanov backed up the proposal with persuasive arguments. There would, he said, be plenty of credit in it for Britain – it would be recognised as a vital contribution to world peace. Also it would show that Britain was not merely a pawn of Washington, but an independent power capable of taking balancing action in future crises. Britain might again find herself in the position of mediator when the boot was on the other foot – when Russia took action over Berlin. It wouldn't be long before the heat was really on there – would Britain then be in a position to act as peacemaker?

Ward was excited by Ivanov's arguments, and probably even contributed to them. He agreed to help Ivanov pass on his thoughts informally to influential circles.

Lord Home afterwards described Ivanov's proposals as 'classic Soviet manœuvres' at subversion. He wrote (a fortnight later): 'I think the Soviet intention was twofold. First it was to drive a wedge between ourselves and our American allies. Second, it was to test our resolve and to lay a bait to our vanity.' There is little doubt that this was Lord Home's opinion throughout the Cuba crisis – certainly he does not seem to have taken Ivanov's overtures very seriously. But in the doubts, hysteria and British feelings of impotence that hung over the Cuba week, it is not surprising that some people, without the benefit of hindsight, thought the idea at least merited attention. An intervention from Britain was after all being quite respectably canvassed in the Press and some Parliamentary circles.

As for Ward, he had no doubts at all. Apart from his pinkish sympathies, he was flattered at having the rôle of international mediator. He would be the man who had enabled the Cuba crisis to be solved. *That* would impress them in Marylebone High Street. The next few days' events revealed much about the personalities and motivations of Ivanov and Ward.

Within a few minutes of the end of his conversation with Ivanov, Ward was on the telephone to the Foreign Office. He does not seem to have been very successful in getting through to its inner sanctums – he spoke to the Resident Clerk. Nevertheless, he outlined what had emerged from his discussion with Ivanov, and was told that the information would be passed on to Sir Harold Caccia, the Permanent Under-Secretary of State.

Not very satisfied with this, Ward began to scatter the seeds of the idea elsewhere. One of his recent patients had been Sir Godfrey Nicholson, M.P., a long-serving Tory baronet. Sir Godfrey, head of a distillery company, was not very high in the Tory hierarchy – he had been a back-bench M.P., with one short break, for more than thirty years without ever having held a ministerial post. But he had been in Parliament long enough to know his way around, and Ward asked if he could help. Sir Godfrey agreed to talk to Ivanov, who went to see him that same (Wednesday) evening. Ivanov explained his 'solution', and asked for some indication that the British Government were working towards negotiations. Within twenty-four hours a report of the conversation had reached Sir Hugh Stephenson, Deputy Under-Secretary at the Foreign Office, who was an old boy of the same school (Winchester) and the same Oxford college (Christ Church) as Sir Godfrey.

At lunch the following day (Thursday) Ward encountered Mr William Shepherd, M.P., another long-serving Tory backbencher, though not yet a baronet, in circumstances that reveal not only the enthusiasm he was devoting to his rôle of mediator, but also his remarkable facility for picking up acquaintances. Mr Shepherd was lunching with a party of doctors at the Kenya Coffee House in Marylebone High Street. (He was interested in medical matters and frequently lunched with doctor friends in the Harley Street/Wimpole Street area.)

On this occasion, the conversation not surprisingly turned from medicine to Cuba. As it happened, two or three of the doctors were Hungarians – refugees from the uprising – and were therefore extremely hostile to the Russian point of view. Suddenly, halfway through the conversation, a man at the neighbouring table turned round and, without invitation, joined in the discussion. It was Dr Ward. He was putting a mildly pro-Russian point of view, and this tended to rile the Hungarians. The conversation became somewhat heated, and Mr Shepherd tried to smooth things over. Ward may have misinterpreted this as a sign of sympathy.

So far as Mr Shepherd could find, none of the doctors was acquainted with Ward, and at no time did he tell him that he was an M.P. Of course, it is quite possible that Ward, an habitué of several of the cafés and restaurants where Mr Shepherd held his luncheon parties, did in fact know who he was, though he never revealed this. Or he may simply have noticed that Shepherd was talking from a standpoint of greater political knowledge than the ordinary man-in-the-street, and simply assumed that he was important. Whatever the reason, when Mr Shepherd left the restaurant he found Ward waiting on the pavement outside, anxious to continue the discussion.

'By this time,' recalled Mr Shepherd afterwards, 'I had taken a strong dislike to him. I found his voice rather irritating. It had phoney, almost homosexual intonation. His whole manner was one to arouse suspicion. But I had become curious. I wanted to find out more.' Mr Shepherd's curiosity – and suspicion – were further aroused by Ward's name-dropping. He mentioned discussions at Cliveden and casually referred to a senior Cabinet Minister. He then asked if Mr Shepherd would like to meet his friend, a Russian attaché, to talk further about Cuba. Shepherd agreed and they exchanged telephone numbers. Next day they arranged, over the telephone, to meet early the following week. It was the classic Ward technique for making acquaintanceships – to arouse interest and curiosity.

Meanwhile, Ward had been hard at work finding other receptive ears for Ivanov. There is no evidence that he contacted Mr Profumo at this time. But he got in touch with Lord Astor and told him that Ivanov was urgently seeking to pass information to the British Government. Could he do anything to help? The solution Lord Astor came up with was, on the face of it, rather surprising.

Arthur Strange Kattendyke David Archibald Gore, the 8th

Earl of Arran, is one of the less conventional peers of the realm. He is known to his many friends as 'Boofy' Gore; to others as 'Goofy Bore'. His contributions to Parliamentary debates, though excellent in effect, have sometimes been rather startling in content. There was, for example, the occasion when he informed the House of Lords during a debate on drunken driving that he had been conducting experiments on himself, deliberately imbibing too much so that his reactions could be tested (this earned him yet another title, 'The Plastered Peer'). And there was the debate when he recounted his own personal investigations into prostitution, in which he had verified the statistic that one of every 544 British women is a whore. He was best known for the zany weekly column he wrote in Britain's largest evening newspaper, the London *Evening News*, the subject matter of which roamed from upper-class sex ('horses lead to divorces') to sly comments about heads of state, which once necessitated an official diplomatic apology to President Kennedy.

But Lord Astor's suggestion to Boofy on the Thursday evening of Cuba week that he should meet Ivanov was perhaps not so eccentric as it seems. A fair proportion of the upper reaches of the Foreign Office had either been contemporaries of Boofy's at Eton or were members of the endless ramifications of his family – among them his first-cousin-once-removed, Sir David Ormsby-Gore, the British Ambassador to America. He had easy access to Lord Home, the Foreign Secretary – they address each other in letters as 'Dear Alec' and 'My dear Boofy'. He was hardly the kind of person to be overawed by dealing with diplomatic attachés – after all, early in his career Boofy had twice been an attaché himself, at the British Legation in Berne and the Embassy in Lisbon, though each appointment had ended rather abruptly. Most important of all he was the sort of person who could be asked to do this kind of thing without embarrassment, and whose motives would be beyond question. Boofy, of course, accepted Lord Astor's suggestion with delight. Ward telephoned him the next day to fix a meeting and was invited to bring Ivanov round to his home in Hertfordshire for a Saturday morning drink.

The Cuba situation had by now become critical. On an

official level, the Russians were trying other face-saving compromises – on Friday they said they would withdraw rockets from Cuba if the West withdrew theirs from Turkey. Meanwhile, Ward, nothing if not persistent, was further extending his unofficial diplomacy. He decided to try another direct approach to the Foreign Office; this time he had an interview with Sir Harold Caccia's private secretary. Ward represented himself as an intermediary between the Russian and British Governments, and kept a note of the precise time he had put forward the Russian 'offer' – 4.30 p.m. on Friday, October 27.

On Saturday there was a strong smell of hydrogen in the air. It was clear that Kennedy was not prepared to accept any deal over the Turkish rockets, and the world seemed on the brink of war. That morning, Lord Home again met the Soviet Chargé d'Affaires, Mr Loginov. Ivanov afterwards said that Loginov had thought Lord Home's reason for summoning him to the Foreign Office was because the back-stairs diplomacy had borne fruit – he fully expected to be told that Britain was prepared to make a deadlock-breaking gesture. He was thrown completely off-balance to find Lord Home stern and intractable, demanding that the Russian rocket bases be removed and making it quite clear that Britain would stand by the Anglo-American Alliance.

At precisely the same time as this stiff interchange was taking place, a somewhat more convivial gathering was discussing the topic of the day at Boofy's home in Hemel Hempstead, Hertfordshire. Ward and Ivanov had turned up there promptly at 11.30 a.m. to find that in deference to his Russian guest, Boofy had got in a bottle of vodka. By the time their business was completed, an hour and three quarters later, the bottle was empty. The Earl, it will be remembered from the drunken driving debate, is something of an expert on liquor capacities, so it was high praise that in the memorandum he subsequently sent to Lord Home, he thought Ivanov's vodka consumption worth recording. Ivanov had drunk at least half the bottle himself, 'while remaining reasonably sober.'

It is clear that Ivanov went out of his way to ingratiate himself with his host. 'Ivanov is a pleasant fellow who gives the impression that he must have been at the Leningrad Charm

School,' the Earl said in his memorandum. Nevertheless, he was a little puzzled why he, a backwoods peer, should have been asked to transmit an apparently important diplomatic message. He believed it was because of Russian ignorance of who and what counts in Britain, comparable only to that of the Nazis and Ribbentrop. 'Throughout our conversation,' he wrote, 'Ivanov kept stressing the major rôle still played by the British aristocracy. To him, the mere fact of being a lord meant that one was in a position to influence events.'

As it happens, Ivanov was perhaps not so very far wrong. Within a few hours, the Earl of Arran's report of the Russian proposition was lying on the desks of the Prime Minister and of a senior Foreign Office official. Dr Ward had opened up the channel to the top.

The world went to bed that night wondering if it would ever wake up. A few hours later, on the Sunday, to the amazement of most people and the extreme annoyance of Captain Ivanov, Khrushchev capitulated. The Cuba crisis was over.

Ivanov, Ward and Boofy had planned to continue their conversation on Sunday evening. Along with about a dozen other people, including the Labour politician Lord Longford, they had been invited to dine with Lord Astor at Cliveden. The conversation became an inquest.

Some of Ivanov's charm seemed to have been worn off by the day's events. 'It was a very chagrined comrade who met us that evening,' the Earl of Arran wrote. 'He kept on saying he couldn't believe it and that he was sure Mr Khrushchev had some counter-demand to make on the Americans. We all felt embarrassed by the man's humiliation.'

Ivanov was still in an angry mood a couple of days later when the meeting with Mr Shepherd, planned the previous week, eventually took place. Mr Shepherd went to Dr Ward's Wimpole Mews flat, where, in addition to Ward and Ivanov, were Christine Keeler and Mandy Rice-Davies. (This meeting later led to a misunderstanding in the House of Commons. In the debate on the Profumo affair of June 17, 1963, Mr Shepherd made an intervention in which he said, '. . . at the end of October I saw all the parties in this case at the flat of Dr Ward, and Miss Keeler was certainly there at the time. . . .' It was generally taken that 'all the parties in this case' meant that Mr Profumo had been there too. Mr Shepherd did not realise this implication until later).

The conversation began curiously. Ivanov asked Shepherd if he was connected with politics. Shepherd, still suspicious about the set-up, and not wishing to reveal his identity, replied 'No.' 'Well then,' said Ivanov, 'we can talk freely.' In fact he talked very freely. He angrily blamed his own Government for the betrayal of Cuba. 'His attitudes,' Shepherd recalls, 'were those of a big-fist Stalinist. When I mentioned the merits of a free society, he got wilder and wilder. He seemed to want to turn the conversation into a shouting match. I didn't want to get involved so I shut up; then he angrily accused me of behaving in a superior manner. I found it surprising that anyone in diplomatic circles should talk as he did.' The two girls joined in the conversation only occasionally, usually in support of Ivanov. When Mr Shepherd left Ward apologised to him for Ivanov's behaviour.

Nothing Mr Shepherd had seen had allayed his suspicions. He began to make inquiries about Ward. And he went to see the girls' former club employer, Mr Murray. A few days later he made a report – verbally – to an acquaintance in the Security Services about the Ward-Ivanov set-up. Nothing seemed to be done about the report at the time, though it is possible it contained nothing that the Security Services did not by then know. (Later, after Mr Profumo's notorious statement to the Commons, Mr Shepherd again passed on his information to Security.)

Ward's actions during Cuba and other curiosities of his behaviour led many people – Mr Shepherd among them – to the conclusion that Ward must have been a Russian agent. There were several bits of information that appeared to support this. For example, Ward seldom seemed to carry a personal cheque book; it might be convenient for a spy not to create any evidence of payments. Later there were also allegations, stemming from Miss Keeler, that Ward had asked her to question Mr Profumo during the time of Cuba about shipments of nuclear warheads to Germany (this will be discussed in Chapter 12). Many incidents of Ward's life, it seemed, could

64

be interpreted in the light of his being a Russian agent, working not primarily on the acquisition of information, but on subversion.

However, the general consensus of opinion among the M.P.s and journalists who subsequently investigated the case (and presumably the Police too, since they did not find evidence to prosecute on any secrets charges) rejected this explanation. As Mr Harold Wilson summed up in the Commons debate of June 17: 'I do not myself think Ward to be a spy. He was too unstable . . .'

Certainly, Ward was not a Russian agent in any formal sense, though he may have been used as a tool by the Russians. His actions over Cuba may now seem strange, but they must have seemed less so at the time when the crisis was at its height, and Britain was waiting impotently to be blown to bits. There was a difference only in degree between the action he took and the actions of the unquestionably honourable men who helped Ward pass on Ivanov's information. Ward, not unintelligent about politics, realised at the time that his activities *could* be intrepreted as an attempt to split the Anglo–American Alliance. He said so at the time in a letter he wrote to a senior Parliamentary figure. But he dismissed it as preposterous that a British intervention could have had this effect.

There are strong indications that Ward, throughout, was acting in good faith, so far as he was able. Even if he had not been, his motives hardly seem to have been those of a professional spy. Given his psychological make-up, he would probably have accepted Ivanov's commission in any case – for quite extraneous reasons.

Perhaps the most revealing and ingenuous comment he made during his excursion into diplomacy was to Mr Shepherd. Ward told him: 'I am just an honest broker. I simply want to see countries brought together.' His attitude seemed precisely analagous to his more orthodox pimping. Whether countries or girls all he wanted to do was to make introductions; that way he could exercise power and gratify his yearning for importance and influence, yet remain basically disinterested. In neither case was he primarily motivated by money or ideology. And although he skated near the borderline of both the vice and the security laws (indeed so far as vice was concerned, the Old Bailey jury decided he had crossed the border) he was not of the stuff that a normal ponce or spy is made of.

When Cuba was all over, Ward could not, of course, keep quiet about the part he had played. He felt the need to tell people about it, and on November 1 he wrote, on a rather slender pretext, to Mr Harold Wilson (the mere fact of writing the letter at all would have been a strange action if Ward had been in the employment of the Russians). The letter, scrawled out on his consulting-room notepaper – Ward never used a typewriter – was mainly a political analysis of the Cuba and post-Cuba situation. It showed him capable of discussing politics at a reasonably sophisticated level, able to argue the kind of ideas that might be found in a *New Statesman* leader. In the part of the letter describing approaches from the Russian Government, he used the phrase, 'I was the intermediary . . .'

Mr Wilson sent a routine reply, filed the letter away and forgot about it. He was later to rediscover it and use the fact that Ward was a 'self-confessed Russian intermediary' with devastating effect in showing to the Commons that although Ward may not have been a spy he was nevertheless a substantial security risk.

But, when it came to exposing security risks, the Labour Party already had another formidable champion. Enter the intrepid Colonel Wigg. . . .

7

Mr Wigg Out-manœuvred

COLONEL GEORGE EDWARD CECIL WIGG has large, alert ears, melancholy eyes with heavy but mobile lids and a prominent nose. The whole demeanour is watchful. He has considerable nervous energy, which for years has been dedicated primarily to a passion which has consumed his waking life: to stop people playing politics with the Army. Few men at Westminster know and understand the Army as intimately as he. He joined the Tanks Corps in 1919 when he was eighteen, stayed in the Army until 1937, and in the Second World War went back, and ended up in 1946 with a senior Staff appointment. In the post-war Labour Government he was Parliamentary Private Secretary to Mr Emanuel Shinwell, who was then the Secretary of State for War. At that time Field Marshal Montgomery was Chief of the Imperial General Staff. Nobody would deliberately have thrown these three men together: the flamboyant and puckish Shinwell, his loyal and dogged aide, and the inflammable and opinionated maestro of the desert campaign. In fact, it turned out to be a potent and coherent combination. Wigg came to revere Shinwell, and rates him one of the fundamental influences on his life. He was also impressed by the Montgomery dynamic, and the Field-Marshal's classic epigram hangs above his desk, to stir if energy flags: 'We do the impossible immediately – the miraculous takes a little longer.'

Every War Minister since Shinwell – John Strachey, Anthony Head, John Hare, Christopher Soames and John Profumo – has had George Wigg's unflickering gaze upon his every action. To some people, this eternal vigilance seemed to be an obsession pursued to the point of crankiness. They underrated the depth of his feeling for the Army, and his grasp of both the military and the political mind, and particularly the constant failures of the one to understand the other.

His zeal disturbed members of his own party as well as the Conservatives. The Labour Party had embraced the nettle of war with some embarrassment. Their abhorrence of it was always much nearer to the surface than with the Conservatives. The idealistic and pacifist section of the Party were unhappy handling the machine of war. Wigg shared in their ultimate hope, but was in no mood to duck the current realities. If it was necessary to maintain the machine, he saw no reason why it should not be as competently managed as possible.

Wigg became alarmed by reports that started to reach him in July 1961 about the Kuwait operation. It was not, however, until July 1962 that he began to receive substantial evidence that reinforced what he had said a year earlier – that the operation had been a wash-out.

It was this operation that first brought Wigg into conflict with John Profumo. Until this time he had rather liked the enthusiastic War Minister, though he felt that his interest in the Army was not as deep-rooted as his own. The result of his investigation into the Kuwait operation was to change his opinion of Profumo. For he believed he was double-crossed by him in a most humiliating way, and he resolved never again to have any dealings with the man. Had the clash between them never happened, the course of the scandal in 1963 might have been less disastrous for the War Minister and taken a different direction altogether. This is how Profumo out-manœuvred Wigg.

In July 1962 a document which became known as the Adam Report was circulating in the Army. It was prepared by Lieut.-Col. J. M. Adam of the Royal Army Medical Corps, and it concerned primarily the medical case history of the operation, although it had great bearing on wider issues.

The main points of the report were that if Kuwait had involved any fighting there would have been heavy casualties from heat exhaustion among the British troops, especially those flown direct from the reserve in the United Kingdom. In the units from England as many as 10 per cent were out of action

68

with heat disorders in the first five days, although they were not engaged in active operations.

To establish the validity of these findings further experiments had been carried out which dramatically proved that without a full programme of acclimatisation, lasting at least a week, troops flown directly to a climate like Kuwait's from England were dangerously vulnerable to heat exhaustion.

There had been inadequate training in heat discipline: many officers had mistakenly restricted the water supplies at Kuwait when it was necessary to drink even beyond the demands of thirst. Much of the clothing and personal equipment had been unsuitable.

That summer, the Recess was hectic for George Wigg. Through his contacts in the Army, he pieced together various extracts of the Adam Report, and added them to what he already knew about the Kuwait operation. He was building up a formidable case.

At the beginning of September there were reports in the *Liverpool Daily Post*, the *Sunday Express* and the *Daily Express* that Mr Wigg had been investigating the Kuwait operation, and had documented evidence of heat exhaustion among the men and mechanical failure in machines. Wigg was worried because the stories appeared to have been planted by him. In fact, somebody who knew about his inquiries had talked to journalists. It distressed him because the reports were inaccurate and his work was not then complete. On September 4 he went to the War Office to see Mr Profumo's Under-Secretary, Mr Ramsden, to discuss his findings and to stress that he had not been responsible for the reports.

Profumo was apparently concerned, at that moment, by the way in which the Ministry of Defence's interference had affected the operation. He told Wigg that he was also anxious that the facts should be straightened out. And he suggested they should work together to ventilate the failings of Kuwait in the House. Wigg readily agreed to the plan. It was arranged that Wigg should raise questions on Kuwait in a general debate on the Army and the R.A.F., which was scheduled for November 23. Wigg's questions were checked with Ramsden so that answers could be prepared that would help to clear up the whole thing. The night before the debate Profumo phoned Wigg at his flat in Victoria to make sure that everything was organised. The watchdog Colonel was happy: he felt that, at last, something constructive could come out of the affair.

It had been arranged on Mr Profumo's suggestion that Mr Wigg should speak first in the debate. A procedural consequence of this was that he was unable to speak again . . . whatever followed. Wigg rose on November 23 as planned and called for an inquiry into the operation. He criticised, among other things, the shortage of basic supplies and said that parched troops had been drinking water from the radiators of vehicles – contaminated by rust and containing, paradoxically in view of the climate, anti-freeze.

Not Mr Profumo, but the Air Minister, Mr Hugh Fraser, was the first to answer Mr Wigg's charges. He said the faults had been grossly exaggerated. Where there had been errors, things had been put right.

Then Mr Profumo rose. It was soon plain to Mr Wigg that the Minister had discarded the agreed plan for the debate. He admitted that the operation had not been perfect. But he said that since Kuwait the purpose of the Government's studies had been to learn the lessons and profit by them. Action had been taken to provide a special diet more suitable for a hot climate. 'The surprise was not that anything went wrong, but that such a large proportion of the planning went as it was intended to.'

The Adam Report was not disclosed. Instead, Mr Profumo said that he had seen letters from two officers, one of whom commanded a unit engaged in the operation, which said that heat casualties had been negligible. Both letters criticised George Wigg for the things he was supposed to have said, but didn't, in the newspaper articles. Wigg, unable, because of procedure, to make a second speech, could not answer back. He had been out-manœuvred. And he was furious.

Three days later, Wigg won a small concession from the Minister – he forced him to publish the letters as a White Paper. But in a lofty written reply to Wigg, Profumo added insult to injury: 'I have now laid these two letters before the

House. I certainly accept the hon. Member's [Wigg's] assurance that the newspaper articles which gave rise to them were not published with his authority. I am satisfied that, as a result of last Friday's debate, the questions raised about the Kuwait operation have been put in their proper perspective and that no further action in this respect is required.'

'Not published with his authority' could be interpreted as an innuendo that the accounts had nevertheless come from Wigg. This added heat to Wigg's intense sense of frustration at the outcome of his efforts to get the deficiencies of the Kuwait operation out into the open. He felt, he said later, 'trussed up and done'. His guns were spiked for further Parliamentary action on Kuwait.

But the double-cross, if such it was, was to rebound on Profumo. Wigg is essentially an honourable man and his natural reaction on hearing of any personal scandal involving one of his Parliamentary colleagues would be to take it to him and, if necessary, tell him what he intended to do about it. When the name of John Hare, the Minister of Labour, cropped up in Wigg's inquiries into the Profumo affair, he made sure the Minister was warned of the gossip and accepted his denial without question. But when Wigg had information that seemed to prove John Profumo's liaison with Keeler and its dangers to security, he broke his rule; he took the counsel of friends who said: 'Don't go to him. He has cheated you once. He may do it again.'

The story moves into late 1962 and, for George Wigg, there was no rest. Two other matters concerned him at that time; one of them was public knowledge and the other one a disturbingly private affair. On October 22 William Vassall had been sentenced to eighteen years' imprisonment at the Old Bailey for spying for the Russians. But the affair by no means ended with the sentence. Certain aspects of the case which had come out during the trial seemed to have deep implications for various Ministers. From the end of October and through the first half of November, the Vassall affair slowly turned from being a sordid spy case into a feud between the Administration and the Press. That was the public issue that occupied

71

Wigg; it seemed entirely separate from the private information that reached him in November, yet the two were to become bound together in a way that made the feud even fiercer.

Vassall, a homosexual, had been compromised by the Russians while he was serving at the British Embassy in Moscow. After Vassall left Moscow the Russians blackmailed him into spying for them. He was working at the Admiralty as clerk to Mr Thomas Galbraith, the Civil Lord. Vassall's trial disclosed that for some time he had been living ostentatiously in an expensive flat well above his income, on the proceeds of his espionage – but this had not made anybody suspicious. The Admiralty, which had had its share of spy incidents, was castigated by the newspapers. The Security Services were also attacked. But soon after the end of the trial, criticism became focused on one man: Mr Galbraith.

What became a witch-hunt began with an article in the *Sunday Express* on October 28, the Sunday of Kennedy's triumph over Cuba. This article devoted most of its attack to the relationship between Mr Galbraith and Vassall, and implied that the Civil Lord had been altogether too familiar with his junior. The following weekend, the *Sunday Pictorial* serialised Vassall's own story, for which they paid about £7,000. ('Even at modern rates of exchange,' commented the *Sunday Telegraph*, 'he will have done better than Judas.') The *Pictorial* had letters, and a postcard, which, it said, 'appear to give a clear picture of the friendly relations between an Admiralty junior clerk and some high officials for whom he worked.' And, the *Pictorial* added: 'Before Vassall was sentenced for spying he talked of the urgent need for an inquiry into sex blackmail of people who work for Government departments. But he warned that such an inquiry – to weed out homosexuals in high office – would be unlikely to succeed. Many of the types who would be vetted are respectable married men holding senior posts.'

In this atmosphere of accusation and innuendo, the Labour Party, with Wigg sharp-shooting at them as well as the Government for the way they were handling the case, pressed the Government to 'discuss the evidence available and what we ought to do about it'. The Prime Minister, in fact, issued an 'interim report' by a Committee of Inquiry, which had been set up to inquire into the case. This report simply contained the full text of twenty-five letters, cables and postcards from Mr Galbraith and his wife to Vassall. Several of the letters began, 'My dear Vassall'. This, to judge from the emphasis given to it by some newspapers, was seen to have some sinister significance, though the letters made dull reading. If they revealed anything at all it was that Vassall was plaguing Mr Galbraith with requests to show off his flat in Dolphin Square, and kow-towing to him whenever the opportunity arose. Mr Galbraith had perhaps been less stiffly formal towards his junior than strict protocol permitted. He had certainly not suspected that his clerk was a Russian spy. Nevertheless, the day after the letters were released, Mr Macmillan accepted Mr Galbraith's resignation.

The papers, dissatisfied with Mr Galbraith's scalp, kept up the attack, on the far more valid line of the failure to detect Vassall's defection sooner. The affair smouldered on, with deeper recriminations flowing between Westminster and Fleet Street.

On November 13 the Prime Minister announced the setting up of a Tribunal, and it was apparent, from its terms of reference, that the Tribunal would be as much concerned with the conduct of the newspapers as the efficacy of the Security Services.

The hostility between even the most dedicated Tory newspapers and the Government was deepening. The Prime Minister himself was all but estranged from Fleet Street. Such was the political climate when another crisis, far more combustible than the Vassall case, and involving many of the same issues, was nearing ignition point.

Once again, the bloodhound on the scent was George Wigg. This time the circumstances of his involvement were extraordinary. It happened on November 11. Wigg, preoccupied with the Vassall affair, left his home in Stoke-on-Trent to attend an Armistice Day service in Stourbridge. Later, on arriving at the home of Councillor Tommy Friend who had invited him for lunch, he was told there had been a phone call for him. He thought the call was from his home as only his wife, Minnie, knew he was with Councillor Friend. He rang her but she said no one had phoned to ask his whereabouts. A little later the caller rang Friend's house again. The voice was unclear; it could have been male or female. And the message was brief. It said: 'Forget about the Vassall case; you want to look at Profumo.' That minute, though puzzled, he attached little significance to the call. It was not until he was driving home that he began to muse over it. He remembered that his wife had said nobody had called to ask where he was. And the thought struck him: 'How the hell did they get the number?'

Although for the moment the other issues predominated in his mind, the phone call became a nagging riddle . . . the kind of mystery that George Wigg could not leave unexplored.

8

Shots in the Dark

CHRISTINE KEELER CROSSED the threshold between nonentity and notoriety with seven shots from a pistol. At about one o'clock in the afternoon of December 14, 1962, a minicab drove up outside 17 Wimpole Mews, Marylebone. John Edgecombe leapt out in a highly agitated state.

Keeler had gone to live with Edgecombe, but had since left him. Now he wanted to get her back.

Edgecombe had already slashed 'Lucky' Gordon's face when he decided to go after Keeler. He rang the bell at Wimpole Mews. Mandy Rice-Davies appeared at the window of the flat on the first floor (there was a garage below). She lied when Edgecombe asked to see Keeler: she had gone to the hairdressers, she said, when Keeler was in fact cowering in a corner of the flat. The lie only excited Edgecombe all the more and, shouting 'I known she is in', he kept ringing the bell and demanding to see her. Eventually Keeler edged to the window and told Edgecombe to cool down and go away.

The pistol in Edgecombe's pocket had been purchased while they were living together in lodgings at Manor Road, Ealing. It was a 'hot' gun for it had been used in a hold-up at Queen's Park and had been bought from a criminal negro. Edgecombe pulled the pistol from his pocket, fired five shots at the locks on the flat door and then two other shots. Both missed. Then he ran off.

The reports of the shooting, Edgecombe's arrest later in the day and the names of the two girls caused only minor interest. They make amusing reading. The *Daily Telegraph*'s was typical: 'Miss Keeler, twenty, a free-lance model, was visiting Miss Marilyn Davies, eighteen, an actress, at Dr Ward's home...' There were other things to worry about: unemployment was growing, the Skybolt had failed in its trials,

75

Macmillan was meeting Kennedy to get an agreement on Polaris so as to maintain Britain's theoretical independence, the Common Market negotiations were locked in higher-calculus bargaining, economically the country was coming to a standstill with the uncertainty caused by the talks. But to one man, involved as he was with the Government's problems, the reports caused a tremor of anxiety. He knew that his ex-mistress was not the most discreet of people. She had, according to many people who have met her, an 'aura of disaster'; she was so irresponsible and irrational that they felt she might be the sort of person who would get herself killed or involved in some other crime. It was not going to be a happy Christmas for John Profumo.

Miss Keeler was in fact monumentally indiscreet. Panicking, and at the same time revelling in the importance of having been shot at, she blabbed everywhere. Perhaps it wouldn't have mattered but for the fact that among the people she talked to were two men who were intelligent enough to see that what she told them was political dynamite. The first was Michael Eddowes, a well-to-do Knightsbridge author, restaurateur and one-time solicitor. He had once before been behind a political controversy, the Timothy Evans case: he had written a book, *A Man on your Conscience*. Eddowes, at sixty, was still a handsome man despite a three-inch scar across his forehead, a legacy of a car-crash two years ago. He didn't need to work; he had an eager interest in politics.

Keeler phoned Eddowes, an old friend, in a panic the night of the shooting and arranged to meet him. She not only asked his advice on Edgecombe but wanted to know how it was likely to affect Profumo. She talked and talked. And, according to Eddowes, the whole story came out: the contrapuntal affairs with the War Minister and the Russian naval attaché, Ivanov, and the crucial tit-bit that Ivanov had asked her to undertake an unlikely mission – to ask John Profumo when the Allies were going to let Germany have nuclear warheads. The likelihood of this mission is discussed later in the story. For the moment the notion can be left unmolested.

On December 22, John Lewis, the ex-M.P. for West Bolton,

went to a tea-party. There were only three people there, Mr Lewis and two young women who worked at Murray's Cabaret Club. Halfway through the tea-party Christine Keeler arrived with one of her boy-friends, Paul Mann, one-time racing driver. Keeler was in an odd mood: she was still worried about the forthcoming Edgecombe trial – Edgecombe had that day appeared in court for a preliminary hearing – but she was enjoying being just a little famous. Once again she talked. But this time her indiscretion, if it were indeed accidental, was to have far more effect than her conversation a week earlier with Eddowes. For, though she did not know it, John Lewis had encountered Stephen Ward before and was deeply suspicious of anything he did.

Late in 1954 Mr Lewis won a divorce from his wife Joy after a costly fifteen-day hearing. One of the witnesses who had been called in support of his wife's evidence was Stephen Ward. Maliciously, Ward had sought to turn the case against Lewis, a fact which did not escape the judge, Mr Justice Sachs. In his summing-up the judge described Ward as 'a far from attractive witness on whose testimony not the slightest reliance could be placed'. But that was not the end of it for Ward later tried to sue Lewis for libel. There wasn't a shred of evidence to support Ward but his action involved Lewis in more legal costs.

Lewis had been through years of litigation in other ways – including the still unsettled libel actions against the *Daily Telegraph* and the *Daily Mail* in which he and his company were awarded the highest libel damages ever, £217,000 (see Chapter 4, page 46). He had no regard for a man who had involved him in actions twice and he was alerted by the story that Keeler had to tell. He did not disclose his interest in Stephen Ward, letting Keeler ramble on with the sordid story. There was no mention at that first meeting of nuclear warheads.

Lewis impressed on her that she must go and see a solicitor; she was in an extremely dangerous situation, he said. If the information fell into the wrong hands there was the possibility of blackmail. Keeler left the party a little later with Paul Mann. Lewis, worried by what the girl had told him, emphasised to a friend of hers that Keeler must contact a solicitor as soon as possible, taking all the evidence with her that she could, including a letter that she had mentioned. In the end, after constant pressure, Keeler finally did go to a solicitor.

It had been a long struggle: Keeler had needed a bulldozer to get her to see that she was the central character in what could be the biggest political scandal of the century. John Lewis, who has a sharp brain and is highly attuned politically, had seen the implications concerning security almost from the start. When, at a later meeting with Keeler, she told him that there had been a request for her to get a secret from the War Minister, he realised just how far the shock waves of the affair could go; because – and only because – of his worry over security he went to George Wigg, an acquaintance of his Parliamentary days.

Only a handful of people at this time were in possession of any of the facts. Many more had heard the rumours, particularly those in the traffic from Westminster to Fleet Street. There was a story about the police raiding a call-girl's den and finding her in bed with a Cabinet Minister; the story had, of course, been hushed up and nothing, they said confidently, would ever appear of it. In any case, Fleet Street and Westminster had already had their fill of rumours: the Vassall case and all its implications had begun to rebound. Nobody felt inclined to make anything but the most perfunctory of inquiries. There was so much else to write about: the unrelenting freeze, the economic malaise, the growing unemployment figures; the Leader of the Opposition was dying, the Prime Minister was in trouble because he had put all his eggs in the Common Market basket and was beginning to lose his grip on it. Even George Wigg, whose antennae usually quivered at the mention of any War Minister, was preoccupied with Vassall and Labour Party manœuvres.

When he was first approached by John Lewis on January 2, George Wigg was inclined to discount Keeler's story. It wasn't until January 7 that Lewis told the M.P. that Keeler had been asked to get a nuclear secret. Then Wigg (though he continued to discount the likelihood of a girl being asked to get such a vital fact, and still does) became aware that the security aspect of the alleged relationship was so potentially dangerous that it would have been irresponsible of him to ignore it.

In the same way as the causes of the failures of the Macmillan Government can be seen in July 1961, they were apparent in a more condensed period in January 1963. Within three days there were three events each potent in its own way. On January 14 General de Gaulle finally declared that Britain was not ready for Europe; the one blow that was needed to provoke rebellion in a Government already shaken by the crises of the winter. On January 15 the Vassall Tribunal began its public hearings at the Board of Trade, so beginning for the Press one of the most disastrous phases of its recent history which ended with two journalists in jail and a complete alienation of Fleet Street and Whitehall. On January 16 early hearings of the Edgecombe case were taking place at Marlborough Street, and Miss Christine Keeler, in a knee-length suede coat, was enjoying posing for the cameramen. And all the time George Wigg was building up his dossier.

Several newspapers were interested in Keeler. The gossip about her, though unsubstantiated, had made it seem that it might be worthwhile to purchase her memoirs when the Edgecombe case was over. In any case there was something attractive about her: she had a figure which made the kind of photograph that helps to lighten the burden of the news, especially at a time when all the news seemed to be so bad; and it wasn't every girl who could provoke the kind of passions that were apparently aroused in this case. Edgecombe had said: 'I love the girl. I was sick in the stomach over her. My sickness in the stomach overcame me and I started firing the gun.' The story was bubbling.

So far Authority, in any of its forms, had not been told the substance of the Keeler story. Michael Eddowes knew, George Wigg knew, so did John Lewis and a handful of cabaret girls. It was not until January 26 that a police officer, interviewing Keeler in connection with the Edgecombe case, became the third person to be informed direct of the incredible tale that she had been asked to discover from Profumo the date on which 'certain atomic secrets' were to be handed to West Germany by the Americans. She said she was asked the question at the time of the Cuba crisis, but she had not put it forward to Mr Profumo.

This was an important step in the translation of the Keeler story from gossip into hard information told to people in a position to take it seriously and act upon it. Two days later Ivanov left Britain in a hurry. He, at least, realised what was coming.

But it was not this information that so alarmed Sir Peter Rawlinson, the Solicitor-General, that he set in motion the first cross-examination of the War Minister on January 28. He had heard some of the gossip of an affair between Keeler and Profumo – just that – and he felt so concerned by it that he told the Attorney-General, Sir John Hobson. Sir John was then cross-examining at the Vassall Tribunal and it was not until after the Tribunal had finished for the day that he could meet Profumo.

He began the inquisition by warning Profumo that it was vitally important that there should be complete frankness. Mr Profumo appeared quite shocked by the gossip: certainly, he said, he had been friendly with the girl but their relationship was completely innocent. Not only had there been no adultery but no sexual impropriety of any sort had taken place. The idea that he had actually known Miss Keeler associated with West Indians was ridiculous.

There was one thing though: he had written a note to Miss Keeler cancelling an engagement the day Sir Norman Brook had warned of his association with Stephen Ward.

The interview ended with the Attorney-General convinced of Profumo's honesty but still worried by the gossip that seemed to be mounting up. He believed there was a danger of some newspaper or magazine publishing the rumours and said it would be a good idea if Profumo went to the best legal adviser available. (Profumo in fact went to Mr Derek Clogg, a solicitor with considerable experience of libel in the offices of Theodore Goddard and Company of New Court in Lincoln's Inn.)

What was the Government's state of knowledge at this time? They had no shred of evidence; their examination of the

Minister had been provoked entirely by rumours. It had established solely this: that Mr Profumo had known Miss Keeler and Dr Ward; that he had once written a note to Miss Keeler; that the relationship was entirely innocent. Surely it was the Vassall case all over again: it was rumour against a Minister's word and, of course, the Minister's word prevailed.

In the next part of the story – before anything was to get into print, and before George Wigg, who was now closely involved in the movement to get Harold Wilson as head of the Party, had completed his investigations sufficiently to pass his dossier forward – it is Fleet Street and its people who play the central characters in the development. On February 1, Mr Macmillan, by now desperately aware of how closely his fortunes had been tied to the collapsed Market and of how he had lost support through his failure to supply an alternative plan, had left for Rome to talk with the Italian Government when Mr Mark Chapman-Walker, general manager of the *News of the World* and former director of research at the Conservative Central Office, made a phone call to his friend John Wyndham, the Prime Minister's wealthy and unpaid principal private secretary. Mr Chapman-Walker, with his only motive, he said, *pro bono publico* had a story to tell which deeply involved the Government. In the afternoon he met Mr Wyndham at Admiralty House and told him of the discoveries of the *News of the World*'s crime reporter, Mr Peter Earle.

Mr Earle had been (he said later) on the trail of Dr Stephen Ward for some ten years. The information however that Mr Chapman-Walker was able to confide to Mr Wyndham was limited: Earle had heard rumours about Mr Profumo's affair and after checking had found that they were apparently true. Miss Keeler had not only slept with Profumo but with Ivanov, the Russian naval attaché. Dr Ward was involved, despite the fact that he had been warned about his association with Ivanov. That was the extent of the paper's knowledge, said Mr Chapman-Walker. They did not know of the existence of any incriminating letters or any photographs.

As soon as Mr Chapman-Walker left Admiralty House, Mr Wyndham moved fast. He immediately informed 'C', the head of the Security Services, with the idea that the Prime

Minister should have a full report as soon as he returned from Rome on February 3. He also went the same afternoon across to the War Office to see Mr Profumo and tell him the details of the *News of the World*'s story. For the second time Mr Profumo had to make categoric denials to a close friend and colleague: he denied all the allegations, repeating the story he had told the Attorney-General four days earlier. Mr Wyndham's advice was that Mr Profumo should either wait to see the Prime Minister himself when he returned and give him a full factual account of the relationship or, if he wanted to shed himself of the tale now, to see Mr Martin Redmayne the Government's Chief Whip. Mr Profumo did more: he not only saw Mr Redmayne but the Solicitor-General, the Attorney-General and 'C'. The pressure on Profumo was building up. To all the people he saw, and in every particular, Mr Profumo continued to deny the allegations. With Mr Redmayne he went further. He asked the Chief Whip whether, like Mr Galbraith when he had been faced with dreadful rumours at the time of the Vassall exposure, he should offer his resignation. The Chief Whip reassured him. If the rumours had any foundation he had no alternative, but if, as he claimed, they were false, then there was no reason whatsoever for his resignation.

The Prime Minister got back from Italy, half an hour behind schedule, on February 3. On the evening of February 4 he was told for the first time by Mr Redmayne of the rumours concerning his Minister. Although Mr Macmillan had at no time seen John Profumo personally, he was satisfied with the accounts he was given of the exchanges which his representatives had had with the Minister and he could see no possible reason to call for his resignation.

The pressures on Mr Macmillan's mind must be understood at this point: what had happened to Mr Galbraith was only a matter of weeks ago. The Prime Minister had felt he was being hard when he accepted Mr Galbraith's resignation and had told him: 'I believe that in the long run this might help you but it will not help me.' Here he had an almost identical situation and this time he chose the opposite course. The rumour seemed thin to him at that time. The Vassall Tribunal, then in its second week, had been demolishing systematically the rumours floated by the newspapers about Mr Galbraith, and especially an allegation in the *Daily Express* that the First Lord of the Admiralty, Lord Carrington, had had eighteeen months' forewarning of a spy in the Navy. This was no time to undermine, however temporarily, the career of another Minister.

That same day the alienation of Fleet Street and the Executive became complete. Two reporters, Reginald Foster of the *Daily Sketch*, and Brendan Mulholland of the *Daily Mail*, were sent to jail by the High Court for refusing to disclose to the Vassall Tribunal the sources of stories they had written about Vassall and Galbraith. Foster's sentence was three months, Mulholland's six. Thus, at a time when Mr Macmillan's standing was eroding within his own party, the support for him in many parts of Fleet Street disappeared.

Even papers loyal to the Conservatives, particularly the *Telegraph* newspapers and the *Daily Mail*, were disaffected. And a heavy groundswell began in favour of Mr Edward Heath, the Lord Privy Seal, for the succession.

It was in this atmosphere that Christine Keeler became aware that she was sitting on a goldmine. She realised that there might be money in the information she had to tell. It was the Manchester office of the *Sunday Pictorial* that was contacted first. The story was outlined to the newspaper and the first money came into the Keeler till. It was a paltry sum compared with the thousands that were to come later: £250. The *Pictorial* had got something of a bargain for not only did they have Keeler's story but they had evidence, the first piece of solid evidence that anyone had had. It was the letter, brief but affectionate, to Keeler signed 'J'. Christine Keeler was installed by the newspaper for safety in a flat in Park West, in Edgware Road, while it delved further into the story, and she was given a further £50.

It did not take Mr Hugh Cudlipp, editorial director of the *Mirror* newspapers, and Mr Reg Payne, editor of the *Sunday Pictorial*, long to evaluate the story. Like the Prime Minister, though for different reasons, they were aware of the Vassall Tribunal. Two journalists were in prison for publishing similar material.

Meanwhile, Stephen Ward had heard of Keeler's activities

83

and had decided to out-manœuvre her. Ward phoned Mr Fred Redman, an assistant editor of the *Pictorial* and, with all the charm and apparent honesty that he could muster, convinced him that certain major facts in the Keeler story were wrong. He then suggested and the newspaper agreed, that his own story should be published in its place. He also stopped Keeler getting anything published in the *News of the World* by talking to the crime reporter, Earle. Keeler was well and truly out-smarted: her story was to have appeared on March 10. There wasn't a line. And on March 17 Ward's story appeared in the two newspapers.

But Keeler was not around to read it. With a girl called Kim Proctor and Paul Mann, and the remains of the *Pictorial* money, Keeler set off for Spain on March 7 to become the missing witness. . . .

It was not until the fourteenth, when the Edgecombe trial opened, that Fleet Street heard of her disappearance. It accelerated the rumour. All that was needed was a missing witness to add to the impression that those powerful people in high places who had sent two of their colleagues to jail in their witch-hunt against the Press, were manipulating justice.

There were stories of an attempt at blackmail. On February 4 Mr Clogg and Profumo's counsel, Mr Mark Littman, told the Attorney-General that there had been an approach to Theodore Goddard and Co. which seemed to be a demand for money. Mr Profumo had insisted that the matter be taken to the Director of Public Prosecutions, but the Director decided that there was not sufficient in the demand to enable action to be taken.

At the same time the story was circulating in Fleet Street that an attempt had been made to hush up the involvement of Ivanov in the affair with the machinery of the 'D' notice. Somebody, they knew not who, had asked the Ministry of Defence to issue a 'D notice' on Ivanov, a request to newspapers not to print items which it would be against the national interest to publish.

But the risk of damnation was too great for the stories to be published. Although one journalist, had, haphazardly, already begun the process of revelation.

9

A Glimpse of the Skeleton

BY THE BEGINNING of March the rumour lay around Westminster like a heavy, inflammable vapour, waiting only for somebody to strike a match to create the explosion. It was certainly a combustible situation. On the one hand there was the gossip, retailing the rumour which by then had acquired substantial form. And on the other hand, there was the Government, knowing what was being said but unable to contain the situation. They were waiting for the rumour to take on tangible form in such a way that it could be challenged, contested and, as they believed, discredited. There was also Mr Profumo, who knew that he had persuaded his colleagues that he was innocent, and that they were prepared to protect him. The firemen awaited the fire with their pumps primed. Who would ignite it?

The Government half expected Fleet Street to do it. They knew that several newspapers had been working on the story with great dedication. It was, though, no Fleet Street crusader that struck in the end, but the tiniest of mice.

In the first week of March, Mr Andrew Roth, an expatriate American journalist, was preparing the next issue of a weekly news-letter called *Westminster Confidential*. This was one of the most elusive political broadsheets in the country: three or four pages of mimeographed foolscap with a circulation of less than 200 (six guineas a year subscription, sold mainly to politicians, embassies and journalists).

Mr Roth had been running a series of items on incidents which seemed to indicate that the Government was accident-prone. That week nothing suitable for that series seemed to have arisen, and instead he was working on the rather hoary old economic idea of the country having a 'floating pound' instead of devaluation. This item collapsed at the last minute.

In its place he decided to print a story about the Profumo rumour. He had first heard the story, in a highly garbled form, at the very beginning of the year – from a journalist working in the Commons Press Gallery for the Soviet news agency, Tass. He had discounted the story then, but by March had heard the much more detailed – and, to him, authenticated – version from a Right-Wing Tory M.P. And so, without much premeditation, Mr Roth put the rumour into print, under the heading 'That Was the Government That Was!' It said:

' "That is certain to bring down the Government!" a Conservative M.P. wailed, " –and what will my wife say?" This combination of tragedy and tragi-comedy came from the efforts of this M.P. to check with a newspaperman on the story which has run like wildfire through Parliament.'

It went on to give details of the rumour – which had now gained some embellishments – of how two girls had come into the limelight because of a shooting incident involving a negro, and that an effort had been made to sell the story to the Sunday newspapers, the *Sunday Pictorial* and *The People* in particular. It continued:

'One of the choicest bits in the stories was a letter, apparently signed "Jack", on the stationery of the Secretary for W⌐r. The allegation by this girl was that not only was this Minister, who has a famous actress as his wife, her client but also the Soviet Military Attaché, apparently a Colonel Ivanov. The famous actress wife, of course, would sue for divorce, the scandal ran. Who was using the girl to "milk" whom of information – the W⌐r Secretary or the Soviet Military Attaché – ran the minds of those primarily interested in security.

'It was probably knowledge about this story as well as the scandal concerning Charles Fletcher-Cooke and his young car-borrowing friend which led the Chief Whip, Brigadier Redmayne, to tell a correspondent with resignation: "We have all the luck!" '

This pinned down, fairly accurately, the state of rumour at this stage – and showed how the kernel of truth had become encrusted with exaggerations.

Not surprisingly, Mr Roth's scarce news-letter was in

86

considerable demand at Westminster within hours of its being released. Photostat copies were made by people who wanted to improve its distribution, of whom some of the most active were Right-Wing Tories. A copy soon arrived on the desk of Mr Redmayne. The Prime Minister then read it and consulted the Attorney-General. His view was that the limited circulation of *Westminster Confidential* did not give adequate grounds for the issue of a writ for libel, and that it did not provide the occasion then being looked for on which the rumour could finally be squashed.

It is worth noting that Right-Wing Tories had been assiduous both in spreading the unprinted rumour and distributing Mr Roth's news-letter. Much later, it was the Right-Wingers who were most anxious to point out what they regarded as the curious failure to take legal action at this point.*

Newspapermen, who lived daily with the problem of the libel laws, were amazed that Mr Roth had survived. Some of them suspected it might be a trap to lure them into printing the story. The failure to sue inevitably left the impression that the Government was not prepared to risk drawing the attention of the whole country to a charge which only a few hundred people in London had seen. The Labour Party, meanwhile, was beginning to wonder how the rumour was going to be answered. As well as Mr Wigg, two other Labour M.P.s knew something of the background to the allegations against Mr Profumo: Mr Richard Crossman and Mrs Barbara Castle. Both of them had good connections with the newspapers, and they knew how far Fleet Street had progressed

* The *New Daily*, a Right-Wing newspaper which has the declared policy of removing the present leaders of the Conservative Party (chiefly because of Mr Macmillan's African policy), published a pamphlet in July 1963, which said of the *Westminster Confidential* case: 'The argument for not taking action over the statement does not hold water. It is a fact that if Mr Brown writes a single letter to a Mr Smith and calls a Mr Robinson a thief, and Mr Robinson comes to see the letter, he can sue the writer for libel and (unless the allegation against him can be proven) obtain heavy damages.' The *New Daily* had not, of course, been party to spreading the rumour, but it relished the opportunity given by the failure to prosecute Mr Roth to speculate on the soundness of the Government's handling of the case.

with its inquiries. As well as being able to appreciate the documentary evidence, Mr Crossman was in a unique position to evaluate the strength of the rumours. During the war he had been director of psychological warfare against Germany, and one of his tasks there had been to manufacture rumours, which were called Sibs. This gave him a deep understanding of two things: how rumour was spread, and how to detect if any of it was true. He knew that the stories about Mr Profumo and Ivanov contained a lot of obvious embroidery, but he was convinced that they had enough substance to justify concern.

There was no question at this stage of any official Labour Party action. Those M.P.s who were watching the situation were making their inquiries privately. But on Sunday, March 10, George Wigg returned from his constituency and decided that he should go to Mr Wilson to tell him his story. He had heard that two Sunday papers were going to reveal what *they* knew. When their stories failed to appear that morning he suspected that for some reason the truth was being bottled up. (At this time his own file compared well with that of any newspaper.)

Mr Wilson was at the house of a friend. When Mr Wigg arrived the room was cleared so that the two could talk privately. Even before taking the case to Mr Wilson, Mr Wigg had been in some torment about whether to act at all. Every instinct in him was against it. But finally it was the nagging worry that there really was a security threat in the situation that made him go on – he was sure that the link between Mr Profumo and Ivanov, however innocent, had been established.

Mr Wilson had first heard the rumours towards the end of February – some weeks after they had reached the Prime Minister. Mr Wigg was able to speak to him with some candour: he had supported with vigour the campaign to elect Mr Wilson leader, and Mr Wilson respected his grasp and experience of defence matters. Mr Wigg stressed in the interview that he was not asking for permission to act, but was seeking advice on how best action might be taken. He said that he was thinking of using the coming debate on the army estimates as a vehicle for airing his anxieties. Mr Wilson advised against this, but emphasised that he must feel absolutely free to do what he thought wise. On his part, Mr Wigg realised that if he mishandled the affair it might rebound and damage Mr Wilson. And so Mr Wigg left that meeting reassured by Mr Wilson's reaction, but still with serious qualms about what he should do next. Dealing with the private life of a Minister was distasteful in any event, and he realised he was exposing himself to the charge of sensationalism if he took up the case. This, of course, was part of Mr Profumo's protection. He knew that if it was simply a charge of sexual indiscretion, no politician on either side would be anxious to pursue it. But the involvement of Ivanov made it rather different. Mr Wigg walked round the squares near his flat in Victoria cross-examining himself. The question that tipped the balance when he asked it was, 'If I don't act and the charges prove to be true at some later date, what sort of a man would I be?' It was the dilemma of the man who jumps in at the deep end because he is fearful of what might happen if he *didn't*.

In this state of mind Mr Wigg sought the guidance of his closest friends. One was an eminent politician, three were senior journalists and another was a television executive. He was advised to consult a lawyer, and this he did. He asked the solicitor if he should go direct to Mr Profumo with the allegations. The lawyer said no, 'he will not be obliged to you and he won't thank you.' Mr Wigg then considered how it might be raised within Parliamentary procedure. He remembered, particularly, what Hugh Gaitskell had told him when he wanted to press the Government in the Vassall case, 'If you feel you should use your parliamentary privilege, do so – *that is what it is given to you for.*'

Wigg accepted that if some action had to be taken, the House of Commons was the proper place for it. Of course, he knew that, should Mr Profumo prove to be innocent, his own parliamentary reputation, to which he was dedicated, would be damaged as surely as the career of the Minister, if the charges were true, would be destroyed. Mr Wigg had good need for an intense personal cross-examination; even though he was eventually proved right, some malodorous things were to be said about him in the next few weeks.

Then, on March 14, the newspapers were at last presented with a reason for giving Miss Keeler prominence. On that day the trial of John Edgecombe opened at the Old Bailey, and the first thing that the prosecution did was to announce that Miss Keeler, the principal witness (she, after all, had provoked the passions), had disappeared, and that the case had to proceed without her. This caused frantic conferences in Fleet Street. It was seriously suspected that she might have been got out of the country to avoid revelations during the trial. There was no evidence of this, but knowing what by then they did, the newspapers felt intense frustration at not being able to convey the full significance of who Miss Keeler was. One newspaper, though, devised a way of sailing closer to the wind than anyone. The *Daily Express*, practised in this type of message-by-code, printed on its front page a large picture of Miss Keeler, and separated from it by only one column there was a main story by its political correspondent, Ian Aitken, saying that Mr Profumo had offered his resignation to the Prime Minister – at some unspecified time, and on the grounds of the coming reorganisation of the defence departments. There was a picture of Mr Profumo with his wife but, of course, no connection was suggested with Miss Keeler. Of the thirteen million readers of the *Express*, not more than a few hundred, mostly in the centre of London, could possibly have seen the significance of the proximity of the two stories. It was as though the *Express* wished to demonstrate, to only very few people, that it really did know of the link between the Minister and the 'model', as Miss Keeler was called.

There was ample reason for calling her a model: a page inside the same issue of the *Express* had a selection of studio pictures of Miss Keeler in several provocative poses, in one as Mr Profumo had first seen her: draped only in a towel. It was soon to become clear that Miss Keeler had the best documented body in the history of political scandal

Apart from the hidden message, there was some substance to the *Express* story. Mr Profumo had – back in February – suggested resignation to Mr Redmayne. The *Express* said that the Prime Minister had refused it. In fact, he had never had the opportunity, although his feeling was opposed to it. Thus the lie had begun to break the surface – cautiously, but the pressures underneath were building up. During this period the rumour was multiplying like a virus in an outbreak of plague, partly because the climate was as suitable for its breeding as a hothouse. The information reaching the newspapers was growing in bulk, too, because of their inquiries into the background of the Edgecombe case – on Friday March 15 Edgecombe, with the charge amended to one of possessing a pistol with intent to endanger life, was sentenced to seven years' imprisonment. At the end of the trial the *Daily Sketch* interviewed the girl who had not got away: Marilyn Rice-Davies. On March 16 they printed a ghosted account by her, under a childish signature, of 'the top-drawer life we had been leading among the Peers and the V.I.P.s'. For the first time in a national newspaper Ivanov was introduced as part of the Keeler story.

Miss Rice-Davies said with wide-eyed enthusiasm: 'He brought round a big pot of fabulous caviare and a bottle of vodka, bowed and said with a grin: "I know the weaknesses of the Capitalists." One well-known man brought a huge bottle of perfume, swathed in wrappers, from Fortnum and Mason's.' (The 'well-known man' was Mr Profumo, but the *Daily Sketch* lawyers would not let that be said.) 'Members of Parliament also joined the discussions and the bridge sessions we had at Wimpole Mews.'

It seemed all very cerebral.

There was more about Ivanov: 'I shall always think highly of Eugene, as we used to call Ivanov. He was suddenly recalled to Moscow just after the shooting at Wimpole Mews, where he had spent much of his spare time. Of course, both Christine and I thought Eugene may have been a spy; but we would never have told him anything even if we HAD any information.'

This story had been heavily bowdlerised. Miss Rice-Davies knew a great deal more, but for the lawyers it came to the decisive question then confronting other newspapers: the unsubstantiated word of one girl against that of a Minister was too big a risk – a risk that might cost £100,000. The same morning that Miss Rice-Davies's story appeared in the *Daily Sketch*, people working on the following morning's Sunday papers heard more. Fleet Street gossip said – and Fleet Street gossip tended to be larger than life – that the *News of the World* had *three* letters from Mr Profumo to Miss Keeler, written on War Office notepaper, and that the *Sunday Pictorial* had a picture of Miss Keeler and Mr Profumo together, and had actually got a story, already in type, of their association. There was an anticlimax when only Ward's glossy account appeared.

On Monday *The Times* printed a remarkable editorial. There is such a feeling of permanence about *The Times* that it gives the impression that whatever an editor might wish to do with it, it will maintain a firm resistance. But inside its anachronistic cloak restless forces were at work. For more than a week before March 18, the letter columns of *The Times* had been awash with indignation. Its provocation had been an editorial on March 7, headlined 'A Proper Defiance', about the jailing of Foster and Mulholland after the Vassall Tribunal (their appeals had just failed). The editorial said: 'However sound in law, the judgment that two journalists must be imprisoned because they refused to disclose their sources of information is against the public interest . . .

'. . . The people are being placed more and more at the mercy of the authority and of the Executive . . . the techniques of power, of political manipulation, of the predatoriness of officialdom, become ever more insidiously efficient . . . No doubt if enough journalists hold fast, the people will wake up in the end to what is at stake and the law will be put right. . . .'

Not even the papers which employed the jailed journalists made such a vehement comment, nor read into the act the sinister intent seen by *The Times*. Certainly, the paper's own readers thought the case exaggerated. On March 9 the first replies were printed. One of them said: 'Public opinion . . . would be more influenced by evidence of concern on the part of the Press by self-discipline to protect the public from abuse than by advocacy by the Press of defiance of the law . . .' For succeeding days this tone continued, until, on March 15, one reader, against the tide, observed: 'The hostility (to the Press) has been fostered and intensified by authoritarian sources. . . . As the freedom of the Press is no more or less than the freedom of the citizen, the Press itself must engage in a massive campaign to re-educate the public to a realisation of the indispensability of preserving, if necessary by a proper defiance, not a claim or a right to freedom but the existence of freedom . . .'

That letter struck a chord in Sir William Haley, the editor of *The Times*, and he went home that weekend to write a reply to his hostile correspondents. On March 18 he snapped back at them with a vengeance. Under the portentous headline of 'It *is* happening here' it said: 'The predominant note in the letters *The Times* has received about the two imprisoned journalists has been that of hostility to the Press. The bitterness has gone far beyond what could be justified by a reasonable reading of the published proceedings of the Vassall Tribunal. It has over-flowed and at times sought to sweep away the principle at stake in these cases . . . what makes the business so grave is the degree of ignorance, complacency and apathy towards the particular dangers perpetually threatening every free society that now stands revealed. There really are people who believe that the encroachments of authority, the corruption of society, and maladministration can safely be left to the powers-that-be to put right . . . the truth is that in a quiet way very much is going seriously wrong.

'The Executive has taken over power from Parliament. It rules, or fails to rule, by a tacit agreement with outside forces in the community that *their* authority also shall not be challenged. The administrators at all levels decide more and more without the citizen having effective redress. . . . And all these hazards are faced by a middle-class that, either through comparative affluence, weariness, or disgust, has thrown in its hand or lost sight of its responsibilities . . . Journalists have no authority beyond that of other citizens. They do have in their hands an instrument which, when courageously and responsibly used, has so far proved in free societies to be the most effective in informing, in promoting discussion, in exposing error and malpractice, and in preserving liberties. . . .'

The editorial warned that if journalists were not prepared to honour the secrecy of their sources, much of their information would dry up.

This had obviously been written with great emotional involvement. Its fire was scattered over a large area, and its target not specific beyond the 'Executive'; it seemed, anyway, that the very facelessness of the enemy was one of its sinister characteristics. Anyone reading it who had just set foot in England would imagine that the country was on the brink of a new kind of Establishment-dictated totalitarianism. Sir William had been watching the erosion of journalistic freedom on the Continent – particularly in France and Germany – with some alarm, and was fearful lest the habit should spread across the Channel. And for a long time in its news columns *The Times* had been at pains to record cases of bureaucracy rampant. Even if the idea was to stamp out the fire before the spark was struck, the case seemed over-stated and over-written.

Of course, passion has always been a requirement for the defence of freedoms: apathy and timidity, the respectable alternatives, lead to defeat by default. An editor capable of speaking out with such fervour was a rare animal in Fleet Street, and the fact that this voice was booming from such an incongruous setting added the more to its effect.

The Times could hardly be regarded as a passive supporter of the administration after this. Nevertheless, it was possible to wish that some of this fire would spill over into the paper's reporting. The threatening encroachment of the Executive had not been exposed in any convincing detail there. The vigilant, crusading journalism which the leader was seeking to protect was a stranger to *The Times*. At this very moment the entire Press was not prepared to dig more deeply into an apparent scandal, and if it was timid then it was soon to have intimidation added to its burden.

There was no mistaking, though, the mood of *The Times* and its editor. Their activity and influence had only just begun. If the majority of the public walked that week in ignorance of the latent storm, the pressures to force out more were becoming harder to resist. One result of the failure to reveal the correct story then was that people who had heard only half-truths or gross elaborations indulged in further embroidered speculations – the idea that Mr Profumo had somehow been connected with Miss Keeler's disappearance was a persistent subject of gossip.

There was more activity in the Labour Party, this time caused by Miss Keeler's disappearance. Miss Alice Bacon, the party's spokesman on Home Affairs, put down a question to the Home Secretary, asking why Miss Keeler was allowed to go abroad when she was a chief prosecution witness, and what police action had been taken to trace her. Seven hours after the question had been put down it was withdrawn. The reason given was that the Home Secretary had no responsibility to cover the case. In fact, what had happened was that Mr Wilson, who knew that Mr Wigg was planning to raise the real issue, asked for the question to be withdrawn.

The newspapers continued to make moves which stopped short of consummation. On March 20 the *Daily Mail* decided to float the resignation of Mr Profumo again. Three columns discreetly separated this story from the one about Miss Keeler's disappearance (which said, coyly, '. . . there is interest among M.P.s of all parties about certain aspects of the case . . .') But if this was superb understatement, the political story by Walter Terry, debating the likelihood of Mr Profumo's departure from office, was a masterly essay in disingenuous comment, concluding: 'Continuous speculation about possible resignation is always irritating for a Government, and naturally embarrassing for the Minister concerned.' He had a point there.

The same day the case of Miss Keeler's absence came before Mr Justice Lyell at the Old Bailey. No order was made for her to appear. A decision on whether she would forfeit her £40 recognisance was postponed. Because of the interest in the matter, the Clerk of the Court took the unusual step of holding a Press conference to explain the Judge's ruling. He said that there was no question of issuing a Bench warrant for Miss Keeler's arrest. 'It will be up to her to decide whether she gives any explanation,' he said. 'If she chooses not to, then it is likely an order can be made to make her pay the £40. If she is never found, then so far as this court is concerned it will be the end of it.'

There was further activity in the Labour Party. Mr Marcus Lipton said that the following Monday he would ask the Attorney-General how many Crown witnesses had failed to appear at the Old Bailey in 1962 and what action was taken against them.

The game of cat-and-mouse was on, with confusion on all sides. The door of the cupboard was slightly open, and the skeleton would fall out in a very few hours.

10

Speak and be Damned

ON THURSDAY MARCH 21 four people, all of them Labour M.P.s, had made up their minds to act. That day the House of Commons was debating the case of the two imprisoned journalists, Reginald Foster and Brendan Mulholland. For Mr Wigg the right moment and the right place had combined. Mr Crossman and Mrs Castle realised this too.

But before they were able to speak, Mr Ben Parkin, the Labour member for Paddington North, decided to tackle the problem in a more oblique way. Mr Parkin was a member of Standing Committee F, which was dealing with the London Government Bill. On March 21 they were in the twenty-first sitting and the last day of the committee stage of the bill – it was, in fact, under the guillotine.

Just before 5 p.m. Mr Parkin started to speak on the subject of the London sewage system, a basic if not necessarily riveting problem. After a few minutes his listeners began to lose track of his speech. Having made some comments about the drainage of storm water, he went off at a tangent: 'We have been told that this has been discussed at Cabinet level. When I referred to that at a previous sitting the hon. Member for Barons Court (Mr Compton Carr) rebuked me for dealing in chit-chat, but of course we are obliged to depend upon chit-chat to some extent.

'There is the case of the missing model. We understand that a model can quite easily be obtained for the convenience of a Minister of the Crown . . .' At this point the Chairman, Sir Samuel Storey, became bewildered. He interrupted: 'I do not think there is anything about a missing model in this Schedule.' Mr Parkin, however, sustained the double-talk: 'No, Sir Samuel, but at the beginning of our discussions there was a model just outside this room and I admired its gracious curves.

97

It was provided by the Ministry of Transport to make it possible for us to understand the complicated proposals for London traffic.

'I have looked in vain for a similar model showing me the Minister's vision of the future when the new type of drainage is installed in London to cope with his conception of an evolving efficiency in living in a built-up area – something which mankind has never yet learned to do in a free and stable community.'

By then Mr Parkin was back on course, but his diversion was not lost on several of the committee members. When he had finished speaking a Press Association reporter, somewhat perplexed, went up to him to check this passage of his speech. Mr Parkin confirmed that he had got it right, without betraying its hidden significance. The reporter phoned over his account to Fleet Street. It did not take long for the code to be deciphered by the news editors who received it.

By the time Mr Parkin left the committee there was a pile of blue cards in the lobby asking him to call various newspapers. But he was going into the Chamber for the debate on the journalists, and the calls were left unanswered. (The only paper which printed his cipher was the *Daily Worker*, whose edition went to press too early to record the more startling events that were still to come that evening.)

One of the people at the committee meeting had been the Minister of Housing, Sir Keith Joseph. He had congratulated Mr Parkin on his speech, evidently unaware of its *double entendre*, and therefore probably unaware of the rumours about Mr Profumo. A week or so later, somewhat embarrassed, he stopped Mr Parkin in one of the lobbies. 'That speech I congratulated you on,' he said, 'you were meaning something quite different.' 'Well, as a matter of fact,' said Parkin, 'Yes.'

The news which engrossed the other papers began just before 11 p.m. when Mr Wigg rose to speak in the debate. He began by examining the relationship between the Executive and the Press: 'The Press can exercise freedom over its criticism of the Executive, the Opposition and hon. Members – but it should do it in such a way that it should have regard to the public good.' He said that although he felt that the instrument of a Tribunal was a bad one, its members had treated the Press as kindly as possible. 'But they had a job to do. They were not there in order to bring the mailed fist of totalitarianism into it, but to do a job that the House of Commons had by unanimous Resolution authorised them to do. If hon. Members now grumble about the results, I ask them where they were on 14th November, when we were raising our voices against this particular form of tribunal.

'So far, so good. Here was a set of rumours that gained and gained in strength, consumed men's reputations – might, in fact, have destroyed them – and which here infringed on the security of the State.

'But are we quite sure that the same thing is not happening again? There is not an hon. Member in the House, nor a journalist in the Press Gallery nor do I believe there is a person in the Public Gallery who, in the last few days, has not heard rumour upon rumour involving a member of the Government front bench.'

Suddenly Mr Wigg's audience suspended the various expressions of relaxation normal at that time of night and began to listen very carefully.

'The Press has got as near as it could – it has shown itself willing to wound but afraid to strike. This all comes about because of the Vassall Tribunal. In actual fact, these great Press lords, these men who control great instruments of public opinion and of power, do not have the guts to discharge the duty that they are now claiming for themselves.

'That being the case, I rightly use the Privilege of the House of Commons – *that is what it is given to me for* – to ask the Home Secretary, who is the senior member of the Government on the Treasury Bench now, to go to the Dispatch Box – he knows that the rumour to which I refer relates to Miss Christine Keeler and Miss Davies and a shooting by a West Indian – and, on behalf of the Government, categorically deny the truth of these rumours.

'On the other hand, if there is anything in them, I urge him to ask the Prime Minister to do what was not done in the Vassall case – set up a Select Committee so that these things can be dissipated, and the honour of the Minister concerned freed from the imputations and innuendoes that are being spread at the present time.

'It is no good for a democratic State that rumours of this kind should spread and be inflated, and go on. Everyone knows what I am referring to, but up to now nobody has brought the matter into the open. I believe that the Vassall Tribunal need never have been set up had the nettle been firmly grasped much earlier on. We have lost some time, and I plead with the Home Secretary to use that Dispatch Box to clear up all the mystery and speculation over this particular case.'

By the time Mr Wigg sat down, at 11.5 p.m., the nature of the whole affair had altered. Mr Profumo's name had still to be mentioned, of course – though few in the Commons that night, as Mr Wigg had suggested, were in doubt about the identity of the Minister. 'We have lost some time,' Mr Wigg had said. All that time the rumour had been festering. Had the wound now been lanced? Could anything stop the truth emerging at last? The alert went out from Westminster to Fleet Street: this might be the night on which the stifled stories could be printed.

A few minutes went by before the rumour was taken up again, this time by Mr Crossman. After dealing with the Vassall Tribunal, he said: 'By this evening a Paris newspaper may have published in full the rumours which have run round this House and the country and are touched upon day by day in the Press. I agree with my hon. Friend the Member for Dudley that it would have been infinitely wiser if we had established a Select Committee ten days ago to go into the rumours and that if we have a 1921 tribunal again we shall not have what we want.' Another Labour Member, Mr Reginald Paget, then intervened to make what in the circumstances seemed one of the most naïve remarks passed on the whole situation: 'What do the rumours amount to?' he asked – and answered: 'They amount to the fact that a Minister is said to be acquainted with an extremely pretty girl. As far as I am concerned, I should have thought that that was a matter for congratulation rather than inquiry.'

As Mr Crossman put it, that was a very interesting way of spreading a rumour.

The debate then returned to its original subject. Both Mr Wigg and Mr Crossman had been very careful about one thing: not to say anything in the House of Commons which would not be repeatable outside it, that there should be no suggestion that their privilege was being abused to mount an attack that would be shielded from fair reply. No Minister, remember, had actually been named.

For forty minutes the subject was not raised again. Then Mrs Castle, towards the end of her speech, took it a stage further – further than either Mr Wigg or Mr Crossman had been prepared to go. She said: 'It would suit the book of many people no doubt to deplore the avidity with which the Press is at this moment pursuing the question of where Miss Christine Keeler has gone, the missing "call girl", the vanished witness. Is it the pursuit of sensationalism for its own sake, or could it be that there is public interest at the back of the agitation by the Press? My hon. and learned Friend, the Member for Northampton (Mr Paget) said that if it is just a case of a Minister having been found with a pretty girl, good luck to him, but what if there is something else of much greater importance? What if it's a question of the perversion of justice that is at stake? The Clerk of the Central Criminal Court, Mr Leslie Boyd, is reported in *The Times* today as saying that: "If any member of the public did know where Miss Keeler was it is his or her duty to inform the police." If accusations are made that there are people in high places who do know and who are not informing the police, is it not a matter of public interest?'

Sir Lionel Heald interrupted: 'Ought not the hon. Lady to make the accusation if she is going to make it?' She said that she hoped that the truth would come out. Mr Paget got up again: 'Surely the hon. Lady should tell us from whom and where the rumour has come other than from herself – and from herself it will appear in every newspaper tomorrow – that people in high places have been in any way responsible for the disappearance of Miss Keeler. I have seen that stated in no newspaper. I have seen it suggested nowhere until this evening.'

'All I can say,' answered Mrs Castle, 'is that my hon. and learned Friend must be the only person in the House who has not heard it mentioned.'

Mr Paget pressed again, but Mrs Castle, like the journalists Foster and Mulholland, said that she had no intention of disclosing her source.

The fact that these exchanges were between two Labour M.P.s was a result of the absence of any joint consultation before the rumour was first raised by Mr Wigg. He, in fact, was disturbed that the disappearance of Miss Keeler had become the dominant issue – it was a red herring, and he knew it. What further alarmed him about this was that it now amounted to an allegation which Mr Profumo could deny with absolute conviction: that he had had anything to do with Miss Keeler's disappearance. Mr Crossman, too, with his wartime experience, knew the dangers of allowing truth to mingle with lies. That point was not lost on Mr Profumo.

The Government now had no alternative but to answer the charges. The two Law Officers, the Attorney-General, Sir John Hobson, and the Solicitor-General, Sir Peter Rawlinson, went to the Chief Whip, Mr Redmayne, to discuss how the allegations could be answered. They knew, of course, that the identity of the Minister concerned could not be concealed, because so many in and outside Westminster knew that it was Mr Profumo.

The Law Officers and the Chief Whip then decided that Mr Profumo should make a personal statement to the House as soon as possible. It was by this time nearing midnight. Mr Macmillan had gone to bed, but he was telephoned, told what the Labour members had said, and that the form of reply suggested was a personal statement. He agreed to this. There was some urgency, because the following day, March 22, was a Friday, when the House started business at 11 a.m. instead of in the afternoon. It was essential to reply to the allegations before the House rose for the weekend.

It was decided that Mr Profumo should be called to Westminster at once; he had to be got out of bed. There was to be a meeting between Mr Profumo and some Ministers as soon as possible.

Meanwhile, the debate on the Press was still going on. At 12.38 a.m., while the meeting was being organised, the Home

Secretary, Mr Brooke, began his winding-up speech for the Government. He said: 'I do not propose to comment on rumours which have been raised under the cloak of privilege and safe from any action at law. The hon. Member for Dudley and hon. Member for Blackburn (Mrs Castle) should seek other means of making these insinuations if they are prepared to substantiate them.' It was already plain where the Government's guns were to be aimed, and at this Mr Wigg began to bristle.

The Leader of the Opposition had not been in the Chamber when the rumours had come up. He spoke at 12.56 a.m. When Mr Brooke sat down, Mr Wilson said: 'I had not intended to intervene in this debate, one good reason being that I have not heard much of it. Having noted the names of the hon. Members who have spoken I think I can form a fairly clear view of what must have been said, and I am sure that the House will understand that, having listened to the speech of the Home Secretary, one has a great temptation – an irresistible one for me – to get to one's feet and say a few words.' Now, this, like Mr Parkin's speech earlier, had several shades of meaning, as did a certain amount of what followed, although Mr Wilson never directly referred to the subject of Mr Profumo: 'The right hon. Gentleman has spoken with great sincerity on the issue that has been debated tonight, and we always expect that from him. We also understand that he has been on duty for a long time today and we understand the difficulties he is having. Thus we appreciate the fact that he is still with us.' This was not lost on the House. Mr Wilson then operated cuttingly on the Home Secretary: 'I cannot feel that his speech has dealt adequately with the subject before us. I have heard many attacks made on the Home Secretary in the past few months, many of them fair and some of them perhaps unfair. He has been accused of many things. I have a great personal regard for the right hon. Gentleman, as I am sure have all hon. Members, but one of the things he has never been accused of is recognising a principle when he sees it.

'I think it fair to say – and his speech tonight is proof of this – that however broad or vital a principle may be we can trust the Home Secretary to reduce it to a narrower issue.'

There were several other playful shots from Mr Wilson – he noted with pleasure that the Attorney-General was there at such a late hour, and he offered sympathy to a Cabinet Minister, Mr Deedes, a kind of super public-relations man for the Government, who was sitting opposite: 'I do not know what his job is. Is it Minister without Portfolio? Whatever it is, he is the propaganda officer for the Government. All of us understand the difficulties with which he is labouring in these circumstances and we have sympathy for him.' This was Mr Wilson at his most caustic.

The debate on the journalists did not end until Mr Wilson sat down at 1.22 a.m. What later became known as the meeting of the five Ministers (a meeting which was to arouse Mr Wilson again) was therefore delayed until just after 1.30 a.m. Then, in the Chief Whip's room, were assembled the five: Mr Deedes; the two Law Officers, Sir John Hobson and Sir Peter Rawlinson; the Leader of the House, Mr Macleod, and the Chief Whip himself, Mr Redmayne. Mr Profumo had with him, at the Attorney-General's suggestion, his solicitor: Mr Derek Clogg, of Theodore Goddard & Co., who had been fetched from his home. Oddly absent was the Home Secretary, Mr Brooke, who was still available in the House when the meeting began. His absence was curious because his office and responsibilities were greatly relevant to the occasion. He was evidently not considered necessary for the meeting; Mr Deedes, whose relevance seemed far less, was. Of course, Mr Brooke had taken no part in the earlier cross-examination of the War Minister; but neither had Mr Deedes.

Mr Brooke's inclusion might have spared his colleagues considerable future embarrassment. The Metropolitan Police, for whom he answers in Parliament, had not thought fit to pass to him the crucial information they gave to the Security Services – that Miss Keeler had told a police officer on January 26 of her association with Profumo and Ivanov. Nevertheless, had Mr Brooke been at the meeting he might have been asked to make inquiries and he would have quickly uncovered the information. Its revelation at that point would have changed the course of events.

The purpose of this meeting was never adequately explained

at the time. It was widely said afterwards that the five Ministers had either been extremely gullible, or had conspired to let their colleague off the hook, knowing already of his guilt. Ministers, of course, and especially Chief Whips, are not usually given to gullibility. The explanation was that the brief the Ministers were working on for the meeting was not to conduct another interrogation, starting from scratch – all that ground had been repeatedly gone over. *It was simply to help him draw up his statement.* Mr Profumo had by that time satisfied all his colleagues, the Law Officers of the Crown and the Security Services that he was innocent of any offence. As was shown by the Government's reaction to the story published by Mr Roth, they had been waiting for the right moment openly to nail the rumour. Now Parliament, not the Press, had provided the opportunity for doing that. They were in fact all deceived, but were not parties to the deception.

One item of knowledge common both to Mr Profumo and his colleagues was that he had written the letter of August 9, 1961, to Miss Keeler. Two things were known about that letter – that it began 'Darling', and that it was then in the possession of the *Sunday Pictorial*. The first fact gave the examiners cause to seek a definition of the relationship, the second fact suggested a sword hanging over Mr Profumo's head which would surely fall if he lied.

It was, however, no deterrent. Mr Profumo explained away 'Darling' by saying that this degree of intimacy was normal in the world in which he moved, and that it was, anyway, a letter breaking off a friendship and therefore demanded a chivalrous generosity. Only the *Sunday Pictorial* had the text of the letter, and the Ministers accepted Mr Profumo's explanation of it without attempting to see it. The meeting then set about drafting the personal statement. With the two Law Officers of the Crown and a solicitor present, there was no paucity of experience for this task. The Solicitor-General warned Mr Profumo: 'You must realise that you are making a statement that there is no truth whatever in any of these allegations. Supposing that there is, for the rest of your life you will be submitting yourself to blackmail.' And Mr Profumo replied: 'I quite realise that, but, as it is all true, I have nothing to fear.'

The impression of Mr Profumo's self-confidence in the Ministers' minds was reinforced by the knowledge that he had instructed his solicitor and counsel to visit the Director of Public Prosecutions, and that he was prepared to say in the statement that he would not hesitate to sue anyone who made further allegations.

The profusion of cooks produced a text of jerky prose, with its continuity somewhat damaged by amendments. But then nobody could expect a statement with such a purpose to possess an elegant flow.

The drafting was completed, and the meeting ended at 3.30 a.m. The Prime Minister had a copy of the statement by 9.30 a.m. He was impressed by its confident ring, and he decided to go to the Commons that morning and indicate, by his presence alongside Mr Profumo, that he accepted his Minister's word. Friday mornings in the Commons are usually desultory and anti-climactic occasions and sparsely attended. This one was historic, and the atmosphere was electric. At 11 a.m. Mr Profumo sat on the Front Bench flanked by the Attorney-General, Sir John Hobson, and the Leader of the House, Mr Macleod. Then Mr Macmillan arrived and took Sir John's place next to Mr Profumo. The big guns were in place. At 11.8 a.m. Mr Profumo rose. He was pale from lack of sleep but self-controlled, though obviously under high internal tension. He spoke slowly and deliberately, and it soon became clear that he was asserting his case with a challenging defiance. This was his statement:

'I understand that in the debate on the Consolidated Fund Bill last night, under protection of Parliamentary privilege, the hon. Gentlemen the Members for Dudley (Mr Wigg) and for Coventry East (Mr Crossman) and the hon. Lady the Member for Blackburn (Mrs Castle) opposite, spoke of rumours connecting a Minister with a Miss Keeler and a recent trial at the Central Criminal Court. It was alleged that people in high places might have been responsible for concealing information concerning the disappearance of a witness and the perversion of justice.

'I understand that my name has been connected with the rumours about the disappearance of Miss Keeler.

'I would like to take this opportunity of making a personal statement about these matters.

'I last saw Miss Keeler in December 1961, and I have not seen her since. I have no idea where she is now. Any suggestion that I was in any way connected with or responsible for her absence from the trial at the Old Bailey is wholly and completely untrue.

'My wife and I first met Miss Keeler at a house party in July 1961, at Cliveden. Among a number of people there was Dr Stephen Ward, whom we already knew slightly, and a Mr Ivanov, who was an attaché at the Russian Embassy.

'The only other occasion that my wife or I met Mr Ivanov was for a moment at the official reception for Major Gagarin at the Soviet Embassy.

'My wife and I had a standing invitation to visit Dr Ward.

'Between July and December 1961, I met Miss Keeler on about half-a-dozen occasions at Dr Ward's flat, when I called to see him and his friends. Miss Keeler and I were on friendly terms. There was no impropriety whatsoever in my acquaintanceship with Miss Keeler.

'Mr Speaker, I have made this personal statement because of what was said in the House last evening by the three hon. Members, and which, of course, was protected by privilege. I shall not hesitate to issue writs for libel and slander if scandalous allegations are made or repeated outside the House.'

This statement contained one of the most barefaced lies uttered in the House of Commons. 'There was no impropriety whatsoever . . .' This was the only specific denial in the whole statement, the only phrase which was unambiguous. But it was enough to bring disaster. That Mr Profumo had maintained his innocence through many interrogations shows the extent of his determination to live with the deceit; that he was prepared to go to the lengths of uttering a contempt of the House, and by doing so also invoke a demonstration of loyalty by the Prime Minister and his colleagues in the Government, suggests that by this time his belief that he could get away with it had superseded all judgment and become a reckless obsession.

Why was a Minister who, for all his faults, knew perfectly well the appalling danger of such a situation, driven to these lengths? It is probable that in his own mind the affair with Miss Keeler did not seem to be more than a sexual adventure of the kind indulged by many men of his age. The nature of the allegations made against him enabled his conscience to subjugate the lesser lie – that he had fornicated – to what he knew to be the larger truths: that he had *not* abetted Miss Keeler's disappearance and had not, as far as he could know, allowed a security leak. It was therefore, ironically, the nature of the charges against him, once they were made, which led to his resolve to lie his way out of his actual sin by being given the opportunity to answer groundless allegations with absolute honesty.

Hence even those of his friends and his colleagues who knew him well, and would probably have detected deceit, were convinced by the force of his denials which, on two out of the three charges (the most serious ones) were perfectly true. Perhaps this also made the lie more easy to live with – after all, a man who was able in the first place to fall victim so easily to lust was not likely to find it an impossible burden of guilt.

Many politicians, higher than he, had in their time been untroubled by liaisons of more intensity and longer duration than this. Mr Profumo knew this, and he also knew that by those standards it was *discovery* that was the crime, not an undetected act. This is, of course, a standard of moral conduct which falls short of that which the public expects in its servants – though they may not demand it of themselves.

In one respect, though, there was a violation of even the laxer tolerances in Mr Profumo's action. Some of the people who could condone the running of a mistress – so long as it remained secret – were influenced in this attitude by the romantic conception of the Edwardian 'blade' in the man. But there was one facet of the blade's make-up, as they saw it, which Mr Profumo had not lived up to: the duty to observe a gentleman's honour and not lie. This not even the Edwardians could forgive.

11

Mr Wigg Meets Dr Ward

AT 11.10 A.M. ON MARCH 22, when Mr Profumo sat down, there were two kinds of people in Westminster: those who believed him and those who didn't. It is difficult to know which was in the majority. From the number who later claimed to have seen through the lie all along it would appear that the sceptics were. But hindsight was then spreading its great wisdom.

If Mr Macmillan and his colleagues were at that time convinced that the truth had been told and malicious rumour silenced, there were undoubtedly many people sitting behind them who didn't share that view. The Right-Wing Conservatives were natural sceptics, but there were others, nearer to power, who had felt that when Mr Wigg had produced the skeleton from the cupboard he had performed a service both to the public and the Conservative Party. They now felt cheated.

Mr Wigg was enraged. Mr Brooke's inference the previous night that privilege had been abused deliberately to wound a Minister, had twice been repeated in Mr Profumo's statement, in the first and last paragraphs. It was a charge that, after all his earlier soul-searching, cut Mr Wigg savagely. Mr Crossman and Mrs Castle felt it too. Despite the extensive code of Parliamentary etiquette, scrupulously administered by the Speaker, political warfare was not always conducted according to the Queensberry rules. No doubt this was only a counter-attack by the Government produced by a conviction in Profumo's word and reinforced by the desire to protect him; but it came near to character assassination. As Mr Wigg was later to tell the House: 'I left with black rage in my heart because I knew what the facts were. I knew the truth . . . I had been trussed up and done again.' [The first time was during the Kuwait debate.] According to tradition, a personal statement could not be debated, but for a brief moment Mr Wigg had wondered whether to rise to attempt a challenge. He saw, however, that it would be pointless and possibly dangerous.

It is only fair to say that not all of the people who disbelieved Mr Profumo's statement had such good grounds for doing so as did Mr Wigg. Few had gone to the trouble he had to find facts for themselves. In the Press Gallery as Mr Profumo was speaking, though, had been many who knew that in their offices was evidence enough to suggest the statement was a lie. But if there were sceptics and cynics in Westminster and Fleet Street, the majority of people outside had the impression that once again, as in the case of Mr Galbraith, a murky rumour had been confounded by the truth.

Mr Profumo's next action could hardly have been more fortuitously effective in presenting to the public an impression of triumphant respectability. That afternoon he and his wife went to the Sandown Park races, and in accordance with a previous appointment, joined the Queen Mother. There they were photographed together. [Looked at later, these photographs suggest to judge by Mr Profumo's face, that he was feeling more defiant than confident, like a man accepting a dare.] The occasion certainly set the seal on what seemed a day of vindication, although it did nothing to pacify Mr Wigg. That night the Profumos went to a dance at Quaglino's given by the Hatch End Tory Party, and had a further morale-boosting reception. It was a victory of virtue over scandal-mongering, or so it appeared.

That night, too, Dr Ward was interviewed by Independent Television News. Indignantly, he said: 'I have just read the statement that he [Mr Profumo] made in the House of Commons this afternoon. It is a dreadful thing that a man should be put in the position of having to do this as a result of entirely baseless rumours and insinuations that have been started by the Press. I know them to be baseless because I was there when the meetings took place and there is absolutely nothing of a sinister nature which can be attached to these occasions.'

Dr Ward, then and later, was a plausible performer on television. It wasn't, though, going to be long before he was contradicting this statement.

On March 23 every paper reported Mr Profumo's statement in full. Those who believed that they had adequate evidence to suggest that it was in part a monstrous lie took care not to commit themselves. The libel threat had struck home. *The Guardian* on the other hand, felt that purity and honour had been reasserted. Its headline said: 'Mr Profumo clears the air.' It concluded its report with an optimism which Mr Profumo, for one, must have felt encouraging: 'That, it seems, is the end of the story, and after the tensions of the last few weeks few, even among Mr Profumo's bitterest opponents will be sorry.' This was hardly designed to assuage Mr Wigg, who was feeling more bitter than ever. Some Conservative M.P.s were after his blood. In common with many people excluded from the truth and convinced by Mr Profumo's denial, they carried on the campaign against what they thought had been abuse of parliamentary privilege. Sympathy for Mr Profumo became associated with distaste for Mr Wigg's tactics, and some of the Tory M.P.s consulted among themselves on whether to raise objections publicly. Nothing, fortunately, came of it.

Mr Wigg, having spent the weekend boiling, had become more determined than ever that Mr Profumo should not be allowed to get away with this lie. On March 25 the B.B.C. made a decision which set in motion a cycle of events which would allow Mr Wigg to be vindicated. They asked him to appear on 'Panorama', with Mr Donald McLachlan, the editor of the *Sunday Telegraph*. He took this opportunity to stress that his action had been dictated entirely by his concern for security, and his apprehension about the activities of Ivanov. He said three things about Ivanov: that he drove a sports car, wore Savile Row suits and visited night spots – to illustrate that this was far from a normal way of life for a Russian in London.

Meanwhile, the same day, the newspapers had finally tracked down the missing Miss Keeler. Teams of reporters, of the type known in Fleet Street as the 'heavy mob', had been despatched all over Europe at the slightest hint that she might be somewhere. Any 'lead' had been followed up. Over the weekend the information available seemed to indicate that she was in Spain. It was there, in Madrid, that she was found, by the

Daily Express. Two of their reporters succeeded in negotiating exclusive access to the re-incarnated celebrity. Safe in a flat from the other Pressmen, Miss Keeler began to tell her story: for £1,400, a sum established after some tenacious bargaining.

The story that appeared in the *Express* on the 26th, occupying most of the front page, was accompanied by pictures in which Miss Keeler, by now established as a goddess of sensuality, appeared in clothes appropriate to the rôle: leather boots up to the knees, a skirt which ended well above the boots, and a tight sweater. The account of her relations with Mr Profumo was innocuous, as respectable as Mr Profumo's own account had been ... 'I have met Mr Profumo on several occasions. He was most courteous and gentlemanly ...'

What she did disclose was how she left the country. She had gone, she said, on March 7, driven by Paul Mann in his red Jaguar and with her friend Kim Proctor. They had been so anxious to reach Spain that, rather than be delayed by staying in hotels, they had slept by the roadside. In two days they had reached Barcelona, and then went on to a small resort called Altea, near Valencia. At the time when she should have been in the Old Bailey witness box, she recalled, she was riding along the beach at Altea on a mule called Pepi. This idyll ended with an invitation to accompany two matadors to Barcelona, where, on the afternoon of Saturday, March 23, she discovered that she had become a celebrity – from a cutting dated March 18, which said that the Home Secretary was going to be asked questions about her disappearance. She had contacted the British Consul in Madrid and decided to stay there for a few days.

That, as far as readers of the *Daily Express* were concerned, was it. They had not, however, had the full £1,400 worth. The *Express* reporters extracted enough from Miss Keeler to write a 'memorandum' of 50,000 words, containing not euphemisms but facts, and representing a complete, unexpurgated, biography.

But if Mr Profumo's threats had intimidated the newspapers, the rumour was unabated. It grew more leprous and defamatory than ever, and spread to every capital in Europe and also to the United States, imported as if in a diplomatic bag, and dominated dinner table gossip. One of its legends was a dinner party, waited upon by a man wearing an iron mask and nothing else. The French, to whom such customs were perhaps more commonplace, were nevertheless shaken by reports of Anglo-Saxon depravity.

On the afternoon of March 26 Dr Ward took a step which was to affect the lives of many people. He had been worrying about what Mr Wigg had said on television, and particularly by implications of security risk. At 5 p.m. Mr Wigg was talking to a political correspondent in the Members Lobby at the House of Commons when he was handed a telephone message. It was from Dr Ward, asking him to ring Paddington 8625.

Mr Wigg decided that it would be wise for the conversation to be monitored, but no sophisticated monitoring equipment existed at Westminster: certainly nothing on the American pattern of a 'tapping' post in the basement with a tape recorder and Security man attached. Improvisation was necessary. In the lower corridor, Mr Wigg remembered, there was a rather curious instrument which had a separate earpiece, as well as the ordinary receiver.

So, with the strange spectacle of Mr Wigg at the receiver and his journalist friend holding the separate attachment to his ear, Dr Ward and Mr Wigg spoke to each other for the first time. Dr Ward pointed out that Mr Wigg's information on Ivanov had been wrong. Instead of a sports car he drove either an Austin A 40 or a Humber Snipe, he said. His suits were not from Savile Row but from John Barker's, just across the road from Millionaire's Row where the Russian Embassy was. And the only night spot that Ivanov had seen, according to Dr Ward, was the Satyr Club, where he had once spent ten minutes.

Mr Wigg asked Dr Ward what his interest had been in Ivanov. He replied that Ivanov had been a friend and that he was no longer in London to defend himself. He was angry about an article in the *Sunday Telegraph* which had asked 'How did Ivanov get so high?' One reason might have been, suggested Dr Ward, that the editor of the *Daily Telegraph* had introduced Ivanov to Ward, and he claimed that the editor,

113

Sir Colin Coote, had been on Christian-name terms with the Russian. (This was hardly sinister: Ivanov was well known in Fleet Street.)

Mr Wigg made it quite clear to Dr Ward that he was concerned only with the security aspect and not with people's private lives. Then it was suggested that the two should meet, and Mr Wigg arranged to meet Dr Ward in the Central Lobby at 6 p.m.

He arrived in a state which Mr Wigg later likened to 'a shivering jelly'. He was obviously in need of spiritual revival, and Mr Wigg took him for a drink in the Harcourt Room. On the way Dr Ward said that he knew many M.P.s including some members of the Government, and that he had often taken Ivanov to the House.

The hospitality in the Harcourt Room had swiftly to be ended because Dr Ward became extremely agitated when an ex-Cabinet Minister entered the room. He covered his face and said: 'I must go, I should never have come here, people I know will recognise me.' Mr Wigg took him to one of the private interview rooms, and then he began to settle down a little. They discussed Ivanov, whom Dr Ward said was a loyal Russian who nevertheless was dedicated to establishing peaceful co-existence.

Some of Dr Ward's self-importance now began to break through, and he described his rôle during the Berlin and Cuba crises. He said that during the Berlin crisis Ivanov had used him to tell senior people at the Foreign Office that the Soviet Union was prepared to adopt a conciliatory attitude over Berlin if the West would give guarantees of the Oder-Neisse line. Whenever Dr Ward was pressed by Mr Wigg to say precisely who the approaches had been made to, he hedged, and simply said that 'very important people' were involved.

He said that Ivanov had been to his parties, but these affairs consisted only of playing bridge and meeting girls – nothing improper ever took place. Coming to what Mr Wigg interpreted as the real purpose of his visit, Dr Ward said that he was sure that the Security authorities had been closely watching Ivanov, and that there could not have been any security risk. The Security Services, he claimed, also knew about Mr

Profumo's visits, and nothing improper happened then, either. He was sure that Mr Profumo had never put himself in a position which would create a security risk. In any case, he claimed to have kept records of Mr Profumo's visits to Miss Keeler and to have passed them on to the Security Services.

He seemed to be upset that Christine Keeler had secured newspaper contracts and he had not. He knew that letters which Mr Profumo had written to Miss Keeler still existed, but that they were quite innocuous.

Some of Miss Keeler's frenetic life was revealed by Dr Ward, a note of reproof in his voice. He said Miss Keeler had played one West Indian lover off against another.

Dr Ward's performance at this stage was something like that of a father distressed by his inability to control his daughters, and at the same time feeling that they had abused the breeding which he had given them. Miss Keeler and Miss Rice-Davies were little girls who had strayed into the shady side of West End life, and their contact with influential people was limited.

The rumours, he said, had ruined his practice – his patients had shrunk in number from sixty a week to four. He had been persecuted by the Press, yet he had got nothing from his attempts to protect Mr Profumo. When he had seen Mr Profumo – only three weeks before – it had been at the Dorchester Hotel – he asked him about Miss Keeler, and, imitating a gesture of Mr Profumo's which Mr Wigg recognised, tapping his forehead with a finger, he said Mr Profumo had told him: 'Christine Keeler? Who's she?' If he really wanted to know, Ward had said, he should consult M.I.5, who would be able to give him the precise dates of his visits to the flat in Wimpole Mews.

Ward said he had last seen Ivanov in December. Here again there was a sign of equivocation, and Mr Wigg had information which contradicted this, suggesting that Dr Ward had, in fact, seen Ivanov shortly before the Russian left London in January. Mr Wigg, assessing Dr Ward carefully, realised that on all the important points he was not prepared to make precise answers: his approach was oblique, carefully opening avenues of evasion.

After three hours Dr Ward left the House at 9 p.m. and Mr Wigg went immediately to see the Leader of the Opposition. He told Mr Wilson that Dr Ward had claimed that he had written to him in November, at the end of the Cuba crisis (Mr Wilson was then the Shadow Foreign Secretary). Mr Wilson had no recollection of the letter. But his secretary went through the filing cabinets and found it under the 'Ws'. It was written in Dr Ward's spidery hand. The phrase 'consultation by appointment only' on his letterhead was crossed out. This was the letter written on November 1, setting out in detail Dr Ward's activities during the Cuban crisis, and explaining his own anxiety to help along peaceful co-existence.

The phrase that lodged in Mr Wilson's mind when he read the letter was '. . . because I was the intermediary . . .' in the passage giving an account of the approaches made on behalf of Ivanov to the Foreign Office.

Here was a man who was a friend of the Secretary of State for War, and also of a member of the Russian Embassy who sought, on some basis, unorthodox diplomatic initiatives. Mr Wilson felt that this had got to be carefully examined by the proper authorities. He asked Mr Wigg to prepare a full report of his talk with Dr Ward, and to annotate his own interpretations. The following day, March 27, Mr Wilson saw Mr Macmillan, and gave him the letter which Dr Ward had written, and explained his anxieties about its implications.

Mr Wilson was about to fly to Washington to meet President Kennedy for the first time as Leader of the Labour Party. Mr Wigg was preparing his account of the talk with Dr Ward and Mr Wilson asked him to take it to Sir Frank Soskice, the Labour Party's lawyer, for his appreciation and advice on what should be done.

When Sir Frank read the document he found the contents more hair-raising than a Mickey Spillane paperback. He was particularly shocked that Mr Profumo should have strayed into such a world. Mr Wigg's annotations were pungent and exclamatory, in the nature of his speech, and peppered the document in parenthesis. Sir Frank thought that they were a little too colourful if the papers were to be handed on, and Mr Wigg produced a bowdlerised version.

When Mr Wilson returned from Washington he was confronted by the same question which had tormented Mr Wigg a few weeks before: was there a *prima facie* case for an inquiry of some form, and if there was how should they press for it? Sir Frank advised that Mr Wigg's document did justify further action, and it was decided that Mr Wigg's expurgated version should be sent to the Prime Minister, through the respective Chief Whips. Mr Wilson was anxious that knowledge of these developments should be kept to as few people as possible – only those who needed to know – and should certainly be concealed from the Press. In the event, the only people who did know were Mr Wigg, Mr Wilson, Sir Frank Soskice, Mr Herbert Bowden, the Labour Chief Whip, the Government's Chief Whip, Mr Redmayne, and Mr Macmillan. The document was sent to Mr Macmillan on April 9, with a covering letter from Mr Wilson.

While these secret steps were being taken, Miss Keeler had begun to discover her celebrity status. She returned to Britain on March 28, arriving at London Airport late at night. When she changed planes from Spain in Paris there had been fights between competing squads of journalists on the tarmac. At London the police were determined to prevent another fracas: Miss Keeler, in dark glasses and suede jacket, received as formidable a plain-clothes escort as any visiting statesman.

The B.B.C. news bulletins misunderstood what was happening, and said that she had been 'mobbed by journalists'. In fact, the reporters did not stand much of a chance of making contact, so numerous was the State bodyguard. The police wanted to see her, of course, because of the unsettled question of her failure to appear at the Old Bailey for the Edgecombe trial.

On April 1 Miss Keeler went before Mr Justice Lyell at the Old Bailey to explain her non-appearance. She was represented by Mr Victor Durand, Q.C., who said that the way in which she had been molested by newspapermen at Paris airport had brought upon her such a degree of punishment that she fully felt the inconvenience she had caused the court. She wished, he said, to proffer her 'humble apologies' for an act of silliness which was perhaps not unique in a person of twenty-one. With her penitence thus established, the Judge ordered Miss Keeler to forfeit the £40 surety she had entered into, and told her that it would have been easy for her to have communicated with the police, wherever she was.

When Miss Keeler left the Old Bailey, the Jamaican Aloysius 'Lucky' Gordon ran forward shouting: 'There she is. I want to see her.' Five constables grabbed him as Miss Keeler was driven away. There was a struggle which ended with Gordon's belongings strewn across the road, his shirt torn, his denture broken and two police helmets on the ground. He had been removed from the court building earlier after shouting: 'I want to be in court. All she has on her face is a big smile. I've got seventeen stitches in mine.'

Gordon's part in Miss Keeler's life and in the larger drama, was far from over. It was, in a sense, only just beginning.

12

Sitting on the Bomb

'I THINK THAT the House must realise this: one word from us
on this side in this House and we should have released an
explosion as great as we have seen in the last fortnight. But we
decided that, although the documents in our possession were,
in a sense, dynamite, and would have touched off such an
explosion, it was our duty, as a responsible Opposition, to
hand over all this information to the Prime Minister, who has
first responsibility for security, and not to make public use
of them.' – Mr Harold Wilson in the Commons on June 17.

Until the beginning of April, the inquiries into the Profumo case had been conducted through three basic channels:
by politicians, the Security Services and the newspapers. All
three by then knew about the same amount: the Press had
detailed but unsubstantiated accounts from Miss Keeler, Miss
Rice-Davies and lesser versions from Dr Ward and others;
the Security Services knew about Ivanov, Dr Ward and Mr
Profumo's association with them, and of Miss Keeler's part;
the Prime Minister and his staff knew about the rumours but
felt that they had been effectively answered by Mr Profumo's
denial; and Mr Wigg and Mr Wilson had their dossier.

There remained to be added a fourth pressure. This began
its course on April 2, when Chief Inspector Samuel Herbert
and Det. Sgt John Burrows, two officers attached to Marylebone Lane Police Station, began investigations into Dr Ward's
activities.

By a piquant chance, the day after the police began their
investigation, the *Sunday Pictorial* (by now re-named the
Sunday Mirror) dropped its own inquiry. On April 3, an
assistant editor of the paper went to the offices of Dr Ward's
solicitor, Mr Nevil Henle, of Coward, Chance and Co., and

handed over the letter which Mr Profumo had written to Miss Keeler on August 9, 1961. It was given to a representative of Mr Profumo's solicitors, Theodore Goddard and Co. Mr Henle later communicated Mr Profumo's gratitude. A photostat copy of the letter was, however, retained in the files of the newspaper – for posterity, presumably.

But if the *Sunday Mirror* thought Miss Keeler to be of no further value to them, the *News of the World* kept closer touch. On April 7 it published the most comprehensive biography of her which had then appeared. There were descriptions of her childhood, and a rather graphic account by Peter Earle, the writer, of his first encounter with Miss Keeler. Before the Edgecombe trial, he said, he had called at her flat. 'She welcomed me at the door, wearing skin-tight jeans and nothing else.' On this evidence he formed the the somewhat uncharitable conclusion that her figure might have been improved if she ate a little more.

By now the material distributed between Fleet Street, Westminster, Scotland Yard and the offices of the Security Services was collectively enough to blow Mr Profumo's statement of March 22 into a thousand discredited fragments. Four statements had been made about the allegation that Miss Keeler had been asked to obtain military information from Mr Profumo: the one taken on January 26 by the police investigating the Edgecombe case, in which Miss Keeler said the request had come from *Dr Ward*; a statement on March 29 by the ex-solicitor, Mr Eddowes, who had been consulted by Miss Keeler after the Edgecombe shooting, saying that it was *Ivanov* who had asked for the information; on March 25 the Security Services had a report from someone else which gave *Dr Ward* again as the source of the request. And finally, on April 4, Miss Keeler had told the same story to Inspector Herbert and Det. Sgt Burrows, again saying that it was *Dr Ward* who had asked. In every case she said that she had never carried out the request.

Nobody had passed on any of these four statements to the Prime Minister; nor had the allegation by the ex-M.P. John Lewis that Miss Keeler had been asked to get nuclear information from Mr Profumo been included in Mr Wigg's memorandum. Mr Wigg thought the idea completely improbable (and continues to do so), and so apparently had the Security Services.

It is worth imagining the kind of conversation which would have resulted had Miss Keeler decided to question Mr Profumo:

Keeler: Oh, by the way, Jack, I hear that there is some idea of increasing the second-strike capability in Germany ...

Profumo: Well, darling, I'm not sure that that would be in accord with the policy of controlled response; after all, Her Majesty's Government is opposed to supplying nuclear warheads to German troops because of the inherent danger of escalation. The Americans felt that the first phase of a conflict should be confined to a conventional response ...

Keeler: Yes, Jack, I agree with the idea of a conventional option, but at a time of great crisis, like this, is the electronic-percussive link system to be trusted?

Profumo: Look here, darling, you shouldn't be worrying your pretty little head about controlled response, you can leave that to me ...

The scene is manifestly absurd. Would a girl who hardly knew one end of a rocket from the other seriously be enlisted to obtain the most esoteric military information in the book?

The question which Dr Ward actually asked Christine Keeler was: 'Ask Jack when the Germans are going to get The Bomb.'

In this form, the question becomes more understandable. For, almost certainly, Dr Ward meant it as a joke, although Christine Keeler was not sure whether Ward was joking or not.

She is not a particularly consistent person, but on this point she always remained steady. She was cross-examined on it many times and her story was almost always the same. In any case, there was no apparent reason why she should not have been telling the truth.

It was during its journey to various points that the story became distorted through misunderstanding. Mr Michael Eddowes, the first of the messengers, is not a simple person;

his political views are complex and sophisticated; he does not think in such terms as 'The Bomb'.

He believed genuinely that Keeler told him that '*Ivanov* asked her to ask Profumo when nuclear warheads were being delivered to the Germans.' And he had a brilliant, though somewhat glib, explanation why the information should have been so vital that Ivanov was willing to risk using such a girl as his Mata Hari: 'It was Cuba time when the question was asked,' he recalled later. 'There had never been a satisfactory explanation for the Russian withdrawal. The question from Ivanov explained it.

'Mr Khrushchev deliberately created the situation to help him over Germany. Geographically, Berlin is to Russia what Cuba is to America. After Cuba, if the Americans ever tried to give Germany nuclear warheads, Mr Khrushchev could react with precisely the same determination as did Mr Kennedy, and force him to withdraw, and the public could be so fair-minded that it would give him support.'

Mr Eddowes regretted that he ever re-told the story. He got nowhere when he tried to pass it on, and he was scorched by the Prime Minister for his efforts to get the story out through Christine Keeler's mother (he visited her at Wraysbury on March 23).*

And what of Mr Lewis, the ex-M.P., who was the second person to whom Keeler told the story? He got the questioner right: Dr Ward. But, once again, his wide political knowledge probably led him to distort accidentally the end of the story. Politicians simply do not think in terms of 'The Bomb' in relation to Germany. Apart from the fact that missiles have taken over from the Bomb, the Germans would never have

* Mr Macmillan said in the House of Commons on June 17 about Mr Eddowes: 'He suggested that Miss Keeler should make a statement saying that Ivanov was her boy friend and that she got information from Mr Profumo and gave it to Ivanov for a joke. Mr Eddowes went on to say that Miss Keeler would have to keep to this story to protect herself. He said that she would get £5,000 to £10,000 when the Press had the story. In that respect, it was an underestimate in my view. Mr Eddowes added – this is what he told the mother – that the Government would be forced to open an inquiry to which Miss Keeler would state these things and turn out a little heroine.'

122

been given such a weapon. Retelling his unrecorded conversations with Miss Keeler to Mr Wigg, another well-informed man, Mr Lewis would have naturally used terms other than 'The Bomb'.

Perhaps the most ironic aspect of the whole sequence of events was that, had Keeler taken Ward's joke seriously and asked Profumo, he would not have known the answer anyway. At that stage, had a decision been made to give Germany nuclear weapons within NATO, only the Prime Minister, and possibly the Foreign Secretary, Lord Home, would have known of such a dangerous move. Profumo was not even in the Cabinet and would have been among the last of the Government to hear.

On that point, a red herring dies.

Mr Macmillan received Mr Wigg's document, with Mr Wilson's covering letter, on April 10. There was on that day something else to occupy his attention; the annual luncheon of the 1922 Committee, which represents the rank and file of the Conservative Party in both the House of Lords and the Commons.

Although the Conservatives did not need to go to the country until, at the latest, the autumn of 1964, there had been a great deal of speculation about whether they would hold a snap election in the late spring or early autumn of 1963, or run to the full term. The unemployment crisis had been slightly lessened by the end of the severe winter, but the economy was notoriously slack and the opinion polls showed Labour to be well ahead of the Government. By this time it was clear that the criticism of the leadership which began with the collapse of the Common Market talks had run out of steam, but if the Prime Minister was not immediately to be replaced, there was the question of whether he would remain to lead the party at the election – whenever the harassed tacticians of the Central Office deemed that to be.

When the Prime Minister spoke to the 1922 Committee that lunchtime he wore the expression of bland optimism which had been such an effective palliative in times of doubt and crisis. There were about him the men whom gossip indicated were candidates for the succession. But Mr Macmillan was on form. He did not trouble to embrace assumptions of electoral defeat in his speech; the note was one of confident prediction. The party was prepared to modernise: Dr Beeching's mayhem with the railways was proof of this. He was equally ruthless with the rumours of his retirement. 'I shall be leading you into the general election, and I shall be with you in the new Parliament,' he said. The ambition was tacitly accepted.

At this time the newspapers and the public were preoccupied by an unprecedented insight into the sexual excesses of an aristocratic marriage: in Edinburgh the litigation between the Duke and Duchess of Argyll had come to an end after three and a half years of progress through the courts. Such a history was unlikely to produce anti-climax, and the summing-up of the Duke's divorce action was appropriately superlative: 65,000 words long – nearly as long as this book – and four and a half hours in the delivery, even though the judge, Lord Wheatley, spoke at a breathless 200 words a minute.

On the basis of the evidence, said Lord Wheatley, the Duchess at forty-nine 'was a completely promiscuous woman whose sexual appetite could only be satisfied by a number of men'. Four of the number were cited but one of them had to remain anonymous. He appeared, at least all of him apart from the head, with the Duchess in a photograph taken by Polaroid camera. Both were nude. The photograph had been one of the exhibits in the case.

The comprehensive summing-up was something in the nature of a condemnation of promiscuity and the tolerance of it which the judge felt was accepted by what he called 'moderns'. Abroad, where the divorce was widely reported, it did nothing to dispel the growing impression that old ideas of British sexuality were to be out of date.

Meanwhile, the political parties were concerned not so much with the headless man as with the dateless election. In the two years before the last election the Conservatives had spent nearly £500,000 on advertising. ('Life's better with the Conservatives – don't let Labour ruin it.') Now, in a drastic reappraisal of attitude, the Labour Party had also decided to go to the hoardings and into the newspapers with the image makers and hidden persuaders. Advertising had, three years before, been anathema to them. Now it was an indispensable ally. Neither party could know that, for a while at least, Christine Keeler would have more effect than any fantasies devised by advertising men.

By now Mr Profumo had, in a sense, been as good as his word. The French magazine *Paris Match* carried a picture of him – a very ordinary picture – and an ambiguous caption. The page was removed from the copies sent to Britain, but Mr Profumo sued the magazine nevertheless. And on April 11 in the High Court he was awarded agreed damages of £50 against the English distributors of the Italian picture magazine *Tempo Illustrato*, which had printed the baseless rumour that Mr Profumo had been in some way involved in Miss Keeler's absence from the Edgecombe trial. It was also said that the article contained 'suggestions that Mr Profumo had been, or might have been, in some improper relationship with Miss Keeler.' The defendants, Continental Publishers and Distributors Ltd, said that they recognised that all such allegations were unjustifiable, and they agreed to pay Mr Profumo's legal costs as well as the damages (which Mr Profumo donated to an Army charity).

A week elapsed between Mr Macmillan receiving Mr Wigg's document and a reply being made. On April 17 the Prime Minister wrote to Mr Wilson:

'My Chief Whip has given to me the letter and enclosure from you dated April 9 and dealing with George Wigg's conversation with a Mr Stephen Ward. I will ask the appropriate authorities to have an examination made of this information and will get in touch with you later on, if this seems necessary.'

The reference to 'a Mr Stephen Ward' irritated Mr Wilson. It gave the impression that Dr Ward was an absolute unknown, although, of course, Mr Macmillan had already seen the letter he had written during the Cuban crisis, and knew of his activities then. Mr Wilson said later that this attitude was 'symptomatic of the Prime Minister's indolent nonchalance'. He was far from satisfied with the reply, but assumed that since the letter was being passed on to the 'appropriate authorities' (it was sent, in fact, to the Security Services) there might be a later reaction. At this time, too, Mr Wigg had gone to Ghana, and it would be difficult to make a response while he was away.

On April 18 Aloysius Gordon entered the story again. Miss Keeler was visiting a flat in Devonshire Street, Marylebone, of a friend called Paula Hamilton-Marshall. As she left at 12.30 a.m. there was a scuffle. Miss Hamilton-Marshall heard screams and phoned the police. Gordon was later arrested. On May 3 he appeared at Marlborough Street Magistrates Court charged with maliciously and intentionally causing grievous bodily harm to Miss Keeler. He was committed for trial at the Old Bailey.

Throughout the rest of April Inspector Herbert and Sgt Burrows were continuing their inquiries into Dr Ward and his world. They interviewed many of his patients, and they took a statement from Marilyn Rice-Davies, who was temporarily in prison at Holloway on a motoring offence. (This involved a fake driving licence and a Jaguar given to her by Peter Rachman.)

Dr Ward was gradually feeling isolated and exposed. Not only had his patients disappeared, but the influential friends in whose patronage he had so luxuriated were deserting him. The world of noble houses, diplomatic parties and political soirées had shrunk to one confined mostly to his own four walls and a few people who still felt that loyalty to him contained no embarrassment. He had been forced to give up the cottage at Cliveden, and with it all the spirited informalities and reflected glory which it provided. He felt deprivation and the kind of social claustrophobia that he had never known before. He was becoming a pariah. There was no scope left for ingratiation. And the police investigation heightened his alarm.

On May 7 he took the first of a series of desperate and impolitic steps. He telephoned Mr Timothy Bligh, the Prime Minister's Principal Private Secretary at Admiralty House, and asked for an interview. Mr Bligh consulted the Prime Minister, who was in some doubt about the wisdom of agreeing to this unusual request. He decided, however, that Dr Ward might have some information with a bearing on security, and that Mr Bligh ought to see him . . . but in the company of a member of the Security Services.

Dr Ward arrived at Admiralty House in his grey Jaguar, and parked it in the courtyard. A girl who was with him went to a pub across the road in Whitehall. The first thing that Dr Ward did when he saw Mr Bligh was to complain about the police inquiries. It was made plain that his complaint was improper, since the investigation had nothing to do with the Government. And then, in a desperate bid to blackmail the Government into calling off the police, Dr Ward let drop the fact that he was in a position to cause them considerable embarrassment. Mr Profumo's statement, he said, had been untrue. That was all – he made no specific allegation, he merely said that the House had been misled.

After Dr Ward left Admiralty House it was decided that Mr Profumo should again be interrogated, but since there was no new charge for him to reply to, it was only his word against that of Dr Ward, and he stuck to his story.

There had been no further letter from the Prime Minister to the Leader of the Opposition. Mr Wigg had returned from Ghana, and the apparent inertia at Admiralty House gave the impression that there was still no inclination to take the security side seriously. On May 13 Mr Wilson wrote again to Mr Macmillan, asking what action was going to be taken. The reply sent the following day, confirmed Mr Wilson's suspicions. It said: 'There seems to be nothing in the papers you sent which requires me to take further action.'

But five days later action was precipitated by Dr Ward. It had become plain to him the police had not been called off as a result of his visit to Admiralty House. On May 19 he wrote to the Home Secretary, making the same demand and repeating that Mr Profumo had been lying. He also wrote to his M.P., Sir W. Wakefield, making the same request and allegations.

Then he took really desperate action. He issued a statement to the newspapers which said 'I have placed before the Home Secretary certain facts of the relationship between Miss Keeler and Mr Profumo, since it is obvious now that my efforts to conceal these facts in the interests of Mr Profumo and the Government have made it appear that I myself have something to hide – which I have not. The result has been that I have been persecuted in a variety of ways, causing damage not only to myself but to my friends and patients – a state of affairs which I propose to tolerate no longer.'

This was, in fact, a summary of the letter he had sent to the Home Secretary. No newspaper could print it, although it served to support the information which some of them already had, for fear of libel. There was still no specific charge but it was obvious that with Dr Ward ready to betray Mr Profumo, with the police investigation on the way to completion, and with the newspapers so much in the know, the bomb was now ticking almost loudly enough to be heard in Admiralty House.

13

Why Macmillan Acted at Last

MR WILSON WAS GROWING RESTLESS. He felt that with Dr Ward firing off allegations all over the place it was time to end the paralysis at Admiralty House. He knew, too, that although the contents of Mr Wigg's dossier and the action that had been taken over it were still unknown outside the original confidants, Dr Ward's activities were becoming known to several members of the Labour Party who were likely to act. Mr Wilson himself received a letter from Dr Ward on May 23, similar in substance to the ones sent to Mr Brooke and the newspapers. He foresaw that it was now hopelessly optimistic to expect the affair to die down without instituting some form of inquiry, as quickly as possible. On May 24 he asked to see Mr Macmillan to express his dissatisfaction with the Prime Minister's unwillingness to act. An appointment was made for the two men to meet on the following Monday, May 27. The same day, May 24, there came the first of the independent steps by Labour M.P.s which Mr Wilson had expected. Mr Parkin was in action again. He put down a question to the Home Secretary, asking:

'What conclusions he has reached about information supplied to him by Dr Stephen Ward and what action he proposes to take following recent Metropolitan Police inquiries to prevent the increase of expensive call-girl organisations.'

May 24 was a Friday, and, as soon as Mr Parkin had put down his question, he left London to spend the weekend at his cottage near Stroud, in Gloucestershire. Not surprisingly, many people tried to reach him that weekend. The cottage was not on the phone, and messages had to be left at the house of a friend nearby. There were about a score of them, but Mr Parkin could not be found.

On Monday Mr Parkin was still away from the House. He had arranged to be 'paired' by another member. Meanwhile, Mr Wilson saw the Prime Minister, as arranged. Also present were Mr Bowden, the Labour Chief Whip, and Mr John Hewitt, the Patronage Secretary.

It was another exasperating encounter for Mr Wilson. Mr Macmillan appeared not to have changed his attitude that any further action seemed unwarranted, and he seemed to attach little weight to Mr Wigg's disclosures. This was altogether too casual for Mr Wilson. He decided to use as an illustration of a similar situation producing a different reaction the case of John Belcher, who had been Parliamentary Secretary at the Board of Trade in Attlee's Government. When allegations about Mr Belcher receiving gifts reached Attlee late one night he had, recalled Mr Wilson, immediately sent for Lord Jowitt, the Lord Chancellor. In the resulting investigation Mr Belcher's staff had been subjected to what Mr Wilson described as a brutal investigation by the police. And although the 'gifts' turned out to be pathetic and trivial – some bananas, drinks and ordinary hospitality – Mr Belcher had been crucified and his career broken.

In choosing to recall this case Mr Wilson had played a subtle psychological stroke. It enabled him to cite the ruthless expedience which Earl Attlee had made a characteristic of his approach to the Prime Ministership. It was, Mr Wilson pointed out, in contrast to the way Mr Macmillan was handling the Profumo case, and in the Belcher case there had been no security anxiety; in this one, he told Mr Macmillan, it was security which primarily concerned him.

Attlee's reputation as a Prime Minister had risen over the years, and his ability to hold in check tempestuous clashes of personality, and to deal ruthlessly with men, regardless of personal relationships, had emerged as one of his principal qualities. Mr Macmillan, mindful that his own rôle might similarly be judged, began to reconsider his attitude. It is, of course, unlikely that Mr Wilson's tactics would, in themselves, have been enough to lodge a grain of doubt in the Prime Minister's mind. Perhaps Mr Macmillan had been stung by the comparison, or perhaps he had not. It may have struck into the subconscious, to have an invisible effect. What is certain is that although Mr Wilson left that interview feeling that not much had been done to increase the sense of urgency in Admiralty House, the Prime Minister had begun to turn the matter over in his mind again. This was decisive.

The balance of decision took another microscopic tilt that day. A minute recording the meeting between Mr Wilson and the Prime Minister was sent, as routine, to the Security authorities. They received it on May 28. Somewhere in that opaque machine the files were brought out into the light of day. And there one of the most implausible pieces of information collected on the case came up: the statement Miss Keeler had made on January 26 about being asked to question Mr Profumo on secret information.

At last the separate strands were coming together; or, to put it another way, the left hand was about to learn what the right hand had known for some time. It is now necessary to re-capitulate and survey the whole machinery of inquiry and political communication, for somewhere there had been a serious breakdown in communications. This was the comparative state of knowledge up to May 28:

The Prime Minister knew from February 4 that rumour alleged that Mr Profumo and Miss Keeler were lovers; that the *News of the World* had a story which alleged that Mr Profumo was sharing his mistress with the Soviet naval attaché; from March 27 he knew from the letter Mr Wilson had given to him that Dr Ward, who presided over whatever kind of relationship Miss Keeler had with Mr Profumo, had acted as an 'honest broker' in unofficial approaches by the Russians to the Foreign Office; from April 10 he had had Mr Wigg's dossier with its detailed description of the activities of Dr Ward and Ivanov, and its picture of the lurid world into which Mr Profumo had apparently strayed, and the relationship Dr Ward claimed with the Security Services; from May 7 he knew that Dr Ward was saying that Mr Profumo had not told the truth in his statement to the House of Commons on March 22; and he knew that the Leader of the Opposition felt strongly that there had been a security *risk* in Mr Profumo's relationship; he knew all this and he knew that Mr Profumo had strenuously denied that he and

Miss Keeler were lovers and that security had in any way been prejudiced.

The police knew from January 26, as a result of their inquiries into the Edgecombe case, that Miss Keeler alleged that she had been asked by Dr Ward to pump Mr Profumo for military information, and that she said she had not done so; from March 24 that Miss Keeler's mother had been approached by Mr Eddowes about her relationship with Mr Profumo and Ivanov; from March 29 that Mr Eddowes alleged that Miss Keeler had been asked by Ivanov to question Mr Profumo about nuclear warheads; and from April 2 how Mr Profumo fitted into Dr Ward's life and what that life consisted of.

The Security Services knew from June 1961, as a result of their surveillance of Ivanov, that the Russian saw a lot of Dr Ward; from July 1961, from Dr Ward himself, that Mr Profumo was a friend of his; that on August 9, 1961, Mr Profumo had been warned of the dangers of associating with Dr Ward; from late in 1962 that Ivanov and Dr Ward had made approaches on behalf of the Soviet Embassy during the Cuban crisis; from January 1963 about Miss Keeler allegedly being asked to obtain nuclear secrets, and the subsequent statements repeating this; from April 10, according to the dossier compiled by Mr Wigg and passed on to them by the Prime Minister, that Dr Ward had been evasive about his interest in Ivanov and sympathetic to Russian interests during both the Berlin and Cuban crises.

Mr Wilson knew from March 10 of Mr Wigg's growing dossier; from March 26 of Dr Ward's activities during the Cuban crisis and all that he had told Mr Wigg; from the middle of May that Dr Ward was ratting on Mr Profumo and making allegations to the Home Office and the newspapers.

This was the situation on May 28, while Mr Macmillan was reassessing the facts. By that evening he had decided that there would have to be an inquiry, and that Lord Dilhorne, the Lord Chancellor, should conduct it. Mr Profumo's days as a Minister were now numbered.

The information about Miss Keeler's January 26 statement reached Mr Macmillan from the Security Services, on May 29, having taken 123 days to do so. This would probably in itself have been enough to set off an inquiry; in the event the

Prime Minister had already done so. Mr Wilson could claim some of the credit for that . . . and, of course, Mr Wigg, whose long, wearing and much-criticised investigation was about to be vindicated.

The Prime Minister communicated his change of attitude to Mr Wilson on May 30. He wrote: 'I have been thinking about our talk on Monday. I am sure in my own mind that the security aspect of the Ward case has been fully and efficiently watched, but I think it important that you should be in no doubt about it.' And he disclosed the Lord Chancellor's inquiry.

This was the last full day of Parliament before Whitsun recess. When Mr Macmillan's note was delivered to Mr Wilson both of them were at Westminster, and both were in the chamber at question time. Mr Wilson scribbled a note to the Prime Minister asking that the Lord Chancellor's inquiry should be announced, in view of the fact that so many people then knew of Dr Ward's allegations. The note was slipped across to Mr Macmillan, but he did not react. Later that evening it was formally acknowledged by the Prime Minister's secretary; Mr Macmillan himself was going to Scotland for a holiday.

There was another incident in the Commons that afternoon, which seemed meaningless at the time. Several M.P.s noticed that in the shadow behind the Speaker's Chair Mr Profumo was in a huddle, first with the Prime Minister and then with Mr Redmayne, the Chief Whip.

The Prime Minister was later criticised for not doing what Mr Wilson had requested: revealing the Lord Chancellor's inquiry when it began. The reason was that, as Mr Macmillan had said in his note to Mr Wilson, he was still confident about the security aspect, and at that stage the inquiry was confined to within the administration itself, for the private consumption of the Prime Minister and Mr Wilson.

Mr Wilson had anyway decided to continue the psychological warfare. Mr Parkin had finally returned to Westminster from his country seat on Tuesday, the 28th. His question and his immediate absence after tabling it, had created something of a panic. As soon as he got back he was met by a

Whip's runner, literally panting. Mr Wilson, he was told, wanted to see him at once.

Mr Wilson explained to him that the part of his question which had referred to 'expensive call-girl organisations' was against his policy of tackling the case from the sexual side. He did not want to institute an inquiry into vice, but into security. He asked Mr Parkin if he would mind withdrawing his question, and Mr Parkin agreed. There was no question of a *diktat;* it was done for the sake of consistent tactics. Mr Wilson then told Mr Wigg that he wanted a question put down, and he felt that it should have the maximum authority behind it. He suggested that it should be tabled by an elder statesman of the Party, Mr Chuter Ede, a former Home Secretary and the man who had set up the Lynskey Tribunal in the Sidney Stanley Case. Mr Ede had a reputation for maintaining the highest standards of Parliamentary and public life. He agreed to the idea, and the new question was drafted in Mr Wilson's office.

All this was happening on May 30; and since the House was about to go into recess there was little time left. Another pressure intervened: it was also the day of the Coronation Cup race at the Epsom meeting (the Derby was run the day before) and Mr Wigg, a considerably experienced student of the turf, had arranged to drive Mr Chuter Ede and his sister down to Epsom for the afternoon.

As they left Westminster Mr Ede gave Mr Wigg a copy of the question as it had been drafted, but since they were anxious to get to Epsom Mr Wigg pushed it into his pocket without looking at it. This had bizarre consequences. Mr Wigg, Mr Ede and his sister were in the grandstand, when a message was relayed over the entire loudspeaker system and consequently over all of Epsom Downs. The voice boomed its incongruous message: 'Would Mr George Wigg please go to the weighing-room?' Somewhat embarrassed, Mr Wigg headed for the weighing-room to find there was a phone call for him from Mr Wilson's office. There, among the saddles, the jockeys and the weighing machines, high Parliamentary business was discussed. But the din was too much, and Mr Wigg went to the telephone in the office of the Clerk of the

Course and phoned back. He was told that the Chuter Ede question was out of order, and he was asked to consult Mr Chuter Ede on the re-drafting. Having done so, he decided to drive straight back to Westminster and check the final version when it was put down.

The original question had said: '. . . to ask the Secretary of State for the Home Department what information he has received from Dr Stephen Ward in connection with inquiries carried out by the Metropolitan Police; and what action he proposes to take.' It was the mention of the police inquiries which put the question out of order. The revised question was tabled at 4.50 p.m. It said: '. . . to ask the Secretary of State for the Home Department what information he has received from Dr Stephen Ward *about a Ministerial statement made to the House on 22nd March* 1963 and what action he proposes to take thereupon.'

This question was intended to harry the government and to step up the war of nerves. The tactics had been approved by the Shadow Cabinet. They were certainly effective.

Mr Macmillan took the night sleeper to Inverness on May 30 leaving Lord Dilhorne to begin his inquiry. On May 31 Lord Dilhorne told Mr Profumo that he would want to see him on the following Thursday, June 6. Soon after learning this, Mr and Mrs Profumo left London to spend Whitsun in Venice. They intended to return on June 5. Over the Whitsun weekend, which brought the first spell of warm weather since the severe winter, there was the first holiday exodus of the year. But Lord Dilhorne was not taking a rest – he was a tireless worker – and he made better progress than he had expected. He sent a telegram to Mr Profumo, via the War Office, saying that he would want to see him a day earlier on Wednesday, June 5.

Mr Profumo had gone to Venice clearly realising that the forces of truth were closing in on him. The lie was becoming impossible to live with. Lord Dilhorne's cable indicated that escape was now impossible. . . . He knew that the Labour Party were pressing for details of Dr Ward's allegations, and he realised that if the cornered Dr Ward was prepared to rat on him his own fate was ineluctable. The first person he had to tell demanded the most painful confession of all: his wife. Until then she, like all Mr Profumo's colleagues, had not known. And so, that weekend Mr Profumo's burden became lighter by one person. The crisis made the beauties of Venice incongruous; the Profumos cut short their holiday and arrived back in London on the Golden Arrow on Whit Monday.

That evening Mr Profumo telephoned Mr Bligh, the Prime Minister's Principal Private Secretary, and said that he wanted to see the Prime Minister because there had been 'a serious development'. It was pointed out that the Prime Minister was in Scotland, and that if the matter was urgent it had better be dealt with at once in London. It was arranged that Mr Profumo should see Mr Bligh at Admiralty House at 10.30 a.m. the following day. When Mr Profumo arrived for this meeting Mr Redmayne, the Chief Whip, was also present.

The 'serious development' was that Mr Profumo had decided to confess that for four months he had been lying to his colleagues, to his wife and to the Law Officers of the Crown. He had lied on the floor of the House of Commons and had so betrayed the display of loyal trust provided by the Prime Minister. He had taken legal action and recovered damages on the basis of those lies.

He tendered his resignation and said that he would apply for the Chiltern Hundreds, the archaic procedure by which he immediately ceased to be a Member of Parliament. His political career was finished and his reputation ruined. Later that day, on the next pre-arranged phone call to the Prime Minister, Mr Bligh told him of Mr Profumo's confession and resignation. When the Prime Minister had left for his holiday he had still felt that the incident, as he then knew it, raised no security issues, and he was convinced that Mr Profumo had been telling the truth all along, a conviction fortified by the successful legal action which had been taken. Now the deception cut deep into the Prime Minister's instinct of trust, the blow was personal and severe. He said that he wanted time to consider his reply, and would dictate it the following morning by telephone.

At Admiralty House, meanwhile, the statement announcing the sensation had to be prepared. This involved Mr Profumo's solicitor, Mr Clogg, and Theodore Goddard & Co., who had been deceived by their client. They were anxious that the statement should clearly absolve them from complicity in the deception. By the morning of Wednesday, June 5, the form of the statement had been settled, and the Prime Minister's reply had been received from Scotland. All that then had to be done was for copies of the confession and reply to be duplicated and released to the world.

While this revelation was on the brink of disclosure Sir William Haley, as if by some clairvoyant urge, was making an uncannily apposite speech at the annual lunch of the Automobile Association. The Press, he said, lived by disclosures, and a healthy society should also live by disclosures: 'We have to fight for more freedom. We need a new attitude on the part of the makers of news – officialdom, Government departments, parish councils, institutions, big business and trade unions – any or all of whom will try to withold news if they can.'

The message was an echo of Sir William's 'It *is* happening here' leader: 'It is easy to understand the reluctance of people in any kind of body to reveal information which will disclose error or weakness, and how they at once hastily arrange a Press conference to sidetrack any real inquiry.' Mr Macmillan's Press secretary, Mr Harold Evans, was at that moment arranging a Press conference for an opposite purpose.

At 2 p.m. the political correspondents had been called to the Conservative Central Office to hear an outline of a report on the health of the Conservative Party machine, which had been a labour of love over many months for the ex-Chancellor of the Exchequer, Mr Selwyn Lloyd. At the end of this conference the lobby correspondents were told that Mr Evans would make an announcement to them at 6 p.m. By 4 p.m. some of them had phoned their editors and told them that their hunch was that announcement concerned Mr Profumo.

At 6 p.m. Mr Evans released Mr Profumo's statement. It said:

Dear Prime Minister,
    You will recollect that on March 22 following certain allegations made in Parliament, I made a personal statement. At that time rumour had charged me with assisting in the

137

disappearance of a witness and with being involved in some possible breach of security.

So serious were these charges that I allowed myself to think that my personal association with that witness, which had also been the subject of rumour, was, by comparison, of minor importance only.

In my statement I said that there had been no impropriety in this association. To my very deep regret I have to admit that this was not true, and that I misled you, and my colleagues, and the House.

I ask you to understand that I did this to protect, as I thought, my wife and family, who were equally misled, as were my professional advisers.

I have come to realise that, by this deception, I have been guilty of a grave misdemeanour, and despite the fact that there is no truth whatever in the other charges, I cannot remain a member of your Administration, nor of the House of Commons. I cannot tell you of my deep remorse for the embarrassment I have caused to you, to my colleagues in the Government, to my constituents and to the party which I have served for the past 25 years.

Yours sincerely, Jack Profumo

The letter was dated June 4 and sent from 3 Chester Terrace, Regent's Park, N.W.1, the Profumos' home.

The Prime Minister's reply, dated June 5, was sent from Ardchattan Priory, Connel, Argyll, the home of Lieut.-Colonel and Mrs R. Campbell-Preston, where he was staying. It was more brief:

Dear Profumo,

The contents of your letter of June 4 have been communicated to me, and I have heard them with deep regret. This is a great tragedy for you, your family, and your friends.

Nevertheless, I am sure you will understand that in the circumstances, I have no alternative but to advise the Queen to accept your resignation.

Yours very sincerely, Harold Macmillan

14

Who Was to Blame?

WHEN THE TRUTH about Mr Profumo was revealed, the reaction to it was so violent that it obscured the real issue: how had he got away with it all this time? The rumour had been breeding for so long that elaborate fantasies were created, some of them wilfully, others the product of misunderstanding. Many adult, mature men of great political experience were prepared to believe the wildest inventions. The sinister and the grotesque found ready ears.

Underneath, interred by mounting deposits of absurdities, somewhere lay the truth.

The first fantasy was the gravest charge of all: that the Prime Minister had known about Mr Profumo's sad affair all along and had, for some lunatic reason, decided to bluff it out. This was quite seriously suggested by some senior members of his own party – if they suggested it without being serious it somehow would have been worse. They believed it. The kindest interpretation that can be put on this story is that it resulted from them receiving only half the information: that they knew that in February the Prime Minister had been told about the rumours, but because no overt action followed he had connived to conceal the truth. Many of Mr Macmillan's enemies saw him as the cartoonists caricatured him: as an Edwardian recluse, remote from reality with government somehow being conducted by others who trouble him as little as possible. And yet they saw the same man capable of compromising his honour, prejudicing his future and jeopardising his government solely to protect an adulterer. Did that fit the Edwardian code? One illusion cancels the other.

In the end the charge against the Prime Minister was just that nobody had told him. A failure of communication. But it did not end with not being told – how anxious was he to *be* told? It is not an entirely passive responsibility. What, then, should have activated his curiosity? The failure was really created by two things: a system and an attitude.

To get the attitude right, it is necessary to recall the time when Mr Macmillan became Prime Minister, just over six years before. He followed, in Eden, a man who had not only been unseated by the political disaster of Suez but a man whose health had been broken by the job. Eden, in turn, had succeeded in Churchill a man of abnormal, Herculean constitution. When Eden broke down it was said the Prime Ministership had grown too big a burden for one man; that it was, in fact, a killing job. It was certainly a wounding one in the way that Eden did it; nobody else could be *his* Foreign Secretary.

Mr Macmillan appraised this argument, that the job was lethal, and saw its flaw: that it depended on the philosophy of the man. He then made a decision that was fundamental to his whole subsequent performance: he would rely absolutely on delegation. He constructed the pyramid of command, carefully chose the men who would form it, laid down the lines of responsibility, and left himself clear for the essence of Prime Ministership: decision-making.

This system seemed to work, and it suited superbly his own abilities and character. It kept his mind uncluttered, and it ensured his physical survival. Where it broke down was in the one area where there was no minister to delegate to: security. Delegation was a sound enough philosophy, and the only viable one. But it required that each department should have not only its administrators but its political heads: men able not only to operate the machine but who knew also the wider canvas of the Cabinet and pressures external to their own ministries.

Mr Macmillan's government had been accident-prone in its handling of security (though it is fair to add that the Labour party had had similar troubles when it was in power). Each spy incident had been followed by an inquiry of some form, and each time communications-failure had played some part, notably in the failure to record and pass on the glaring character defects of Houghton, the Portland Base traitor. Each case had led to some minor tightening up, but it was always the policy of the stable door. The Profumo case, involving not a security

140

leak but a security risk, made the security issue a political one more than one of actual security techniques (though it suggested that the resources for surveillance were not all that they might have been). There was a great deal of confusion in the way of seeing the new security problem clearly: many people mixed it up with external intelligence. But it was a defect of *political structure.*

Certainly, the head of the Security Services had direct access to the Prime Minister. But this meant that he went to see Mr Macmillan only when he felt that there was need to: that depended on his own evaluation and judgment, yet he was unaware of what political pressure there might be. It was plainly a one-dimensional rôle, which anyway carried enough administrative burden without requiring political instincts as well. Mr Macmillan's Achilles heel was that he had no Minister of Security. This was a controversial idea, but it had been around for years. Mr Wilson subscribed to it. Yet Mr Macmillan was wary of it. There was in his make-up a genuine fear, perhaps a little old-fashioned, of creating within the executive a monolith security organisation which, by reason of its essentially covert nature, might become a law unto itself. He was always at pains to emphasise that a free society had to be wary about how much rope it allowed its Security Services. He said, after the Profumo revelation: 'There is, of course, unfortunately under modern conditions, where so much is known of the ways in which private weaknesses can be played upon, a wide range of behaviour which is properly a matter of security. But if the private lives of Ministers and of senior officials are to be the subject of continual supervision day and night, then all I can say is that we shall have a society very different from this one and, I venture to suggest, more open to abuse and tyranny than would justify any possible gain to security in the ordinary sense.' This may be admirable sentiment, but it was only sentiment. The point which it avoided was that anybody whose office or responsibility in any way involved the security of the state must accept, surely, that their freedom has to be circumscribed by degrees appropriate to their responsibility. This is far from being the creed of McCarthyism, which Mr Macmillan rightly feared.

In any case, Mr Macmillan's case could hardly hold water as an argument against having a Minister of Security: this would give him more of a safeguard rather than less.

But there was another, more practical obstruction to the idea of a new Minister. It was that whichever politician was chosen for the job, he would have to commit virtual and instantaneous political suicide, or at least a form of self-denial extremely rare among politicians. He would have to submerge completely from public life. He could not go before the House of Commons and brag about his department's successes. His appearances would be confined entirely to answering criticisms of failure. Wherever this man of advanced humility was to be found, it seemed that it was not among Mr Macmillan's colleagues.

The Prime Minister's dependence on *ad hoc* contact with the head of Security Services introduced two entirely subjective conditions: the will in the Prime Minister himself to question and to seek the answer; and the will in the head of the Security Services to tell. Each would decide independently. The Security man would, for example, obviously trouble the Prime Minister only with items which he thought he should know – yet he could not possibly foresee all the situations when this would be necessary. From a day or so after January 26 the Security Services had had Miss Keeler's statement, but obviously decided that there was no reason for it to go to Admiralty House. Sir Norman Brook had made a minute of his warning to Mr Profumo in 1961 and he, only a door away from the Prime Minister, had not felt that it merited passing on. With the information they had, they were probably right. Had they been in the Prime Minister's chair they might have seen it differently, certainly after the events of February 4.

There was no question of dereliction of duty; there was simply not the channel of communication which enabled each fully to appreciate the other's problem. When Mr Macmillan was, on May 27, finally provoked into instituting an inquiry, the results came soon enough. But the machine had to be kicked.

But apart from the failure of the system, there was a failure of attitude. By February the Prime Minister's mind was virtually sealed against the impact of rumour. This was for immensely human reasons.

The rumour then was only the equivalent of Fleet Street tittle-tattle, to which he was allergic. And yet the rumour had been taken to Admiralty House out of a sense of duty, not as a piece of idle gossip. Mr Chapman-Walker, who took it, had the kind of relationship with Mr Wyndham, who received it, which enabled the matter to be discussed without awkwardness, and the motives for taking it there to be above question.

When it got to the Prime Minister three days later, Mr Profumo had been interrogated four times. Knowing both the sketchy nature of the charges and the force of Mr Profumo's denials, did it really merit a less sceptical reception from the Prime Minister? Compared with the major business of state, which then was to find a new course for Britain after our rejection by Europe, the failure to press the rumour further is proof of, if anything, a sane sense of proportion. His resistance to rumour was not at this stage critical. It was perhaps later to prove too obdurate, but at this time there was no cause for him to be diverted from his principal tasks.

Nor was there any cause for him to alter his attitude at the time of the March 22 denial. It was not, in fact, until Mr Wilson's approaches, and Mr Wigg's dossier, that the resistance to the rumour went beyond wisdom. Here, for the first time in his own experience, the Prime Minister had set out for him the substance of the anxieties on the security issue.

At first, this made little impression on him. His letter to Mr Wilson on May 14 had said: 'There seems to be nothing in the papers you sent which requires me to take any action.' Mr Wilson thought otherwise, and his conviction could hardly have been a partisan one, since he had taken great care to handle the whole matter with restraint. Perhaps, once again, the Vassall case was casting its shadows over the Prime Minister's vision. He could recall Mr George Brown's words when pressing in the Commons for a larger scale inquiry: 'We cannot leave the Vassall case where it is. There are other letters in existence, copies of which I and, no doubt, others have seen, the originals of which are in the hands of what are called "the authorities", which indicate a degree of ministerial responsibility which goes far beyond the ordinary business of a Minister in charge, being responsible for everything which goes on in his Department.' Here was Mr Brown, dedicated to everything opposed to autocracy, complaining that what transpired to be an innocuous correspondence had been Ministerial indulgence. This was over-statement and misjudgment. It had led to the Prime Minister accepting a resignation – Mr Galbraith's – which he knew was not justified. Five months later he was determined not to make the same mistake again. What he did not know was that though the situations appeared to be superficially similar, they differed in the most critical way: the first set of charges had been proved false, the second were true. The reaction from the one was obscuring the dangers of the other. Mr Macmillan was guilty not of negligence, but inertia. The reasons for it were manifestly human. Wilful myopia was not in his nature.

It was, in fact, the very *humanity* in Mr Macmillan's approach that let him down: the humanity of not wanting to pursue distasteful rumours; the humanity of not wanting to confront Mr Profumo personally with the charges; the humanity of accepting absolutely the word of a Minister; and the humanity of wanting to restrain the infringement of individual liberties.

It is dangerous to say that a Prime Minister cannot afford these humanities. It was proved equally dangerous to assume that rumours are never true, and that personal relationships do not sometimes have to be challenged beyond what is normally comfortable and right.

The other serious charge concerned the meeting between Mr Profumo and the five Ministers on March 22. The same people prepared to believe that the Prime Minister was guilty of conspiracy to conceal the truth were also ready to believe the same of the Ministers – and present it as fact.

The whole aura of that meeting was fragile, of course. It created more suspicions than it could possibly allay, when it became known. It was almost designed to be misunderstood. Little was done to put the picture right when it was, quite rightly, under attack, and the fantasy was allowed to survive by default.

It was easy to see the fact that two of the five Ministers who were at school with Mr Profumo would suggest comradely collusion. This again was due to the readiness to accept the superficial and damaging interpretation rather than the real one, which was that the intimacy of the relationship enabled franker assessment. A knowledge of the participants in this encounter – of Mr Macleod for example – instantly condemns to the absurd the idea that an alibi was 'cooked up' in full knowledge that the truth was otherwise. But the major misunderstanding of this meeting was caused because its brief was not made clear – that it was to compose an answer to allegations, rather than once again go over the already exhausted area of interrogation.

It was a clumsy device, but not a corrupt one.

The man who in the end carried the can – he had to – was the Prime Minister. The time for his defence was about to begin. The depth of the crisis confronting him was greatly magnified by the extended paralysis of action. If Mr Profumo's bluff had been called at the beginning of February – the 'if' was no consolation – the culpability of others could never have been questioned, the rumour would have died before it assumed malignant proportions and chain reaction would have been prevented. Mr Profumo himself would have fallen, but would later have been able to obtain charitable pardon as a man who owned up when accused, and resume a limited public life although political office would never again have been possible. As it was, Admiralty House itself seemed about to fall about Mr Macmillan's ears.

15

The Taste of Vindication

'Three hostile newspapers are more to be feared than a thousand bayonets.' (Napoleon)

THE CONFESSION BROUGHT a sense of vindication to Fleet Street, and the taste of it was invigorating. The reputation of the Press had been at its nadir; discredited by the performance of some of their representatives before the Vassall Tribunal, the papers had lost their nerve and confidence as they sat on the Profumo story. Now, suddenly, they could say, 'We knew all along.' It would have been more satisfying to have been able to say, 'We told you so'. Only *Westminster Confidential* could do that.

While some could claim to have known a great deal, others were apparently as surprised by the revelation as their readers. *The Guardian* had been aloof and self-righteous all along. First it had wondered, deprecatingly, why some other newspapers had been giving so much attention to Miss Keeler. Then it had been censorious over the innuendoes. Now, confronted by the truth, it wished quickly to be rid of the affair. On Thursday morning, June 6, its editorial said: 'It would be as well if the Profumo disaster could be allowed to sink as quickly as possible into oblivion, security permitting.' That was quite a saving clause.

There was, though, at this point a real danger that, exalted by the outcome, some newspapers would embark on a mission of retribution, provoked as much by a sense of revenge over the Vassall Tribunal as by a mission of legitimate exposure.

As if deliberately arranged to increase the momentum of developments, another element of the drama was taking place at the Old Bailey. Miss Keeler was giving evidence in the trial of 'Lucky' Gordon.

Miss Keeler, whose public rôle was just becoming fully appreciated, had made a grand entrance: she arrived at the Old Bailey in a chauffeur-driven Rolls Royce. Her outfit, a shirt and slim skirt, was in two shades of mauve. The poise in front of the cameras was consummate. There was just the right suggestion of contrition in the face to avoid any sense of the flagrant.

For twenty minutes she gave evidence. She had, she said, first met Gordon in March 1961. She denied both that she had ever lived with him and that she was pregnant by him. But she alleged that during the period she had been seeing Gordon she had been in fear.

Just after Miss Keeler left the witness box came the first sensation: Gordon sat up suddenly in the dock and shouted; 'I have discharged counsel and want to cross-examine the witness.'

The Judge, Commissioner Sir Ernest Goodman Roberts, Q.C., looked surprised, then told him: 'You have not dispensed with counsel at the moment. If you desire to do so now you can, but you will not be allowed to cross-examine the last witness, as her evidence has been finished. Do you say you wish to withdraw instructions from your counsel?'

Gordon said he did.

Gordon asked for the documents involved in the case, and the Judge consented, and then adjourned the court for fifteen minutes to allow Gordon to study the papers. He told him once again: 'Miss Keeler's evidence is over. It cannot now be re-opened.'

But when the court resumed, the Judge had found a compromise. Gordon could ask Miss Keeler questions through him. Dr Ward was introduced into the case, rather obliquely, when Gordon said: 'I would like to ask her if she asked me to find a coloured girl for *her brother Stephen* so we could make up a foursome.' Miss Keeler asked the judge if it was necessary to answer this question. He said it was, and she agreed that the suggestion was true. There was no explanation of the 'brother Stephen', but it was enough both to confuse and alert the court.

When the logic of Gordon's questions seemed to be confused the Judge asked if there were more to come. Gordon replied: 'I want to question her to prove that everything she's been saying in the box including this charge is a pack of lies.'

The Judge advised Gordon to confine his questions to the attack.

The trial fell into further chaos when Gordon told the Judge that Miss Keeler had given him venereal disease. At this Miss Keeler leapt up and shouted: 'It is completely untrue what he is saying and the Press are writing it down. Why don't you check up with the doctor?' She was in tears, and an usher had to take her out of the court.

Gordon then said: 'This is more or less a put-up case by Dr Stephen Ward, who is known as a crank. I want to show that what took place that particular night was a put-up thing.'

The Judge found it difficult to prevent Gordon going off at a tangent, usually in the direction of Dr Ward. He said repeatedly that Miss Keeler had not been beaten up, but had fallen over a suitcase. And then in an argument about new witnesses which Gordon asked to be called, the Judge said that the only witnesses who might be material were two men called Comarchio and Fenton. Their names were called, but there was no answer.

After the court rose on June 6 the police attempted to find Comarchio and Fenton, but when the trial resumed the following morning they had not succeeded in doing so. The jury were out for only ten minutes, and found Gordon guilty of assault, but not of wounding with intent to cause grievous bodily harm. Sentencing him to three years' imprisonment, the Judge said: 'You terrorised Miss Keeler over a period of time and she was very frightened of you. You have a terrible record, and I am sorry that under present regulations you are not liable for deportation.'

(It was Gordon's third conviction for violence in six years. Under the Commonwealth Immigrants Act, 1962, no offender who has been resident in England for five years or more could be deported.)

June 6 was also the day on which Mr Selwyn Lloyd's report on the Tory Party organisation was published. In a few days a situation was to emerge for which Mr Lloyd could not have calculated. He was the architect for a reconstruction in which the foundations had suddenly started to subside.

Dr Ward, meanwhile, had not been idle. He had offered to be interviewed by B.B.C. television. But, after an internal wrangle, the Corporation decided not to put him on the air. He went, instead, to commercial television on the weekly current affairs programme 'This Week' at 9.15 that night. Asked point-blank if he had been running a call-girl ring, he said, 'Certainly not.' As usual, he appeared comfortably articulate.

Mr Macleod was in Washington, where, speaking at the Washington Press Club, he said: 'I was, and am, a personal friend of Jack and Valerie Profumo, and I think it is a tragedy that this should have happened.' Set against some later remarks, this was regarded by some people to have been a tactical error. It was, nevertheless, an act of courageous charity.

For a brief while on the Saturday morning there was a sense of anti-climax, but the relaxation of tension was short lived. Dr Ward phoned Scotland Yard and said: 'I'm thinking of leaving the country for a few days. Have you any objections?' He was told that it would be wise for him to get a solicitor.

The chain reaction was continuing, and the affair had passed from the political to the criminal arena.

At noon Dr Ward was walking, alone, along a road that was strangely distant from his milieu: at Watford, Hertfordshire. Inspector Herbert and Sgt Burrows drove up and stopped 200 yards from the house at which Dr Ward was a weekend guest. There he was arrested . . . wearing light blue trousers, an open-necked shirt, dark glasses – and carpet slippers. He was driven to Marylebone Lane police station, but for five hours no charge was made. Finally, just before 6 p.m., the charge, with all the archaic precision of the law, was read to him: 'That he, being a man, did on divers dates between January 1, 1961, and June 8, 1963, knowingly live wholly or in part on the earnings of prostitution at 17 Wimpole Mews, London W., contrary to Section 30 of the Sexual Offences Act, 1956'. He was detained in custody over the weekend.

On Saturday night Mr Macmillan and Lady Dorothy ate roast ox and drank beer at a Conservative rally at Strathallan Castle, near Gleneagles. Dressed in the casual tweeds of dated cut that were an obligatory part of his off-duty *persona*, he appeared imperturbable. Of the situation, he said, 'Tragically, there hangs over the whole affair like a dark cloud the shadow ... of a political speech.'

He refused to do the Twist, and explained: 'They may call me a twister but I don't do the Twist.' He was in bed at the Gleneagles Hotel by 11.30. He could have been forgiven for thinking that his display of equanimity had begun to calm the reactions.

But when he awoke on the Sunday morning the mood had changed. It was the worst Press in his career as Prime Minister. The *Sunday Telegraph* was the most critical. The fact that the *Telegraph* had turned against the leadership had complex roots. Firstly the *Telegraph* was further to the right than any other paper – though in this case the *Sunday Telegraph*'s bluntness about Mr Macmillan went a good deal further than the *Daily Telegraph* was prepared to go at the time. Secondly, Mr Macmillan's policies were more to the left than the *Telegraph*'s: particularly on Africa. Thirdly, the *Telegraph* had been stung by the Vassall Tribunal. Against this, the *Telegraph* had shared and encouraged Mr Macmillan's enthusiasm for the Common Market.

But apart from the hostility of the editorial pages, there were two further revelations. The *News of the World* ran the first part of Miss Keeler's 'Confessions', which detailed her assignations with Mr Profumo and other colourful sides of her life. The *Sunday Mirror* printed a photostat of the letter Mr Profumo had written to Miss Keeler on August 9, 1961.

The *News of the World* had paid £23,000 for Miss Keeler's story. It began, in teasing outline, on the front page, and continued on two further pages inside. Miss Keeler was photographed nude, shielded by the pelvic form of a modern chair.

The account began with the swimming pool encounter at Cliveden, described Lord Astor in familiar terms – 'Bill Astor, which is what we called him' – Ivanov – 'he was a MAN' – and Dr Ward – 'an extrovert, always eager to attract attention to me and to him'. And it concluded with the promise: 'more revelations next week'. That day's revelations were enough to sell 250,000 extra copies of the *News of the World*.

There was a ring of high magnanimity about the *Sunday Mirror*'s commentary to the letter; it almost sounded like an apology. What the *Mirror* had to explain was why it hadn't published the letter when it first had it early in the year, when it could have brought the whole affair into the open. It gave two reasons:

1. 'The Editor was not satisfied that this letter constituted evidence of any substantial nature. It was effusive but not conclusive.'

2. 'Publication of the letter might have ruined the public career of a Minister on "evidence" from a young woman who clearly would not have produced the letter if Mr Profumo's interests were uppermost in her consideration.'

The failure to publish the letter was later called, by Lord Francis Williams in the *New Statesman*, a 'dereliction of journalistic duty.' This was easy enough to say with the benefit of hindsight, but the question was: had Mr Profumo not been forced into the open by other pressures, would *any* newspaper have exposed him?

On June 9 the Prime Minister might have wondered the same thing. There was, patently, a full morning's reading for him. He stayed inside the hotel. In the afternoon he and Lady Dorothy played their final round of golf at Gleneagles. Photographers on the course once again captured the apparent single-minded dedication to the game in hand: the Prime Minister wore a shapeless windcheater, flat cap and plus-fours. Normally the Macmillans visited Gleneagles only once a year. This time, as they finished their game, Lady Dorothy said to David and Duncan McIntyre, their regular caddies: 'We may be back again in the autumn'.

The Perth-London sleeper express stopped at Gleneagles at 9.26 p.m. The Prime Minister said goodbye to Lady Dorothy, who was staying in the North, and was on his way to face the biggest threat to his premiership.

In the parochial preoccupations of the time, Mr Macmillan's

first act on his return seemed irrelevant. He announced that Lord Hailsham would be sent to Moscow, to negotiate a nuclear Test Ban treaty. But if other people had lost their sense of balance, Mr Macmillan had not. A ban on nuclear testing had been an objective of his policy over a long period: not only would it be a great factor in stabilising the Cold War after the brinkmanship of Cuba; it would also be a considerable electoral asset. While the underground explosions in the Tory Party were all that Britain had ears for, the Prime Minister was looking beyond what he hoped would be a short-term crisis.

Lord Hailsham called to see Mr Macmillan to discuss his mission. Then followed Mr Butler, who had been running things in the Prime Minister's absence. He stayed for 75 minutes, and there was no doubt about the subject of that conversation.

The pace was quickening significantly. In the afternoon the party seismologists, Lord Poole and Mr Redmayne, went to Admiralty House. Lord Poole had just been appointed by Mr Macmillan as joint chairman of the Conservative Party with Mr Macleod. His expertise in handling the Tory election machine was one reason for his recall. Another, until now less urgent, reason was that he had the stature of a kingmaker for the day when the leadership succession had to be settled.

Lord Poole and Mr Redmayne had had plenty to occupy them over the weekend. When Parliament was sitting the feeling of the backbenchers on a given issue could be gauged in half an hour, by talking to no more than twenty M.P.s. With the house dispersed during recess, which it then was, the same operation was vastly more complex. However, at a pre-weekend conference with regional Whips, Mr Redmayne had seen lists of the potential rebels and developed a plan for staving off insurrection.

The first public act was to reveal Lord Dilhorne's inquiry.

On Monday night the Prime Minister emerged from private conference to public appearance. He spoke at a dinner at the University of Sussex, which was celebrating its formal opening that week. He still appeared unflappable. But while he was on his way again to Brighton, *The Times* volcano was active. Sir William Haley was writing another leader. To establish its connection with the earlier one, it, too, contained an imperative 'is' in the headline: the phrase that appeared on Tuesday, June 11 was 'It *is* a moral issue'. Its basic argument was a curious one. It equated moral decline with the country's growing affluence. The Tory policy had brought the nation 'spiritually and psychologically to a low ebb'.

This intervention had more effect than any other newspaper comment in the crisis. Its flavour of outraged rectitude was the voice for a reaction that had so far had no spokesman; the moral impact of the situation had until then been underrated. As *Punch* was later to observe, 'Whenever sexual morality becomes the *leitmotif* of public discussion reason flies out of the window.' *The Times* leader was obviously going to provoke a complex and emotional response. But its implicit condemnation of Macmillan affluence was equally significant: it wounded the leadership at a sensitive point.

A significant absentee from London at this time was Mr Wilson: he had left for a week in Moscow over the weekend, with the Shadow Foreign Secretary, Mr Patrick Gordon Walker. By a fortuitous tradition, the Opposition was free to determine the subject of debate when the House of Commons resumed after recess: this time the following Monday, June 17. There was no doubt about the subject Mr Wilson decided on.

He was at pains, though, to emphasise that Labour would not ask the House, or the country, to indulge in a moral inquest. The real issue was, he said, security and that would be what the Opposition would concentrate their fire power on. There was some advantage in being in Moscow during that week: direct involvement in the hysterical reactions was avoided, and this made objectivity easier to achieve. Nevertheless, there was some sense of news starvation among Mr Wilson's entourage. On one occasion a political correspondent accompanying the party was awakened at 1 a.m. in his hotel by a furious thumping on the door. He thought that either he had photographed an illegal object and was to be removed to the Lubienka Prison in nearby Red Square, or, more appealingly, that a Russian version of Christine Keeler was going to attempt to compromise him (there had been some cases of this during a visit of British businessmen). But when he opened the door it was to find some of Mr Wilson's lieutenants, who had heard that he had a cache of the latest British papers. Some of Mr Wilson's advisers found the tactics for the coming debate difficult. Should they go all out to unseat the Prime Minister, or try to go just far enough to embarrass him? The root of the dilemma was to decide who would be more of a threat at the next election, a possibly discredited Prime Minister or a new and younger man, purged of association with the affair? It was decided to 'cut Mr Macmillan about the face a bit, but avoid an execution'.

Meanwhile back at the scene of the crime, Lord Poole and Mr Redmayne had sensed that reactions were forming a definite geography. At the Tory Central Office in Smith Square, fretting officials were saying 'the main trouble is going to be in the sticks'.

The provinces, where the nonconformist element was strongest, were going to be the hardest to calm down. In the South, and particularly the blasé Home Counties, there was less sensitivity.

The big question had become: when will the Cabinet meet? This was complicated by the fact that some Ministers were away. Mr Macleod was still in America; Mr Brooke was in the Channel Islands; Lord Home was on holiday in Scotland; Mr Heath was due to fly to Norway. But the situation was serious and urgent. A Cabinet meeting was fixed for 10.30 a.m. on Wednesday, June 12. The missing Ministers had abruptly to cut short their visits and Mr Heath postponed his.

But beforehand, Mr Macmillan wanted to sense the mood of the senior Cabinet Ministers. On Tuesday evening the 'Inner Cabinet', lacking only Mr Macleod, went to Admiralty House: Mr Butler, Lord Home, Lord Hailsham, Mr Maudling, and Mr Heath – all of them possible Prime Ministerial candidates if Mr Macmillan should be unable to persuade his colleagues of his case. In addition, Lord Dilhorne was there, with the first copy of his report, only just completed, and Sir John Hobson, the Attorney-General, and Mr Redmayne. The meeting lasted two hours, both Mr Macmillan's wish to get the top men behind him, and their anxiety to be reassured, seemed to have been satisfied.

Then Mr Macmillan, for whom there was little pause, went to Buckingham Palace for his regular weekly audience with the Queen. It lasted longer than usual: sixty-five minutes. There had been embarrassment at the Palace over the fact that Dr Ward had drawn several portraits of members of the Royal Family: though a slender and remote connection with the affair, it had caused displeasure.

Wednesday's Cabinet meeting was brought forward from 10.30 to 10 a.m. because the Prime Minister, still caught hopping between crisis and pre-arranged ceremonial, had to go to Victoria station at noon to welcome the President of India, who was arriving on a State visit. As a result, Mr Macleod, whose Boeing airliner had landed at London Airport only shortly before 10, missed the first minutes of the meeting. With Mr Macleod in his place, twenty of the twenty-one members of the Cabinet were there. The absentee was Mr John Hare, the Minister of Labour, who was convalescing at his home in Essex after an attack of pleurisy.

Admiralty House, the temporary home of the Prime Minister, while No. 10 Downing Street was being renovated, found full Cabinet meetings difficult to accommodate. The improvised Cabinet Room was once the music room of Admiralty House in more leisured days when British sea power dominated the globe. Now it allowed hardly any space to move: the table took up most of the room. The meeting was overlooked by Sir Robert Walpole, whose portrait hung above the carved marble fireplace.

The cobbled courtyard of Admiralty House was thick with reporters and photographers, waiting to read and record significance in the set of a mouth, the speed of a step, the cast of an eye. And so they came out in bunches. Sir Keith Joseph, the Minister of Housing, said, somewhat plaintively: 'Please let me go, I have to go to a lunch.' Mr Soames, the Minister of Agriculture, looking thoroughly flapped, lost his chauffeur and disappeared up Whitehall. (This symptom of tension was to recur: Lord Poole lost his chauffeur the following day.) Mr Macmillan, in tails for the formal engagement, found his car without trouble and sped off to Victoria. But, once there, he revealed preoccupation by forgetting to remove his top hat for the first few bars of the National Anthem.

Signs were read into the faces. And particularly into the fact that the last to leave, by half an hour, were Mr Henry Brooke, Mr Enoch Powell, the Minister of Health, and Lord Dilhorne. At lunchtime, though, it seemed that the Cabinet was holding together. The political correspondents of the evening newspapers, who had to form conclusions at roughly the same speed as does a theatre critic for a daily newspaper, were digging for signals. They were in no doubt that the Prime Minister, rather than the Tory Party, was the first survival to be reckoned. Had his story, and the Dilhorne Report, convinced the Cabinet that the Government could get through the debates the following Monday?

In fact, there had been a general feeling of disgust at the Cabinet meeting: disgust at a Minister's mendacity and abuse of the loyalty of his colleagues, and disgust at the moral depravity involved. But the evening newspapers, and the television and radio news bulletins, had no hint of deep discord among the Ministers over the leadership, and certainly no news of anything approaching a revolt.

But while they were saying this, a different story was being told – and written.

The change of view was bizarre. It was succinctly evident from two headlines from Thursday's editions of the *Daily Telegraph*. The first edition headline said: 'A Cabinet Rallied by P.M. No Resignation at Profumo Meeting. Silence Before the Commons Storm'. This edition reaching the extremities of the island, went to press at about 10 p.m. But by the London edition, printed in the early hours, the headlines had been transformed: 'Cabinet Divided On Profumo. Four Ministers Question Leadership. Mr Powell Gravely Disturbed'. What had happened was not that a Minister had suddenly leaked the situation to the *Telegraph*. In Fleet Street each paper receives copies of the first editions of all other papers, on an unofficial but mutually tolerated network. On this Wednesday night, when the frenetic comparison was conducted between the hours of 10 and 11 p.m., the *Telegraph* had found that *The Times* and the *Daily Express* had accounts saying that Mr Powell had not been satisfied with the Prime Minister's explanation and was on the brink of resignation. Other resignations, said the stories, were also looming: Mr Brooke (who, in fact, had not said one word during the Cabinet meeting), Sir Keith Joseph and Sir Edward Boyle, Minister of Education.

By midnight, the *Daily Mail*, whose first edition shared the impression of Cabinet solidarity with the *Telegraph*, had got denials from Sir Keith Joseph and Mr Brooke; Sir Edward Boyle was spending the night at the Carlton Club and saying nothing. Mr Powell was in Wolverhampton that night for a routine meeting at his constituency party headquarters. He was pursued from there to his suburban home for comment, but remained silent. He slipped from the back door of his house, hopped over the garden fence and escaped from an exit to the road, fifty yards away. He had booked a sleeper on the 12.10 a.m. train from Wolverhampton to Paddington, but he suspected, rightly, that the newspaper men had found out. So, instead, he was driven to Birmingham to pick up the train there. But the determined Pressmen, who had got on the train, caught him. They stayed with him, fruitlessly, to London.

How did the story of a *putsch* get about? *The Times*'s story, by tradition anonymous, was by its political correspondent, David Wood. The *Express*'s story was not by its staff political correspondent, Ian Aitken, but by Henry Fairlie, an experienced political commentator and analyst who had been writing weekly articles for the Beaverbrook paper. It was said that Wood and Fairlie had talked to Mr Nigel Birch, a declared and dedicated opponent of Mr Macmillan on the Tory backbenches. With Mr Powell and Mr Thorneycroft, Mr Birch had resigned from the Macmillan Government in 1958 over its inflationary economic policy. Mr Birch was also an unswerving defender of the axed Chancellor, Mr Selwyn Lloyd. Wood said later that he had tried to reach Mr Birch for his view of the Cabinet situation, but had failed. And Mr Birch had denied that the story came from him, adding, ominously, 'I support Mr Powell and I will speak in the House on Monday.' The story certainly came from enemies of the Prime Minister, but not from 'the mind of one man,' as the *Daily Mail* subsequently claimed. It was the view of a group of Tory backbenchers.

Putsch or not, the Cabinet did not find it easy to resolve the problems. On Thursday morning they met again. There were no resignations, although when he came out Mr Powell looked like a man wracked with internal conflicts. That morning, also, *The Times* leader of Tuesday brought its inevitable response, though the volume of it was exceptional: it printed two and a half columns of readers' letters, and in a new leader, headlined 'A matter of conscience', the paper said, 'Rarely on any public issue have the letters and telephone calls been so largely one way'. The one way was against Mr Macmillan. An irony to which the editorial did not refer was the fact that many of the letters had addresses suggesting the squirearchy and urban middle-class, the very people who three months earlier had been castigating the Press in the same columns so much to the alarm of *The Times* that they had provoked the 'It *is* happening here' broadside.

But *The Times* was arousing not only its readers. On Thursday night Lord Hailsham became the first Cabinet Minister to speak publicly on the crisis. He appeared, passionate with rage, on the B.B.C. television programme 'Gallery'. When his interviewer, Robert MacKenzie, quoted *The Times* at him Lord Hailsham snapped with explosive articulation: '*The Times* is an anti-Conservative newspaper led by an anti-Conservative editor.' And in a comment which contrasted with that of Mr Macleod in Washington the previous week, he said of Mr Profumo: 'A great party is not to be brought down because of a scandal by a woman of easy virtue and a proved liar.'

Because of the intimacy and vigour of Lord Hailsham's peformance the interview got great attention in the papers on Friday morning. But a speech made the same night, not in front of television cameras, by Mr Selwyn Lloyd, was more direct and more meaningful. He was talking at a dinner for Conservatives from the Don Valley, in the West Riding of Yorkshire. In a statement which contained as much calculation as Lord Hailsham's did passionate spontaneity, he said, 'The country is asking for courageous and confident leadership not based on expediency but upon obedience to high moral standards and irreproachable behaviour in high places.' The message of that was pretty clear.

On Friday, Mr Eddowes came publicly into the story for the first time, and in a way that made sensational headlines. The previous day he had written to Mr Macmillan pointing out the statement he had made to the police of March 29. On Friday he released the text of his letter to the *Evening Standard*. He said again that Miss Keeler had told him, after the Edgecombe shooting, that she had been asked to get secrets from Mr Profumo for Ivanov. Since the affair had come into the open, said Mr Eddowes, no indication had been given that his information had reached the Prime Minister. He had therefore made it public.

There was no doubt about it being taken seriously: Mr Brooke, who had gone back to the Channel Islands after the Cabinet meetings, left there again at 1 a.m. on Friday, scooped up by a Naval frigate, appropriately named the *Wakeful*. From Portsmouth he was rushed to London, where he was able later to give the Prime Minister the full background to Mr Eddowes's activities in March. Mr Macmillan had to delay his departure for Chequers, where he was going to prepare his speech for the debate on Monday. He finally left Admiralty House at 8 p.m.

Miss Keeler, meantime, had achieved new distinction. She appeared as the cover girl of a journal in which women figure extremely rarely: *The Economist*. She occupied the same position in the *Investor's Chronicle*. The fiscal impact of the affair had been taking a neurotic course.

As *The Economist* observed, the Prime Minister's own fortunes were indivisible from those of the stockmarket: a fact that was to be born out by the precision with which share prices followed Mr Macmillan's destiny.

At the weekend Mr Powell made a speech which gave the share prospects a slightly healthier glow. He made it finally clear that he was not leading a revolt: the Prime Minister had the right to put his case first. At the same time a new tactic to protect the Prime Minister emerged, having been cooked up at Conservative Central Office and fed to some political correspondents. It was the thesis that if Mr Macmillan were swept out of office, the Queen might have to send for Mr Wilson and ask him to form a Labour Government. This was something of a *canard*, but desperate men resorted to desperate ideas. On Monday morning, an emergency meeting of the 1922 Committee had been organised by its chairman, Major Morrison, in a last-ditch attempt to steady the ranks before the debate in the afternoon. (A three-line whip, the mandatory summons to attend, had been issued by both main parties.) The spectre of Parliamentary dissolution was produced. More important, the impression was given that if the Party that night supported Mr Macmillan at the division, they could tacitly assume that he would not remain in office for much longer.

The effect of this was about to be put to the test.

16

The Prime Minister's Case

'MY SPIRIT IS NOT BROKEN, but my zest has gone,' Mr Macmillan told a colleague on June 17. In a few hours' time he had to face perhaps the toughest debate of his career. This confession of damaged morale was not a good omen. For the twelve days since Mr Profumo's confession the attacks on the Prime Minister had grown in force, stopped short of absolute condemnation only by the knowledge that he had not yet been able to make his defence. But the impression had been solidly planted that he had no convincing case to present. All the time the rumours had been multiplying in a dangerous and malignant way.

But Mr Macmillan knew that his prosecutors had one vulnerable point: they lacked intimate knowledge of his handling of the affair, and therefore they did not know if he could pull some revelation out of the hat which would excuse what then appeared to be inexcusable. Mr Wigg and Mr Wilson, and some of their colleagues, had substantial evidence. But even they could not be sure that the Prime Minister would not once again display his legendary resource and present a plausible case.

When he drove to the House of Commons that afternoon Mr Macmillan knew that he faced a prejudiced jury. The galleries were jammed with people who knew that the Prime Minister was at bay, and many of them expected to see a killing before the day was out. In the Strangers' Gallery women pre-dominated, and for many of them it seemed a dress rehearsal for the Ascot races, being held that week.

The three-line whips had done their job: M.P.s spilled over into the gangways and squatted at the Bar of the House. At 3.26 p.m., with four minutes to spare, the Prime Minister took his seat, obviously lacking his normal composure, looking pale and burdened. Two minutes later Mr Wilson arrived, quietly predatory and carrying an ominous file.

At 3.33 p.m. Mr Wilson rose, paused to savour the hanging silence, and then began, in confident and incisive style: 'This is a debate without precedent in the annals of this House. It arises from disclosures which have shocked the moral conscience of the nation. There is clear evidence of a sordid underworld network, the extent of which cannot yet be measured and which we cannot debate today because of proceedings elsewhere' (the Ward case was *sub judice*).

There was a spark of compassion for Mr Profumo – 'the personal and family tragedy of a man lately our colleague' – and then, dealing with the Minister's mendacity, he got straight away to his principal target: '. . . whether any other Minister in any sense connived at this action through foreknowledge or, being in a position to ascertain the truth, failed to take the steps that were necessary to fulfil the duty that he owed to the House.'

And he asked whether the Minister's association with 'this squalid network' had led to either a security leak, or at best, a security risk. While Labour had been investigating the case, he said, they had done everything in their power to prevent it becoming a matter of public discussion or a matter for party controversy.

It was clear, even at this point, that Mr Wilson's tactic was to present a cold, dispassionate case-history, as far as he knew it. There was to be none of the astringent Wilson wit that had made him one of the most lethal debaters in the Commons. He read flatly from a manuscript, in deadpan and dull tones. Parts of the dossier were revealed: the encounter between Mr Wigg and Dr Ward and the record of it – 'a nauseating document, taking the lid off a corner of the London underworld of vice, dope, marijuana, blackmail and counter-blackmail, violence, petty crime . . .' – the submission of it to the Prime Minister and Mr Wilson's dissatisfaction with his reply, and then the first personal assault on Mr Macmillan: 'After the Vassall case he felt that he could not stand another serious security case involving a ministerial resignation, and he gambled desperately and hoped that nothing would ever come out. For political reasons he was gambling with national security. I think that this is why he was at such pains to demonstrate to me his unflappability and his unconcern.'

Soviet espionage, said Mr Wilson, was not only directed to securing secrets: it was also concerned to create a lack of confidence in our Security Services in the United States. (Fuchs, Burgess and Maclean and the Lonsdale case had all, certainly, been quoted by Americans, demonstrating a mounting dissatisfaction with the British Security Services' performance.)

And then he came to the Dilhorne report, a copy of which he had read when he returned from Moscow two days earlier. (He was the only member of the Opposition to have seen it, although he discussed it with the Deputy Leader, Mr George Brown). He could not, he said, quote from it because it was not to be made public. He could not therefore use any facts from it. But 'I am sure that the Prime Minister will agree that I cannot be muzzled or gagged by the fact that I have seen it.'

Mr Wilson said that he would put some questions to the Prime Minister on the basis of knowledge otherwise available to him.

'This means that I have already put to the Prime Minister, and will be putting to him, some questions to which I now know the answer on the basis of the Lord Chancellor's report. I will not give the answers. I will leave it to the Prime Minister to give the answers, because it is right that he should decide how much of the Lord Chancellor's Report can be disclosed.'

There were five questions. First, why, when Ivanov's activities had been detected, was he not declared *persona non grata* by the Government? Then next, a request to know the date on which a 'full security watch' had been placed on Dr Ward's flat. 'He knows,' said the Labour leader tantalisingly, 'that I know the answer to that question.'

The three final questions were later to be answered: when had Mr Macmillan first heard the rumours; who told him; and had he instructed the Security Services to check Mr Profumo's early statements with Miss Keeler?

If they had told him it would have meant that he had been an accessory to Mr Profumo's deceit on March 22. 'Frankly,' he

163

said, 'I find it quite impossible to believe that the right hon. Gentleman could be guilty of that.

'Either the Security Services knew and deliberately withheld that information from him, in which case heads have to roll, or they did not know. If they did not know – it is a fair question to ask why they did not know, whether they should not have been on to it – something follows from that. It follows that they could not have been monitoring, they could not have been watching, the effects of the Profumo-Keeler relationship.'

He said again that it would be impossible to know if there had been any breach of security, and that the first the Security Services knew about the security risk was when a Sunday newspaper told them. 'If this is true this would imply that the £60 million,* spent on these services have been less productive in this vitally important case than the security services of the *News of the World.'*

He dealt, contemptuously, with the early morning cross-examination of Mr Profumo on March 22; he lashed the efforts to exploit the notoriety of Miss Keeler – 'There is something utterly nauseating about a system of society which pays a harlot twenty-five times as much as it pays its Prime Minister, 250 times as much as it pays its Members of Parliament, and 500 times as much as it pays some of its ministers of religion.'

Mr Wilson's speech ended, rather rhetorically for him, on the moral issue: 'The sickness of an unrepresentative sector of our society should not detract from the robust ability of our people as a whole to face the challenge of the future.' But the inspiration and the leadership had to come 'here, in this House'. And he sat down. The whole performance had been the essence of restraint.

It was 4.25 p.m. Had Mr Macmillan got the answers? Listening to Mr Wilson he had been nervously restless, dabbing his face occasionally with a handkerchief. He knew that Mr Wilson's controlled performance had had a considerable impact. When he rose his eyelids seemed heavier than

* This was an estimate of the total spent in Mr Macmillan's period of office. In the estimate for 1963, the allocation to the 'security services' rose by £1 million to £8 million.

ever. His handkerchief, normally immaculate in his breast pocket, was clutched in his hand.

Two weeks before he had scored a notable debating victory over the Opposition in a parliamentary brawl over the case of the deported Nigerian, Chief Enaharo. The Labour speakers, particularly Mr George Brown, had employed verbal pugilism, an art in which Mr Macmillan was a heavyweight, and he had left Mr Brown badly bruised. The Labour Party's mistake had been to 'mix it' with a pro. This time, continuing their carefully planned psychological assault, the Labour tacticians had told the Members to stay absolutely silent during Mr Macmillan's speech. For the Prime Minister, who often found inspiration in 'bouncing off' hostile reactions, this would be unnerving. It would – and it did – handicap his ability to *ad lib*, which was suffering anyway from the departure of his zest.

As if to explain his pallor he dealt immediately with the personal impact of the affair: 'On me, as head of the Administration, what has happened has inflicted a deep, bitter, and lasting wound. I do not remember in the whole of my life, or even in the political history of the past, a case of a Minister of the Crown who has told a deliberate lie to his wife, to his legal advisers, to his ministerial colleagues, not once but over and over again, who has then repeated this lie to the House of Commons as a personal statement which, as the right hon. Gentleman reminded us, implies that it is privileged, and has subsequently taken legal action and recovered damages on the basis of a falsehood. This is almost unbelievable, but it is true.'

The wound was clear, the sorrow evident. 'I find it difficult to tell the House what a blow it has been to me, for it seems to have undermined one of the very foundations upon which political life must be conducted.' He continued this note of personal conscience-baring by detailing the standards by which he should be judged: 'There is the question of good faith; there is the question of justice, and there is the question of good judgment. I know that I have acted honourably; I believe that I have acted justly, and I hope that when it has heard my account the House will consider that I have acted with proper diligence and prudence.' His posture was one of an appeal for fair verdict. Carefully he reconstructed what had happened after he returned from Rome to be first told of the rumours. There was a stir when he revealed the warning that Sir Norman Brook had given Mr Profumo in 1961, and that he had not been told at the time. 'I do not complain of it,' he said carefully, 'I merely state the fact that the minute that Sir Norman recorded makes no reference to his having informed me.' This dispelled, he said, the charge widely made, that he had known of Mr Profumo's association with Dr Ward since 1961.

'This is the first charge of dilatoriness of duty that has been brought against me and it is completely untrue.' He denied the story that the Security men had seen Mr Profumo enter and leave Dr Ward's house and that they saw Ivanov enter and leave the house. He then came to one of the questions on which he was most vulnerable; why he had not personally questioned Mr Profumo. The Prime Minister said: 'I did not do so for two reasons. First, I thought he would have spoken more freely to the Chief Whip and the Law Officers than to me, his political chief. Secondly, for me personally to carry out an examination of this kind, in the probing detail necessary, would have made it difficult, if not impossible, to have had – however innocent – a social relation with him.'

This picture of sensitivity in personal relationships, with a distaste for inquisition, drew fire later in the debate. It turned out to be one of the weakest points in his case and it was viewed with alarm on his own backbenches. He confessed that his attitude had been significantly influenced by the Vassall case, as he said: 'I must confess frankly to the House that, in considering what I should do the Vassall case, the effect which it had upon Mr Galbraith was certainly in my mind. I have been reproached for accepting the resignation of my hon. Friend when I did, when rather similar rumours were circulating and when nothing was specifically stated but only hinted at. Indeed, I told him at the time that I believed that in the long run his resignation might help him, and would not help me.'

The reluctance to press Mr Profumo further was evident again when the Prime Minister went on to describe what happened after the rumours had been brought into the open in the Commons on March 21. There was laughter when he said that the Profumo solicitor, Mr Clogg, had been sent for to make sure that the War Minister's personal statement, then being drafted, would be 'correct in every particular'. The laughter continued when he described the acceptance of Mr Profumo's explanation of the letter to Miss Keeler which began 'Darling'. The Prime Minister, as if to assert its remoteness from his own experience, explained: 'I believe that that might be accepted – I do not live among young people fairly widely.' It was said with the same sense of Olympian curiosity as when a judge inquires: 'What *is* rock and roll?'

There was no doubt, though, that apart from this readiness to accept the 'Darling' as an innocent prefix, the part of the Profumo defence which had for the Prime Minister and the Government clinched its persuasiveness had been his threat to take libel action against any further development of the rumours. As for his presence next to Mr Profumo as the lies had been uttered, the Prime Minister exposed again the depth of his wounds: 'I could not believe that a man would be so foolish, even if so wicked, not only to lie to colleagues in the House but be prepared to issue a writ in respect of a libel which he must know to be true. So any doubts I may have had' (this was his only suggestion that he had entertained any) 'were removed. I thought it right to come to the House, and I do not reproach myself for that, to sit beside a colleague of my Administration while he made a personal statement refuting the damaging and scandalous remarks made about him.' On his own backbenches there was plain dissatisfaction, the suspicions of Ministerial gullibility had not been placated. And on the Labour benches there was a feeling of incredulity.

But the most surprised reaction came when, after Mr Macmillan had detailed the three separate statements made by Miss Keeler – on January 26, March 25 and April 4 – that she had been asked by Dr Ward to obtain military information from Mr Profumo, the reports had not been passed on to him. There was a cry from the backbenches: 'Nobody ever tells me nuffin!' The Prime Minister's case by this time was built largely on the idea of his detachment from the handling of the affair.

When this shock had subsided, Mr Macmillan dealt with Mr Wilson's first visit to see him about the case, on March 27

. . . taking care to point out that this had been five days *after* the lying statement: 'I am not complaining that he did not come earlier – if he thought that these security things were so dangerous . . . if I am accused of dilatoriness I am entitled to observe that the right hon. Gentleman's description of Mr Ward as a "self-confessed intermediary of the Russians" – if he thought him to be that – should have led him to have forwarded the letter to me. But he did not.' This was plainly a desperate and unconvincing debating point.

Mr Macmillan made another attempt to score a point off Mr Wilson: describing Dr Ward's statement to Mr Wigg, which had been passed on by Mr Wilson – 'a long memorandum' – he said: 'It is interesting to note that, among other allegations – and I hope I am correct in this – it included the statement that there was no impropriety in the association between Mr Profumo and Miss Keeler.' (This was at the period, immediately after the March 22 statement, when Dr Ward, as he had done on the ITN bulletin, maintained that the statement was, *as far as he knew*, absolutely true. His change of mind – and heart – was then yet to come. In any case, Mr Wigg had stressed that Dr Ward's word was suspect.)

Mr Macmillan, ruffled and sometimes indistinct, and trying to gauge the impact of his case, then told of the phase after the March 22 statement. He said that after Dr Ward's statement was sent to him by the Leader of the Opposition which, he said, did not question Mr Profumo's honour, 'no other communications were sent to me by the police or security authorities to the date of his confession that would have led me to doubt the truth of his statement.'

He had been on his feet for just short of an hour. At the end, he returned to his opening, personal theme: 'I have told the House in great detail the whole story of this affair as far as I was concerned with it. I think that I have omitted nothing of importance – I hope not. I have certainly avoided nothing. I said at the beginning that it was my duty to act honourably, to act justly, and to act prudently. My colleagues have been deceived, and I have been deceived, grossly deceived – and the House has been deceived – but we have not been parties to deception, and I claim that upon a fair view of the facts as I have set them out I am entitled to the sympathetic understanding and confidence of the House and of the country.'

The appeal was direct, and almost plaintive. He looked injured – but not broken. The applause from his own benches was mechanical, and obligatory in sound, rather than effusive.

It had been a bad Macmillan speech, without the easy, aggressive panache that he usually mustered, and it had not been enough to remove doubts about the result of the debate, or his own future. It had been enough to reveal the spiritual damage of the betrayal, and it had cleared up most of the questions except the most important one: Why, when one part of Whitehall had, at least four months ago, gathered enough evidence seriously to question the truth of Mr Profumo's denials – why hadn't the Prime Minister been *told*?

Did this amount to culpability on his part? Was it negligence, gullibility and nonchalance carried too far? Or was it merely betrayal by a colleague and incompetence by his servants?

These were the questions that had to be decided in the mind of each Conservative M.P. in the four-and-a-half hours left before the vote. As Mr Grimond, the Liberal leader, got up to speak, the Tory backbenchers filtered out into the lobbies, anxious still to be persuaded, or to persuade themselves, that they should vote for the Prime Minister; or deciding that minds already made up to oppose him had no course to be altered. At this point Major Morrison, Mr Redmayne, Lord Poole and all the Whips could not be sure that their intense persuasion had worked.

And so Mr Grimond's audience was depleted not because of any disrespect for his oratory – it was as pertinent and sensible as usual – but because of the conscience-tearing of the Tory Party. Of suggestions that the Tories would be held together by the unwritten assurance that the Prime Minister would be sacrificed after a decent interval, Mr Grimond said, 'This would be the most cynical outcome of all. This really would be putting party before country in a despicable manner. If the Government have a contribution to offer this country, let them offer it, but if their party, at the back of its mind, has made up its mind that the Prime Minister must go, the time for him to go is now.'

Mr Macmillan, sitting there and hearing this, and at the same time seeing the thinning chamber, must indeed have wondered how many of his party agreed with Mr Grimond.

The principal combatants had been in the arena. But there were two more speakers to come who, for different reasons, would have a captive audience. One was Mr Nigel Birch. After his activities during the previous week he was seen as the leading spokesman for the already committed critics of the Prime Minister within his own party. The other was Mr Wigg, by now dubbed 'the do-it-yourself M.I.5'.

The debate was two and three quarter hours old when Mr Birch rose. An elegant figure, his speeches were renowned for equally painstaking composition. Phrases and ideas for them came frequently to him in the night. On this occasion his nocturnal inspiration must have been particularly fertile. No leader could have been knifed by a more exquisitely honed blade, even if in this case the victim had no reason to be taken by surprise: the thrust was firmly in the chest, not the back. It was done quickly. He said:

'What seems to me to be the real issue is whether it was right to accept Profumo's personal statement. There are two aspects here. There is, first, the moral aspect of accepting that part of the statement which Profumo himself subsequently denied and there is a second issue of whether the Prime Minister in this case acted with good sense and with competence.

'I will deal with these two issues in order. First, there is the question of accepting Profumo's statement. We know a deal more now about Profumo than we did at the time of the statement, but we have all known him pretty well for a number of years in this House. I must say that he never struck me as a man at all like a cloistered monk; and Miss Keeler was a professional prostitute.

'There seems to me to be a certain basic improbability about the proposition that their relationship was purely platonic. What are whores about? Yet Profumo's word was accepted. It was accepted from a colleague. Would that word have been accepted if Profumo had not been a colleague or even if he had been a political opponent? Everyone must, I think, make his own judgment about that.

170

'He was not a man who was ever likely to tell the absolute truth in a tight corner, and at the time the statement was made he was in a very tight corner indeed. There are people – and it is to the credit of our poor, suffering humanity that it is so – who will tell the whole truth about themselves whatever the consequences may be. Of such are saints and martyrs, but most of us are not like that. Most people in a tight corner either prevaricate – if anyone is interested in prevarication they will find the *locus classicus* in the evidence given before the Bank Rate Tribunal by the Leader of the Opposition – or, as in this case, they lie.

'This lie was accepted. I have meditated very deeply on this, and though I have given some rather rough reasons for not accepting that Profumo's statement was credible, I have after deep consideration come to the conclusion that my right hon. Friend did absolutely genuinely believe it.

'Profumo on his own admission had been guilty of a very considerable indiscretion, for a Minister at any rate. He was not a particularly successful Minister. He had no great place in this House or in the country. I cannot really see that the Prime Minister was under any obligation whatever to retain his services, nor do I think that getting rid of Mr Profumo would, in fact, have made the political situation any worse than it then was. On the other hand, to retain him entailed a colossal risk and a colossal gamble.

'The conclusion that I draw from that is that the course adopted by my right hon. Friend the Prime Minister could have been adopted only by someone who genuinely and completely believed the statements of Profumo, and therefore, I absolutely acquit my right hon. Friend of any sort of dishonour. On the other hand, on the question of competence and good sense I cannot think that the verdict can be favourable.

'What is to happen now? I cannot myself see at all that we can go on acting as if nothing had happened. We cannot just have business as usual. I myself feel that the time will come very soon when my right hon. Friend ought to make way for a much younger colleague. I feel that that ought to happen. I certainly will not quote at him the savage words of Cromwell,

171

but perhaps some of the words of Browning might be appropriate in his poem on "The Lost Leader", in which he wrote:
' ". . . let him never come back to us!
There would be doubt, hesitation and pain.
Forced praise on our part – the glimmer of twilight,
Never glad confident morning again!"
' "Never glad confident morning again!" – so I hope that the change will not be too long delayed.
'Ahead of us we have a Division. We have the statement of my right hon. and noble Friend Lord Hailsham, in a personal assurance on television, that a Whip is not a summons to vote but a summons to attend. I call the Whips to witness that I at any rate have attended.'

The Whips could have been forgiven for shuddering. As Mr Birch eased his tall frame back on to the bench the full venom of the Browning verse was sinking in. His flair for the apposite ode had never been more lethal. On such occasions, whatever the justice of the case, one speech can by its power seem afterwards to be the true flavour in the after-taste. This was it, and inevitably 'The Lost Leader' was the kind of phrase headlines are made of. Mr Birch had spoken for only thirteen minutes, but it had been enough. Mr Wigg, who followed precisely at 6.30 p.m., conceded that he could not hope to emulate 'the graceful oratory of the right hon. Member for Flint'. But he was in his style, every bit as potent, and less discriminating in his targets. The first was Lord Hailsham's television performance. 'I would not pretend for one moment to be a Christian. If some of the ideas of Christianity which we have heard from Lord Hailsham are representative, then I confess that I am a pagan, for the Christianity that I learned at my mother's knee taught me that it was something which had to do with redemption and that there was not one Mary but two and that Jesus loved them both. To use this occasion or any other when the Tory Party is in a jam to pour moralising phrases, humbug and cant from their mouths is something that I cannot take.'

Mr Wigg went on: 'It gives me a queasy feeling in the stomach when I hear Lord Hailsham. Let me say, frankly, that if the moment ever comes when I see Lord Hailsham on one side of the road and John Profumo on the other, it is to

John Profumo that I will go. I would prefer him, the sinner, to the sinister saint of Lord Hailsham's type pouring forth his smears, cant and humbug.'

There was more of this, winding up with the challenge: 'Whether I am in order or not, I call Lord Hailsham a lying humbug.' For a personal attack on another Member of the Commons it would have been electric enough; for an attack on a member of the Upper House it was almost unprecedented.

Mr Wigg was a man provoked. There had been the injury to him and his colleagues who had first brought the skeleton out of the cupboard, what he called the 'deliberate and calculated smear' on them for bringing out the rumour under privilege, a smear put into Mr Profumo's first statement by its drafters.

'The mistake which John Profumo made – his only mistake – was the one which is unforgivable to the party opposite: he did not get away with it, he got found out,' rasped Mr Wigg.

He went through the by now familiar timetable of his inquiries, and then turned again to Mr Profumo, this time on his record as Minister of War.

'Who chose him? Who put him into that job? He was put into that job by the Prime Minister to carry out a specific task, a task which Members who know anything about defence and who care for the defence of this country, would not have carried out. What he had to do was to get 165,000 men by 1st January and it did not matter twopence how he did it. What he did was to lower standards and he lowered the rejection rate from seventy per cent to forty per cent. I do not say that he did not care anything about the Army, but it was not as much as I do, or he would not have done it.'

He acquitted the Premier of any act of dishonour, but concluded: '. . . the story he has told this afternoon is a record of incompetence that requires that he should resign, and the whole of his Administration with him.' Mr Wigg sat down at 6.52 p.m.

The key points, for and against, had already been made.

The closing speech for the Opposition was by the Deputy Leader, Mr George Brown. Because he had just returned from the United States there had been some doubt about whether he could be sufficiently briefed for the rôle. Until just before the

173

debate it had been suggested that Mr Wilson might make a symmetrical performance and wind up as well, or that the Shadow Foreign Secretary, Mr Patrick Gordon-Walker, who had been with Mr Wilson in Moscow, might do it. Mr Brown's tactical error in the Vassall debate had caused the doubts.

This time, though, the mood was different, and Mr Brown knew his ground. He made a careful reinforcement of the criticisms already made, divided into three parts: what had happened, why and how it happened and what should have been done about it. Mr Macmillan, who had been out of the Chamber for the first minute of Mr Brown's speech, returned to hear Mr Brown say that even if the Prime Minister had not known what had happened he could not be absolved.

The case-history was gone through again, and then Mr Brown dealt with the nature of the inquiry which he felt ought to be instituted: he called for a Select Committee of the House. (A method criticised for the inherent dangers of partisan thinking.)

At 9.37 p.m., just over six hours after Mr Macmillan's opening speech, Mr Macleod began the Government's concluding speech. He was, of course, speaking as a Minister personally implicated in one of the central areas of the controversy: the meeting which drafted the lying statement of March 22. And it was on this that he first sought to reassure the House.

'One point was raised (in drafting the statement) by Mr Profumo . . . he asked why it was necessary that he should say in the statement that he was on friendly terms with Miss Keeler, as this, to quote his own words, "sounded so awful". We insisted that that must be included because it was part of the truth, and an important part, as he had consistently said.'

There could be two charges brought against the Ministers who questioned Mr Profumo, said Mr Macleod: that either they were conspiring knaves or that they were gullible fools. He dismissed the first, then of the 'Darling' letter, which he had read in the *Sunday Mirror*, he repeated the *Mirror*'s own description of it – 'effusive but not conclusive' – and said that he felt that the knowledge that the letter might or would appear would support Mr Profumo's story 'because it is inconceivable, or would seem so, that he would attempt to deceive the House

174

knowing that his deception was almost sure to be found out'. The trouble was that the inconceivable had happened.

Mr Macleod's was a spiritless performance, circumscribed in its effectiveness by his own involvement. His speech left the Tories feeling exasperated, and the Socialists confident.

And so, at 9.59. p.m. came the vote, and even then nobody could predict whether Mr Macmillan, or even his Government could survive the night. There was plain disquiet among the Tory backbenchers. They had not felt that the Government's case had been a confident one. Many M.P.s were trying to make up their own minds by sounding other people's. They found their colleagues just as unresolved.

Nobody expected the party to commit suicide. It was the margin of the Government majority which would be critical and decisive. Twenty abstentions would be safe. Thirty would be alarming, and more would be disastrous. Then the figures came. The party had just held together: there were twenty-seven abstentions, reducing the Government majority to sixty-nine, and anything under seventy was a threat to the leadership. The work of Major Morrison and the persuaders of the 1922 committee, more than the Whips, had clinched it, though hair-raisingly.

But it was not a result that the party managers could meet with equanimity. There had been serious erosion. They knew then, too, what was not to leak out until later: that but for the implicit impression that the leadership change would be faced, the majority might have been cut by nearly thirty more. In that case the Prime Minister would have gone within hours of the debate.

Mr Macmillan, when the figures were announced, looked dejected. He found no consolation from the newspapers the next morning. 'Premier likely to resign soon' headlined the *Daily Telegraph*; 'Mac: the end' predicted the *Daily Mail*, with brutal economy. *The Times* found the explanations inadequate, and the Prime Minister's case at its weakest on the grounds of judgment . . . 'the questions of justice and good judgment interlock.' Prime Ministers, it said, sometimes have need to be harsh. Judgment had gone wrong: 'It is not unfair to ask whether it did not go even more seriously wrong earlier when

175

Mr Profumo was appointed.' A headline in the *Daily Mirror* said: 'His future, short of a miracle, will be brief'.

Some people, though, still believed in miracles, if not in rumours.

17

Macmillan Fights for Survival

IN THE PURSUIT of Mr Macmillan's head the Tory Party lost its own. As soon as the vote was announced at Westminster on Monday night the blood-lust began. By Tuesday morning there was hardly a Conservative backbencher who was not prepared to say that the Prime Minister should go. It was the biggest threat that Mr Macmillan's leadership had ever faced. There was sheer panic, and because the threat lacked coherence it was all the more dangerous – not only to the leadership but to the whole party.

The onslaught had no rationale: its only object was blood. That most hysterical of compulsions was at work – self-preservation. The spectre of a general election suddenly loomed close, an election in which nearly every Tory seat was a marginal one, and the simple, ruthless expedient seemed to be to get the leader out. For whom, it was not possible then to see.

Here were the Tories doing what even Mr Wilson did not want: attempting a ritual assassination of Mr Macmillan. Of course, the Labour Party's psychological warfare, schemed by Mr Crossman and Mr Wilson, had been victorious. The Tories were swamped by defeatism.

One reason for the party's neurosis was that some of the people supposed to hold it together had themselves been compromised by their part in earlier events. Backbenchers were in no mood to be tranquillised by the Whips, since the Chief Whip had figured in the now suspect meeting of the five Ministers (whose brief had not even then been explained) and also in most of the interrogations of Mr Profumo. Mr Macleod, the joint chairman, was also burdened with his part in the meeting.

The one man who might be able to lead the rabble, blinded by rage, up a dark alley until it could cool off was Lord Poole.

If the throne was threatened, the kingmaker had to protect it until a new incumbent could be selected.

Lord Poole knew that the panic was more than indecorous; the great need was for time – time not only to avoid having the Prime Minister's career ended by an incident which would leave it tarnished, but time in which to allow the amorphous machinery of selection for the succession to complete each cycle of its intricate operation. In such a crisis the covert nature of Tory kingmaking was a liability. There was no declared ballot as in the Labour Party. The invisible processes conducted in the Carlton Club and the other sanctums of inner lobbying could not be hurried. Questions had to be asked, canvassing diligently conducted to reach the furthermost areas. Then these opinions had to be analysed and adjusted on the fulcrum of power. No crude democratic processes were possible, completed in a week or two.

But time was needed for another reason. The panic was dangerously short-sighted. The real issues compelling a re-appraisal of leadership were those which would be conceded even by the leader himself: they were relevant to the future rather than to the past.

In any case, the power of the backbench M.P.s immediately to despatch the leader had been eroded by the increased power of Prime Minister and Cabinet. The Cabinet was more able to behave according to mature motives. And the Cabinet at that stage was not prepared to kill.

By Tuesday afternoon the Prime Minister's own psychology began to affect the situation. Resilience had always been one of his qualities, but it had never had such demands made upon it. At this point it began to return. The howl of the mob infuriated him – and it brought the resolve he needed to fight back. As he saw the chaos he thumped his desk, fist clenched, and said: 'I'll not have this.' As a tactician he was unequalled in his party; and now, with his strength returning, he saw that if he could hang on for a day it would be as good as a week – and that might be as good as a year. Twenty-four hours would be enough to set in motion a force which he knew could thwart his enemies: sentiment.

The public, but more particularly the constituency parties,

were insulated from the burgeoning rumours and self-destruction of Westminster. To them the spectacle of the mob appeared degrading, and the Prime Minister seemed that magnet for British sympathy: the underdog. And so the most curious stage of the week's chemistry began to form and take effect. The panic of the Members was being corrected by the revulsion it created: in the constituencies there was emerging a determination not to have a Prime Minister brought down for such ignoble motives.

It was a splendid spectacle, and Mr Macmillan had an instinct for it. The 'sticks' which a week earlier had been the hotbed of revolt were now his saviour. He knew, too, that there was no simple path to the choice of a new Prime Minister. When the succession had been canvassed in February, after the collapse of the Common Market talks and at the depth of the unemployment crisis, the party had been unable to make up its mind between Mr Maudling and Mr Heath. Now the choice was more complicated. In February there seemed no division on one issue: the new leader had to be a man born in the twentieth century. This time, because of the nature of the crisis, there was a strong lobby for a father figure rather than a Kennedy equivalent. And this need introduced two candidates automatically: Mr Butler, unscathed, as usual, by involvement in the Profumo affair, the real architect of modern Conservatism, the man who had rebuilt the party after the 1945 annihilation, hitherto always the bridesmaid and never the bride. Would his instinct for avoiding commital become a virtue now? His co-runner was Lord Hailsham, similarly unmarked by a drop of slime, responsible for at least one election victory, a man of unchallengeable rectitude. And if it was really a Leader of the Opposition that was being chosen, could there be a more tenacious debater? But Lord Hailsham's support had begun to waver after his television appearance, not because anyone doubted the sincerity of his remarks, but because of the very emotion which they contained. Should a potential Prime Minister blow his top on television?

In the months since February Mr Heath had gradually dropped out of the race. He was the first of the grammar-school meritocracy to get near to the top of the Conservative Party.

179

Why he had fallen back provides an insight into the fundamentals of the Tory power game. There was a strange, irrational reason: he was unmarried. Now nobody can underrate the power of women in the Conservative Party; indeed the women of the party were madly for Mr Heath. For the other senior Cabinet posts, Foreign Secretary or Chancellor, marriage had never seemed a prerequisite. But a Prime Minister, apparently, had to have a mate. Another reason was that Mr Heath had fallen out of the public eye. Buried in the depths of the Foreign Office the image had begun to fade. It was not his fault: he was doing his job. But the bargaining table at Brussels had been dearly forsaken.

It was also said against Mr Heath that one of the reasons for his impact at Brussels told against him as a Prime Ministerial candidate: anyone able so completely to absorb detail could not possibly delegate. This was indeed a curious charge. A delegator would have been no good at Brussels. Because Mr Heath had realised that, he was consequently accused of being unable to suit technique to situation. And, as the Profumo affair had surely shown, delegation can be carried too far. Nevertheless, Mr Heath was out.

This left Mr Maudling representing the New Frontier: 'let's get this country moving again.' Mr Maudling's public image was his liability: the jowls were a little thick for a man of forty-six; the smile was easy, perhaps too easy; but the real burden was the sum of several things, a feeling of endemic lethargy.

But this was caricature rather than justice. As Chancellor his budget had had the wisdom to be unspectacular when there was a demand for the opposite. Instead it was sound and well in control, and it had started to do the right things – not as fast as many would have liked, but to be moving in the right direction alone was something.

These were the candidates. By June 19 it was Mr Butler who had the support of the Cabinet, Lord Hailsham who still had solid backing from the party machine, and Mr Maudling with practically solid support from the backbench M.P.s. On those terms Mr Maudling was in front, without having put any effort into it; Mr Butler was backed by the Cabinet because he seemed made for the situation; and Lord Hailsham had some influential young men from the think division behind him. But this didn't account for the prospective candidates, and it didn't account for the grass roots. The prospective candidates certainly wanted Mr Macmillan out, but who they wanted in was less clear. The constituencies, in varying degrees, wanted Mr Macmillan to stay afloat.

Thus was exposed the bare machinery of opinion and selection: somebody had to allow the backing to harden, then weigh each against the other, then advise on what shifts of allegiance would be realistic, then assess again, and then recommend. The process allowed for some pressure grouping, and it had to allow for smoke signals and jungle drums to be observed. A week earlier, if the Prime Minister had really been compromised, Mr Butler would have waltzed home. Now with the issues obscured by muddy water, no candidate had a clear enough lead to justify short-circuiting the selection machinery.

One ironic result of all this was that the Conservative Party was left in a state of embittered division like that which had compounded the suicide of the Labour Party over unilateralism in 1959. Mr Gaitskell, alas, was not there to savour the sweetness of it.

There was no doubt that the popular support for Mr Macmillan was strengthening by the hour, and mainly because of one idea: that it would be cruel justice for him to be deposed by Miss Keeler. The absurdity of the idea certainly fired him. He told more than one person that week: 'I will not be brought down by that girl.' This was, though, a gross over-simplification, created by emotion to appeal to emotion. It was not Miss Keeler who threatened him; she had not been *his* mistress. The real charge against Mr Macmillan, by now obscured by the flood of moral cant and political skulduggery, was that it had taken 123 days for one document to pass from the Security authorities to Admiralty House.

The 1922 Committee was to meet on Thursday, June 20. This was expected to be critical in deciding the effectiveness of Mr Macmillan's Praetorian guard. The pledge given on Monday, however strong, that the Prime Minister would remain in office only for a decent interval, would not be enough it seemed. Some hard commitment would be demanded.

But what happened proved the impotence of backbench opinion, and the 1922 Committee in particular. When they met, the M.P.s were virtually tied up and gagged: not by the overt efforts of Major Morrison, the chairman, or his assistants, but by the speech of one man, Sir Derek Walker Smith. He executed a superb confidence trick by once again producing the dissolution threat. His speech was an academic treatise on the constitutional possibilities should the Prime Minister be forced into resignation – with emphasis on the dangers which had been suggested the previous Monday. They were just as much of a red herring as they had been then.

It was gullible but typical of the Members to accept this thesis (their critical faculties were probably beaten to pulp) for it abused the facts of the Queen's constitutional position. Although the monarch's rôle in modern politics is not an entirely passive one, before the Queen could possibly call on Mr Wilson to form a new Government the Tory Party would either have to be without agreement on a new leader, or split by civil war into two disparate, mutually destructive and utterly irreconcilable factions. Even in their present madness the party was not prepared to commit suicide.

Sir Derek spoke for fifteen minutes, and since the meeting lasted only half an hour he successfully diverted any threat to the leadership. Moreover, although meetings of the 1922 Committee were supposed to be private (a condition reduced to a pretence), Sir Derek later repeated the substance of his statement for the B.B.C.

The impression was, not surprisingly, that, unsure of their own grip, the Committee's managers had found a spokesman to put the hierarchy's line across for them. Sir Derek refuted this. In a letter to *The Times* he later said: 'I formed my intention and gave notice of it entirely on my initiative and responsibility; and I did so because I thought it was the right thing to do.' It was, for Mr Macmillan and the party managers, a fortuitous thought, because it worked. The charge was diverted. There was no doubt about what the backbenchers wanted. They simply had no means of getting it.

On Saturday, June 22 Lord Poole chose publicly to administer sobriety to the party. Speaking to Conservative officials in Manchester, he said: 'I can tell the Conservative Party one thing certain about the next General Election. If they throw out, or seem to have thrown out, the Prime Minister as a direct result of the Profumo affair there will be such a revulsion of feeling in the country as a whole that they will not need to speculate much about the result of the next General Election, or perhaps the one after that.'

This was the appeal for time. He continued: 'Mr Macmillan has the right, and he has the duty, to make his own decisions in his own way. Moreover, he is entitled to make them calmly and unhurriedly. We can be sure that in his final judgment he will be governed by one thing alone: the national interests.' Lord Poole, of course, was taking great care to speak for the survival of the party, rather than for the Prime Minister alone. The inference was that, given time, Mr Macmillan would go. There was no attempt to determine the date, nor imply that he would remain for the next election. The threat of ten years of opposition was typical of the over-statement thought necessary to marshal the dissidents.

The fête season was upon the politicians. That day Mr Macmillan was fulfilling his duty at his own constituency, Bromley. What he said dovetailed with Lord Poole's words: 'In forty years' political life I have tried to do my best both for my party and for my country. I will not make my whole life worthless or meaningless by being untrue to those convictions, either through panic or obstinacy.' Message very clear. And then: 'I think you know me well enough to realise that any decisions which I have taken, or have to take, will be taken in the spirit in which I have tried to serve the country all these years.'

He was digging in. And two days later *The Times* showed the extent of his recovery. It printed fifteen letters under the heading 'Mr Macmillan's Leadership'. Only two of them were hostile to the Prime Minister. One of them said, tartly, that the Tory M.P.s had lost their chance to change the leadership. The other had more unfashionable reasons for wanting to see the back of Mr Macmillan. 'We remember the reduction of our country to the status of a defenceless American satellite, the "wind of change" speech with its inflammatory effect on

Black African extremism, and the betrayal of our kinsmen in Africa . . . it is vital that rank-and-file Conservatives awaken to the seeds of rottenness in Conservatism as it stands today.' The address declared its interest. It was from the Chairman of an organisation called The True Tories – the gunboat wing of the party. There was another significance to the addresses of the letters. None came from a point farther north than Sudbury, in Suffolk, and there was a bias in favour of Sudbury: two of the letters were from there, one from 'Elm Hall' and the other from 'Great Waldingfield Hall'. It looked like a plot from the shires.

The next calendar event was the June 27 meeting of the 1922 Committee. After the previous week's diversion, the mood this time was less disciplined. There were condemnations of Sir Derek Walker-Smith's performance, particularly about the fact that his B.B.C. statement had obscured from the public the real feelings of the majority of M.P.s about the leadership. Sir Derek defended himself. And there was still uncertainty about the consequences of a resignation by Mr Macmillan, showing that some M.P.s had still not done their homework about the constitutional precedents.

In spite of the temper of the meeting, it was plain that the backbenchers knew that the timing was now wrong for a more belligerent line: the swell from the constituencies had started to take effect. In this atmosphere the issue might have lain sullenly dormant, awaiting the right moment, but for a totally un-expected intervention by the Prime Minister himself.

Soon after the June 17 debate Mr Geoffrey Cox, the editor of *Independent Television News*, had submitted a request to Admiralty House to film an interview with the Prime Minister.

At first nothing happened. Then the word came that Mr Macmillan would co-operate. Finally the date was made for Friday June 28 – in Wolverhampton, where the Premier was visiting Mr Powell's constituency. The interview was recorded in the afternoon. Before it went on the screen it had advance publicity from the B.B.C. They announced it on their news bulletins, so important was it reckoned to be. It lived up to the promise. The Prime Minister made an obviously calculated and defiant stand against the tide. 'All being well,' he said, 'if I keep my health and strength, I hope to lead the party into the election . . . of course, I must have the support of the party, and I think I have it.'

Naturally, the ambiguity allowed an escape. The Prime Minister was too old a hand to be absolutely unequivocal: there was room for interpretation as well as exasperation. His attitude could, damagingly, be seen as the 'Adenauer inclination' the desire to retain power beyond the wish of his party. Dr Adenauer's ability to do so was based on subservience beneath. Mr Macmillan dare not reckon on that, in spite of the stifling of the 1922 Committee. But perhaps the most important step in the interview had been a pronouncement on the coming Test Ban talks.

This looked very much like the line not only for personal survival but for election policy. The audacity of the statement was breathtaking. Many of the M.P.s were made furious by it: but they knew that they had no answer to it then. They had been brilliantly out-manœuvred.

Another factor which had helped to stave off any assassination attempts was the meeting of the Prime Minister and President Kennedy that weekend. The President stayed for twenty-four hours, during which Mr Macmillan asserted objections to the American proposal of a mixed-manned nuclear surface fleet for N.A.T.O., which contained the politically explosive possibility of Germans getting near atomic weapons for the first time. The Americans had to concede the suspension of the idea, which was seen as a tactical victory for the Premier. The Americans were, in fact, so soured by this setback that they later leaked a story alleging that the British negotiators had been badly briefed and that Mr Macmillan himself seemed not to have his mind focused on the issue.

Two weeks after the Profumo debate, to many people's surprise, Mr Macmillan was still Prime Minister. Indeed, in spite of the fresh stir caused by his television statement, the Tory Party began, on the surface at least, to look a little less factious. This was not so much because there were fewer divisions, but because, with sanity re-established, the manœuvring had, in the traditional Conservative manner, gone underground.

With the coming of July the situation was still that Mr

185

Macmillan's chances of leading his party into another election looked slim. But there was one side-effect, possibly a calculated one, of his vow to do so. To the party workers in the constituencies, there seemed to be a rudder again.

Although the leadership struggle became respectable, there was no respite from the warfare of Westminster debate for the Prime Minister. July opened with another security controversy: there almost seemed to be one for every month of the year. Harold Philby, a Middle-East correspondent for *The Observer* and *The Economist*, had been missing for six months after disappearing one night in Beirut. Now, on July 1, Mr Edward Heath told the House of Commons that Philby had been the Third Man in the Burgess and Maclean spy sensation of 1951 – the man who had tipped off the two Foreign Office agents that M.I.5 were closing in on them, and so provoked their flight behind the Iron Curtain.

Mr Heath's statement fell rather short of his usual lucid performance. It left several key questions about Philby unanswered: First, how the Security Services had finally resolved that Philby was guilty. (In 1955 Mr Macmillan, then Foreign Secretary, had firmly denied a suggestion from the Labour M.P. Mr Marcus Lipton that Philby had been the Third Man.) Second, how Philby had made a 'confession' and yet had disappeared. And then there was the question of Philby's employment as a journalist, after he had left a post at the Foreign Office. Mr Heath's statement failed to mention, as the editor of *The Observer*, Mr David Astor, had to point out, that Philby had been recommended to the paper by the Foreign Office.

Why the Government had suddenly produced the Philby statement, when it created more questions than it answered, was simple: an American magazine had got the story. Otherwise, considering the lack of precision in Mr Heath's explanation, it was unlikely that anything would have come out at that time.

Although Mr Macmillan was carrying the private strain of his fight for survival on top of the public strain of dealing with situations like the Philby case, his performance under this pressure was formidable for a man of sixty-nine. In a clash with

Mr Wilson over Philby he gave as good as he got. This was no fading Parliamentarian, with a grip eroded by a struggle for power. The strength of his performance was not lost on his own benches, nor on the Opposition.

As for the two principal heirs, neither had made an overt move to assert their ambitions. There were no opportunist thrusts while the fever was at its height: both Mr Maudling and Mr Butler were too shrewd to make that kind of miscalculation. But a decent interval had passed. And the sudden strokes came within hours – on Saturday, July 6. In the morning Mr Butler arrived at London Airport with a considerable personal victory in his brief-case: the successful conclusion of the conference at Victoria Falls to dismantle the Central African Federation.

It had been one of those seemingly insuperable diplomatic tasks in which all Mr Butler's subtleties as a negotiator could be brought into play. At the beginning it had seemed unlikely that anybody could reconcile a problem involving such extreme points of view. It was even likely that the result could be a descent into another Congo. But the Butler technique had charmed and won. Of course, demolition was one thing, reconstruction another, and the future of Central Africa still contained plenty of latent strife.

At London Airport Mr Butler made sure that the extent of the success was lost on no one: 'We achieved all our aims, which is saying a lot.' He pointed out, immodestly, that one reason for the outcome of the conference had been the careful preparation that had gone into it.

Africa had been the graveyard of many an Englishman, and many a politician's ambition. Several of the aspirants to Mr Macmillan's throne had been despatched there since his decisive 'wind of change' speech, rather like a tribal rite to prove manhood. Not all of them had returned with reputations consolidated, and none of them with such a fortuitously timed victory as Mr Butler's. It demonstrated exactly the qualities which his supporters, in the Cabinet and in the party's annexes of power, urged were most necessary to meet the demands of the succession.

Mr Maudling had no African trophy to exhibit; he chose

instead to deal with the length of the Tory teeth. Once again a summer fête provided a platform for another round in the struggle, this time at Sawston, in Cambridgeshire. Mr Maudling said that if the Conservatives had fallen behind it was not because their opponents had gained ground, but because the Conservatives had lost it, and they must win it back. This contained no striking profundity, but the method advocated for recovery was significant: 'We have not been successful in obtaining the allegiance of the younger generation of voters, because we have not yet found a way of talking to them in language they understand or in terms of the ideals they cherish.'

His message was the equivalent of the vicar who adopts rock 'n roll for his services: the Tories had to get 'with it', with the inference that a man of Mr Maudling's spritely age of forty-six was more likely to know the steps than a hard-arteried sixty-nine-year-old.

This was the kind of talk *his* backers wanted. They were largely on the back benches, where the membership had been regenerated by infusions of younger men from the 1955 and 1959 elections: of the 365 Tory M.P.s, 128 were between forty and fifty, and another fifty-seven were still in their thirties. The party was becoming markedly separated from Mr Macmillan's generation: members who shared with him the scar tissue of the First World War were thinning out. The surge for Mr Maudling was from twentieth-century men. Not that the majority of them had been conspicuously nonconformist: many had been surprisingly timid on issues where their youth might have divided them from the party's policy.

But if the younger backbenchers liked Mr Maudling's message, their support alone was not enough. It was clear, though, that the contest had been narrowed to one between the older, and consummately experienced, party-builder and trouble-shooter, and the younger man whose capacity for premiership was difficult to gauge. With such a choice, the Tory inclination was traditionally towards the older man. But this time the paradox was that tradition, in many ways, was a dirty word.

By the second week of July there was one of those shifts of feeling, at first slow, then gradually accelerating, that happen in a prolonged contest. The front-runner, Mr Maudling, began to lose support. Perhaps his speech had been too overt a move, or perhaps its content had been more closely examined and found wanting. For whatever reason, his campaign was losing stamina and conviction.

It was a notorious truism that the front-runner always came unseated: Mr Butler had done so the last time. It was also true that by counting heads in Parliament Mr Maudling still had a clear majority. But if each individual head were asked why it so voted, the reasons were found to be far from lucid. In fact the very asking of the question seemed to invoke doubt. Some of this individual reassessment, as opposed to the earlier collective enthusiasm, was responsible for the desertion of the Maudling bandwagon, and it was changing the balance of allegiances.

It was also clear that the contest was not going to be precipitated. Mr Maudling's and Mr Butler's supporters were nearing stalemate. This pleased at least one of Mr Macmillan's tactical advisers: Lord Beaverbrook.

Here was one of the most resourceful but under-employed political minds in the country. After years of exclusion from the centre of the arena, Beaverbrook had, at eighty-four, found a man to advise and support again. Although his newspapers had tenaciously opposed Mr Macmillan's Common Market policy, and sung 'Glory, glory Hallelujah' when it collapsed, Beaverbrook had always liked Macmillan, and Macmillan in turn was fascinated by the enormous reserves of political cunning which the old maestro still exhibited. Beaverbrook's crusader went to the rescue of Mr Macmillan as soon as the hordes were surrounding him on June 18, and ever since they had been behind him, poking caustic fun at Mr Maudling and reinforcing the reaction of sympathy for the underdog. It was said that the support for Mr Butler in the Cabinet had been encouraged by Beaverbrook to force the stalemate, although how this could have been so neatly arranged was not clear. It had however, happened. And the final stroke, guaranteed to sustain Mr Macmillan in power, came when the *Sunday Express* nominated Lord Avon for the succession.

There now came into sight the vehicle which all along Mr Macmillan had seen would provide the valedictory honour which he felt was his due: the prospect of a partial ban on nucleartesting. It had been his initiative, and his idea.

But even Mr Macmillan, with his sense of the melodramatic, could not have foreseen how precise would be the timing of his final coup. On Thursday, July 25 the Test Ban treaty was agreed and initialled at 5.15 p.m. At 6.10 p.m. the Prime Minister confronted the 1922 Committee, which some people still imagined was about to turn him out.

Of all the rôles that Harold Macmillan had played, and they were many, this performance as Pearl White was masterly: as the 1922 Committee bore down the track emitting shrill whistles, up dashed Lord Hailsham, with the ink hardly dry on the Test Ban treaty, and cut the Prime Minister from his bonds. Saved again, Mr Macmillan told the erstwhile insurrectionists: 'You will expect me to say something about my position. My sole motive is to serve the party and the country – and when I go it will be after consultation with those people whose views I hold in the highest regard.' When he left the 1922 Committee conceded applause.

By 11 p.m. that night, when the Prime Minister entered the Chamber at Westminster formally to read the announcement of the Test Ban agreement, he spoke from spiritual strength. 'The House will, I know, understand my own feelings on seeing at last the result of efforts made over many years, and hopes long deferred. . . .' The other struggle, his personal one, was over after six frenetic weeks. Whenever he now chose to go, it would not be at the dictation of Miss Keeler.

One result of the Prime Minister's fight, common to all victors who have come near to defeat, was that most of his enemies had been smoked out and stood exposed. And an enemy visible is more easily out-manœuvred. The assault had come more from within his own party than from the Opposition.

There was never much mystery about the motives of the Right Wing. But the discontent among the younger M.P.s was something he could not ignore. There was also Mr Maudling.

In no sense an enemy of the Prime Minister – he owed his position to Mr Macmillan and knew it – he had nevertheless made a severe tactical error.

As Mr Wigg had said of the Press Barons, Mr Maudling had been willing to wound but afraid to strike. He had at first, wisely, been reluctant to make any move at all. But when his backers did approach he could have indicated that although he was prepared to be supported in the long run, his loyalty was to the Prime Minister until the party had returned to sanity and the real issues – the future policies of Conservatism – and that this was the wrong time to move. Either that, or he could have chosen all-out assault. He did neither, and paid the price.

Outside Westminster and the party, Mr Macmillan had declared opponents in two Conservative newspapers: the *Sunday Telegraph* and *The Times*. The *Telegraph* quiesced a little, showing the realism that all opportunists require. It made it clear that being a Conservative newspaper did not preclude what it felt to be rational and constructive criticism of the leadership. *The Times* relapsed into a patently sullen phase: the Prime Minister rubbed home his conviction in affluence by giving it a new name, 'The Good Life', and implying, with the inevitable pun, that *The Times* was behind the times.

Was the Prime Minister's motive for keeping office as magnanimous as he suggested: selflessly to preserve the interests of party and nation? In one respect he gave cause for doubt. At no time, either during the post-Common Market crisis in February or throughout the Profumo crisis, had he done what he was in a unique position to do – chosen an heir for himself and opened up the opportunity for him. In February he could have done this for Mr Heath, to whom, of all the younger candidates, he was most disposed. But Mr Heath was condemned to the chasms of the Foreign Office, instead of employing his dynamic in more public work.

This virtual exile seemed to have a psychological effect on Mr Heath as was shown by his maladroit performance over Philby. He was, of course, bound to benefit from a Cabinet reconstruction, but that would be too late to give him the chance of ultimate power. Mr Macmillan had withheld his patronage when it would have been most effective . . . and most deserved.

He could not then complain if the choice of his successor was not according to his own preference, for he had forfeited that right.

18

Guilty Until Proved Innocent

IT WAS TYPICAL of the lunatic values of the whole affair that Stephen Ward should be made a martyr by his death. The penalty he exacted on himself was greater than that which could have been administered by the law, and in paying it he swung public opinion, in all its perversity, on to his side. He left an impression that he had been the victim of a revengeful executive, rather than a man allowed a fair trial.

But before ever he had taken the fatal overdose of Nembutal he had paid the penalty that made the future for him seem intolerable. The world he had constructed for himself over the years, founded on wits and contagious charm, had been proved perishable in the glare of publicity. It was something he could not bear to realise – or to lose. When the jury filed back into the court to deliver their verdict the dock was empty. Ward lay in a coma, with no will left to live. Melodrama had been against the jury all along. When the trial opened in the No 1 Court at the Old Bailey on Monday, July 22, they had been asked by the Judge to extract from a fevered picture the decipherable truths; to disregard all the ramifications which had rippled out across the worlds of politics, society and crime and examine only the charges facing Ward. It was an impossible request.

The charges against him were five:

1. That between June 1, 1961, and August 31, 1962, he knowingly lived wholly or in part on the earnings of prostitution.

2. Between September 1, 1962, and December 1962 he knowingly lived wholly or in part on the earnings of prostitution.

3. Between January 1, 1963, and June 8, 1963, he lived wholly or in part on the earnings of prostitution.

4. Between May 1, 1961, and June 30, 1961, he incited Christine Keeler to procure a girl under the age of twenty-one to have unlawful sexual intercourse with a third person.

5. On January 3, 1963, he attempted to procure a girl under the age of twenty-one to have unlawful sexual intercourse with a third person.

These were the charges in law. But was this a trial based on crime or on morality? From the beginning it was apparent that the jury would have to get clear in their minds the difference between promiscuity and prostitution. The battle between Crown and defence was to be fought close to this narrow border every day.

This introduced the refined semantics at the very root of the law: when did sin become crime? Because, within the liberal definitions of 1963, sin was held to be a crime only against God – and private behaviour was becoming entirely a matter of conscience: the law left people a large margin for error. The charges against Stephen Ward concerned acts held to be criminal; but it was hazardous, subjective ground.

When Mr Mervyn Griffith-Jones rose to make the opening speech for the Crown it was obvious that since the magistrate's court hearing the prosecution had realised that in dealing with the libertine world of Ward a new definition of prostitution was essential. He provided this one:

'A prostitute is not necessarily the kind of woman that one pictures when one uses that word. It is not necessary for her to ply her trade on the street corner, or, as is perhaps more customary since a recent Act, to set up as a call girl and make herself available when telephoned.' He was pointing out that the oldest profession founded its resilience on adaptability.

'Prostitution is a matter of law and, for the purposes of this case, is where a woman offers her body for sexual intercourse – that is normal sexual intercourse – or for any acts of lewdness for money.' (In cases of living off immoral earnings the difficulty was always to prove that money had changed hands for this purpose.)

Mr Griffith-Jones explained that on the final two counts which involved inciting or attempting to procure a girl under twenty-one to have unlawful sexual intercourse with a third person the effective words were 'a third person'. In enlarging on this he recognised how near the case was hovering to promiscuity: 'If it were not for that, any young man who tried to get a girl to go to bed with him would be committing a criminal offence. Quite obviously that would be absurd and that is not what is alleged in this case. No doubt it can be argued on behalf of the defence that that is what it comes to, but it is not so, as you will see.'

Mr Griffith-Jones had indeed anticipated part of the tactics of the defence counsel, Mr James Burge.

Later in his opening speech Mr Griffith-Jones went on to the psychology of prostitution; speaking of the relationship between Ward and Miss Keeler, he said that Ward had given her 'moral instruction' by telling her that she was not really a prostitute and should not regard herself as one. And as long as she had not got a prostitute's mentality in the sense that she was not on the streets it was not wrong to go to bed with another man and get paid for it.

All through the trial this was the territory which Mr Burge disputed. The margin between prostitution and promiscuity became particularly fine on the question of presents, and both Miss Keeler and Miss Rice-Davies had received plenty of those. (Peter Rachman's benefactions to Miss Rice-Davies had been particularly lavish.)

Miss Keeler was the third witness called. Those in the court who saw her for the first time were sharply reminded that there were two kinds of people: the real ones and the versions of them which appeared in photographs. In the case of Miss Keeler, presence was revelationary. In her pictures, for example, there was no sense of size; if anything she looked tall. In the intimidating scale of the Old Bailey she seemed small – about 5 feet 3 inches, but she wore very high heels. The face, its bone structure so photogenic, looked mask-like in the flesh – *la belle dame sans merci*. The cheekbones were high, eyes slanting and heavy with make-up, and long, light-brown-reddish hair falling to the shoulders. The identifying pout was in place as she walked up to the curious witness-box, which looked like a discarded sedan. Her back was to the jury. (It seemed, all through the trial, a distinct disadvantage that the jury were denied the scrutiny of witnesses' faces; they must have developed an instinct for reading meaning into backs.) Her effect in the box was calculated. The clothes were related not to the styles of the season – by that rule she was unfashionable – but to her figure. She wore a yellowy gold sheath dress, which closely fitted her natural bosom line, tiny waist and sloping shoulders. Over this was a cloak of the same fabric, which was flung off with panache to reveal bare arms. In defying the fashion writers she represented man's physical fantasy of the sexy, the romantic, the faintly mysterious, the accessible. By this time she had refined the image of the goddess of sensuality to a range of subtle nuances. (It had been Mandy Rice-Davies who said she would go down in history as another Lady Hamilton, but in fact it was Christine Keeler who took that rôle; Miss Rice-Davies was, if anything, more of a Nell Gwynne.)

Nevertheless, Miss Keeler gave the feeling of being a slightly synthetic creation, with a carefully modulated voice, rehearsed gestures not quite correctly timed. She went through the now familiar recital of names, and the confusion of addresses and dates, and she lost control only once, on a vulnerable point, to cry: 'I would like to say I am not a prostitute and never have been.' Definition was at issue again. It was, in fact, true of the trial that the only girls who *looked* like prostitutes were the two who confessed to being so: 'Ronna' Ricardo and Vickie Barrett.

Mandy Rice-Davies, who appeared the following day, made a different kind of impact. She wore a simple, grey dress and a hat of red petals, and unlike Miss Keeler she had a simple spontaneity. There could have been no more disarming a display of this than when she was asked why she had included the name of Douglas Fairbanks, Jr, among her lovers. 'Because I don't like him,' she said, and it was plainly true.

Miss Keeler's voice had been lost in the atrocious acoustics of the No. 1 Court. Miss Rice-Davies's voice bubbled up and conquered the architecture. She seemed not bright enough to be a liar, and the drift of the questioning obviously eluded her. Her face, with a suspicion of coming fatness, was pale, like Keeler's, and her eyes had the same heavy make-up, which began to run when a hot sun came through the skylight of the court.

Different degrees of worldliness became apparent as the trial went on. The public gallery, agape with appetite, was there to learn; the jury, trying its best to be inscrutable, was obviously for the first time face to face with a *demi-monde* it was a stranger to; the Judge, Mr Justice Marshall, ready to rebuke any lapse into flippancy and determined to preserve the dignity of the law in such a labyrinth of amorality; only on the Press benches was there an air of cynicism.

When Mr Griffith-Jones pressed Miss Rice-Davies about her relationship with a man named Ropner, there was another insight into her attitude: 'I did not fancy him,' she said, which in the context meant that she was exercising selectivity in choosing her partners. At this point it was certainly arguable whether the liaisons fell within the compass of prostitution. It was more a highly developed form of promiscuity, demanding perhaps of the girls some discrimination. Was it really profligate behaviour?

There was certainly a great distance between the attitudes of Miss Keeler and Miss Rice-Davies and that of a professed prostitute like Miss Ricardo. She was asked bluntly by Mr Griffith-Jones how she made a living. Her face dipped, there was a pause, and then the voice broke through: 'By prostitution.' It had been a surgical question. Another prostitute by confession, Vickie Barrett, gave evidence on the third day. She had not appeared in the magistrates' court hearing and, indeed, the circumstances of her eventual appearance were extraordinary. According to the police, she had been arrested on a soliciting charge and while she was being questioned a diary containing Ward's telephone number had been found in her handbag. This was at 2 a.m. on July 4 at Notting Hill police station. Detective-Inspector Herbert had been called to Notting Hill and took from Miss Barrett a statement which, if true, was one of the firmest pieces of evidence in the prosecution's case. Miss Barrett said that for two and a half months she had visited Ward's flat two or three times a week. He had first picked her up in Oxford Street and driven her back to his flat in Bryanston Mews. There was a man waiting in the bedroom; Ward had given her a contraceptive and told her to strip and go to bed with the man. While they had intercourse, she said, Ward made coffee in another room. Ward had told her that the man had already paid him. This had happened with a different man the following week.

Ward also asked her, she said, to provide a service for his friends who had strange tastes; they were middle-aged or elderly men who required not normal sexual intercourse but beatings with either a cane or a horsewhip. Mr Griffith-Jones asked: 'For the whipping, what is the market price?'

'£1 a stroke,' said Miss Barrett.

Naturally, this bizarre recital peeled further scales from the eyes of the unworldly. (Added to the previously unfolded repertoire of copulation *à quatre* and two-way mirrors the world of normality seemed to be receding as the No. 1 Court became instructed in the commerce of Port Said.)

For the prosecution Miss Barrett seemed a fortuitous discovery. She had none of the preening arrogance of Christine Keeler or Mandy Rice-Davies, and she was not completely contradicting earlier stories, as had Miss Ricardo. Mr Burge naturally viewed her arrival with scepticism, but amid all the collapsing depositions and confessed lies here seemed a witness of comparative reliability; although consistency had yet to be tested.

For the first few days, Ward, sitting in the dock sketching witnesses apparently dispassionately, seemed to be some kind of court recorder instead of the accused man. He managed to give the impression that the whole saga was foreign to him: compared with his mannered ease, the procession of girls seemed incongruous. Was this the ringmaster of social decay and sexual depravity? Had those sensitive hands plunged to odious arts? Every day, entering and leaving the Old Bailey, he had run a gauntlet of blatantly adulatory scrutiny from women of all ages. Any one of them, it seemed, would have gone readily to his harem.

But gradually his composure began to crack.

On the fourth day Mr Burge opened the defence. He was a large, caustic man. During the prosecution's case he had been constantly alert, swooping in with questions and, once or twice, catching Mr Griffith-Jones on the wrong foot. It was obviously impossible to present Ward as a man of reasonable morals. And so Mr Burge presented him as a libertine but not, in his submission, a criminal. It was, he said, impossible in such a highly publicised case to expect the jury to dismiss from their minds all the stories that had appeared, within the law – but prejudicial – before the trial. And here he made a vital point: that against this background Ward had to prove his innocence, rather than the prosecution having to prove his guilt. 'When he comes to give his evidence,' said Mr Burge, 'you will hear of the two lives of Stephen Ward. You will hear first, and this is accepted, that he is a skilled and successful osteopath earning substantial sums of money.

'And you will hear of his second life, a life that may not appeal to you and quite clearly does not appeal to many people, that of a bohemian, a man who is a talented artist and who will not flinch from telling you that he is very highly sexed indeed and has had affairs with a great many women.'

This was the tenor of the whole afternoon, as Mr Burge put Ward into the witness-box and led him through his dichotomous life. Ward, said Mr Burge, was a 'connoisseur of lovemaking.' Depravity was not contested; prostitution was.

The next day, turned over to Mr Griffith-Jones for cross-examination, Ward lost control of himself for the first time. He said that Vickie Barrett had been lying – 'and why she is lying we must find out'. A little later he banged his fists on the ledge of the witness-box and said: 'Anyone who comes in from the street and comes forward into this court can come and say I am lying. In a general atmosphere of villainy surrounding this case almost anyone comes forward and makes suggestions.' Then, pulling himself short, he apologised to Mr Justice Marshall for the outburst.

There was no doubt that the most articulate, if not the most plausible, witness of all was Stephen Ward himself. At one point, though, the glib self-confession went too far for the Judge, who interrupted: 'Are you seriously comparing the true conception of love with the kind of thing that we have been investigating over the past five days?' 'No, I am not.' 'Don't you think it better not to use the term?' Ward, repentant, said: 'I regret having used it, My Lord.' The Judge was not prepared to allow his standards to be violated by those of another world.

When the court resumed on Monday for the sixth day of the trial, Mr Burge made his closing speech, and attempted to draw together into some logic all the confusing strands of the case. If the trial was concerned with establishing only that Ward led a thoroughly immoral life, he said, the jury's task would be a simple one. Then, putting his finger on an issue which by then was growing in importance, he said: 'If you were there to make sure that the public conscience that was shocked by a major scandal should be appeased so that the penalty should be paid and the whole episode forgotten, then you could hardly find a more suitable subject for expiation than the accused, who has admitted that he is a loose-liver and his conduct is such as to deprive him of any sympathy from any quarter.'

The picture of Ward at fifty with girls thirty years younger was, Mr Burge saw, possibly an offensive one. But 'because they were seventeen or eighteen and the accused was fifty, it does not mean everything he did was from a corrupt and repulsive motive, and everything they did was out of complete innocence. You can have a girl of eighteen, or even younger, who is highly sophisticated and experienced. You can have a a man of fifty who never seems to grow old, and certainly whatever one says about the accused, he certainly has the secret of eternal youth in one respect, and he likes young girls. Don't get the idea that these girls are innocent young things and that Ward is a depraved old man.'

Describing Miss Barrett, who by then was reckoned by many experienced observers to be the principal anchor of the prosecution's case, Mr Burge said: 'Although she might have been quite ingenuous and soft and appealing as a young woman in the witness-box, if a woman is a prostitute she is doing it as a business. However soft she appeared, there may be a hard little heart there ticking over inside.'

And of Miss Ricardo: 'Whatever she is, or whatever she says, there is one thing that cannot be denied, and that is that she is a woman of the most enormous courage, because she came here and went back on certain evidence she had given at the magistrates' court. One can only assume that she, at least, is not prepared to go as far as to tell lies against this man at the Central Criminal Court, realising what it may mean.'*

Mr Burge ended his speech by returning to Ward's motivation: 'Did he lead this life for fun or for profit? – that is the key to this case.'

Mr Griffith-Jones saw no shades between black and white when he made his closing speech – none of the greys of the 'dissolute life' or the 'highly-sexed bohemian'. Ward was, in the rather Edwardian vocabulary of Mr Griffith-Jones, 'a thoroughly filthy fellow'. Later he was a 'wicked, wicked creature'.

Mr Justice Marshall began his summing-up on Tuesday, July 30. By far the most important part of this rested once again on explaining definitions in law.

First, the Judge explained how a man should be deemed to be living off immoral earnings; it was no part of the prosecution's case, he said, that Ward had been living *wholly* on these earnings; what they had to prove was that he had lived *in part* on them.

If only a fraction of his income was produced in this way it would be sufficient. The law laid down no specific percentage. It was not only a degree of support from prostitutes which had to be proved, but also assistance to them in plying their trade.

Here the Judge had a recent precedent of great importance: the case in 1961 of a prosecution against a man who published

* Miss Ricardo had retracted three statements she had made to the police which were given as evidence in the magistrates' court. In an affidavit she had sworn on July 20 she said: 'I never paid Ward any money received from men with whom I have had intercourse . . . the statements which I have made to the police were untrue. I made them because I did not want my young sister to go to a remand home or my baby taken away from me. Mr Herbert told me they would take my sister away and take my baby if I didn't make the statements.' When Detective-Inspector Herbert was questioned by the Judge he said that there was no truth at all in the allegation that he had brought pressures on Miss Ricardo to incriminate Ward.

a magazine called *The Ladies Directory*. This had, in fact, been a catalogue in which, under various euphemisms, prostitutes advertised themselves and their services, with pictures.

On conviction, the publisher had appealed before the Court of Criminal Appeal. There Mr Justice Ashworth had laid down: 'If a man knowingly assists a prostitute with the direct object of enabling her to carry on her trade, and knowingly lives wholly or in part on the earnings of prostitutes *which he assists*, he is in our view guilty of the offences under the 1956 Act.' This judgment had been upheld in the ultimate appeal by the publisher to the House of Lords, and it had therefore become the definitive ruling on the position of Ward. *Assistance* had to be proved.

Mr Justice Marshall explained: 'A person may be fairly said to be living on the earnings of prostitution if he is paid by prostitutes for goods and services supplied by him to them for the purpose of their prostitution, which they would not be supplied with but for the fact they were prostitutes.'

He then passed on to the difficulties of proving that a man had been living on the earnings of prostitution.

'Prostitutes, so dependent on the assistance of such people as touts, suppliers of accommodation where they can pursue their trade – they would be the last persons you may think to provide evidence which would deprive themselves of such assistance, and Parliament has recognised this fact.' The Judge was coming to what turned out to be the most crucial part of his explanation.

It concerned Section 30 of the Sexual Offences Act of 1956. Assuming that *association* with prostitutes had been established and a man who habitually *consorts* with prostitutes was automatically presumed to be knowingly taking at least a part of his income from them – the burden was on the accused to *prove that he had not received immoral earnings*. This had to be proved on 'the balance of probabilities'. The Judge elaborated: 'This is one of those rare cases, there are a few more, where a recognition of the difficulties of proof has caused Parliament to lay down that when once certain facts have been proved, there is a presumption that the case has been made out for living on immoral earnings *unless the defence proves to the contrary.'*

This was a vital point, because it represented an inversion of the normal basis of British law that a man is innocent until proved guilty, that the onus was on the prosecution to establish and prove guilt, rather than on the accused to do the opposite, as in this case.

Now came the third point of definition: what in the eyes of the law was a prostitute?

This was no less difficult a piece of semantics; the jury found that they had entered one of the most complex areas of the law. It was made particularly tortuous by the timing of the trial, for one part of the law's interpretation of prostitution happened then to be under appeal: that part which covered the area beyond normal sexual intercourse, where a woman submitted her body to obscene acts other than normal intercourse 'to satisfy an abnormal sexual appetite.'

This was, as the Judge pointed out, directly germane to part of the evidence of Vickie Barrett. On July 17 the Court of Criminal Appeal had upheld this definition in the case of a man called Webb, who had been convicted on prostitution charges. Webb had run an establishment called an Institute of Massage, and it had been proved at this trial that on one, and possibly two, occasions men went to the institute and were masturbated by a woman. But the Webb case was now due for hearing before the Appeal Committee of the House of Lords.

Since this meant that there was not what Mr Justice Marshall called 'the final and most authoritative view upon this aspect of prostitution,' he told the jury to put out of their minds the question of 'any abnormal sexual activity' and base their decision 'as to whether these young women were or are prostitutes only on whether you are satisfied that they offered their bodies *indiscriminately for payment in return for normal sexual intercourse.'*

Thus was the act of prostitution for this case confined in a crucial way to normal intercourse.

As far as the jury was concerned, all the orgiastic proclivities which had been suggested as a part of the Ward *demimonde* were to be disregarded. A girl could, as Vickie Barrett had said she had done, dress in high-heeled shoes and underwear and whip middle-aged men at the rate of £1 a stroke, and stay beyond the law. Only the evidence in which she alleged normal intercourse, with contraceptives and premises supplied by Ward, was relevant. As Havelock Ellis observed, sexual flagellation among adults might be a traditional British perversion, stemming in the *psyche* from early experiences at the hands of schoolmasters, and here it was, for the moment anyway, perfectly legal while fornication was not. To foreign observers of the British paradox this was confirmation of the national peculiarities which they had long suspected.

There were three paramount legal points for the jury to decide: first, whether it had been established that Ward had *associated* with prostitutes or *assisted* prostitution; second, if satisfied on circumstantial evidence that he had, whether he had proved, *on the balance of probability*, that he had not received any income from them; and third, that acts of normal intercourse had been performed under his patronage.

The Judge listed these three vital considerations:

1. Were Christine Keeler and Mandy Rice-Davies prostitutes within the definition?

2. Did Ward know this?

3. Did he knowingly receive from them direct, or from someone who paid him direct, other than the girls, money for the introduction and the facilities for sexual intercourse which he provided?

Having thus set this out, the Judge turned to the question of the almost total lack of defence witnesses: 'There may be many reasons why he [Ward] has been abandoned in his extremity. You must not guess at them, but this thing is clear: If Stephen Ward was telling the truth in the witness-box there are in this city many witnesses of high estate and low who could have come and testified support of his evidence.'

Nobody in the court knew it then, but the effect of this on Ward was probably considerable. It pointed to what had been increasingly apparent to him for months: the journey from court jester to social outcast.

But when he left the court that day legal opinion was that

204

he still had a chance. Lawyers felt that the Judge's opinion on Vickie Barrett, still to come, would be vital.

That night Stephen Ward went to bed for the last time – with the fatal overdose of Nembutal slowly softening his brain. The next day the Judge decided that since the case for the defence was completed the trial should continue. And then he dealt with the evidence of Vickie Barrett.

He recalled the discovery by the police of Dr Ward's name in her diary. 'You would think,' he said, 'that it was the duty of the police to pursue and investigate, and they did. It was only then that the question about her connection with Ward came out.

'Miss Barrett had not attracted the attention of those interests who were getting, for various reasons of publicity and otherwise, at such witnesses as Keeler and Rice-Davies. There was no question of her being offered any money for any story she knew anything about. By the merest chance – justice often turns on chance – here there comes out this story, if you accept her evidence.'

Justice often turns on chance. Was Vickie Barrett to be the agent of justice? The Judge said – and this was vitally important – that there was evidence from witnesses other than Vickie Barrett which seemed to confirm a number of parts of her evidence and which, if the jury accepted it, they could regard together as some of the corroboration of her evidence which he had emphasised they needed.

At 2.32 p.m. on Wednesday the Judge completed his summing-up. The decision was now in the hands of the jury, and the lawyers' forecasts of their verdict were conflicting.

They were faced not only with the problem of assessing evidence of a highly contradictory nature, but also with points of law which were difficult enough for a trained legal mind to retain. By fateful coincidence the House of Lords had that same day dismissed the appeal in the Webb case, thus upholding the ruling that prostitution embraced flagellation, although the Ward jury had, of course, still to disregard this.

For more than two hours the Old Bailey lapsed into tense expectation. Ward lay in a coma at St Stephens' Hospital in the Fulham Road. At that time he was expected to recover.

Throughout the trial the jury had been straining to follow every nuance of argument. There was one woman among them, middle-aged and crisply turned out, with a hat worthy of the Conservative annual conference. Of the men, all quietly dressed, three were about thirty; three between thirty and forty; and the rest forty-plus.

At about 5 p.m. they returned: not with a verdict but with a long note, which took the Judge three minutes to read. It was seeking a direction, and although it was not read out, the Judge's answer revealed that they were seeking guidance on the *presumption of guilt*, the most unfamiliar point of law.

The Judge's direction was not reported in any of the newspapers the following morning. This may have been partly because of its complexity, at a time when the newspapers were already swamped with legal argument. Or it might have been because the verdict and Ward's illness dominated the interest. And yet this was perhaps the most illuminating event in the whole trial, for it helped to show how the jury's mind was working, and it explained the verdict that they later reached.

This is what the Judge said:

'If you are agreed and satisfied on either of these two counts [there were two undisclosed alternatives on the jury's paper] that Stephen Ward has been proved by the prosecution to be living with a person who has been proved to your satisfaction to be a prostitute, then the burden has shifted on him to prove to your satisfaction on the balance of probabilities that he was not living on the earnings of prostitution.

'That is the first thing. If you are not satisfied that he was living with a prostitute or in fact that he was habitually in the company of a prostitute or that it has been proved that he exercised control, direction or influence over a prostitute in any way that shows he has been aiding and abetting prostitution, if you are not satisfied with either one of those three, then you must, of course, go back and be satisfied that all four points I have made have been established.'

He then gave these four points:

'First of all that he was knowingly assisting prostitutes in the plying of their trade;

'Second, that such assistance was in goods and services supplied by him for the purposes of prostitution – it does not have to be exclusively so.

'Three, that he would not have supplied them but for the fact that they were prostitutes.

'And four, that he did receive payment for such assistance from their earnings.

'You must be satisfied on all four of those by proof through the prostitutes on the evidence. All those four things must be established to your satisfaction.

'If, however, the alternative position arises, and you are satisfied that the prosecution has proved that he was living with a prostitute or exercised control, then that is sufficient and you must consider the evidence and say whether you are satisfied that he has proved on the balance of probabilities that in fact he was not living on the earnings of prostitution.'

Once again, if the *association* was established then it was up to the defence successfully to contest the *assumption of guilt*.

After this direction the jury again retired, at 5.16 p.m. They returned at 7.9 p.m., having considered their verdict for four hours and thirty-six minutes.

The end was anti-climactic. Few of the spectators remained at the cockpit. The jury had disregarded Vickie Barrett's evidence: they found Ward not guilty of living off her immoral earnings, and not guilty on the two procurement charges. But they found him guilty on the first two charges: of living off the immoral earnings of Christine Keeler and Mandy Rice-Davies. Thus, on that admittedly tenuous and delicate *balance of probabilities* the scale of justice had tipped against Stephen Ward.

The defence had failed to prove to the jury's satisfaction that he was *not* living in part on immoral earnings. The jury had also decided another thing: that in their view Christine Keeler and Mandy Rice-Davies *were* prostitutes, whatever the moral instruction from their keeper had been.

The Judge never delivered a sentence. The case of *Regina v. Ward* was closed, the file marked: 'Deceased, August 3.'

What purpose had the trial served? Had justice been done or was Stephen Ward a sacrificial offering by a society panicked into demanding a moral catharsis? The law had been working at the limits of its compass, at the edge where standards of behaviour were most in dispute. The Profumo affair had brought into the open a great warfare of attitudes, which had started to rage as the frontiers of permissiveness had begun to shift. It overlapped public and political morality. And there was at the heart of it the issue of double standards: not simply the double standards of private and public life, but also the conflicting standards of the gathering libertine wave and the puritan reaction which it provoked.

The ease with which girls could pass from suburbia into the promiscuity belt of London was alarming: Christine Keeler and Mandy Rice-Davies could have been anybody's daughters.

Poor Mr Profumo had opened the floodgates to all these fears and conflicts: he must have looked on with the bewilderment which overtakes a man when he pulls one brick from a wall and the whole house collapses. Something was wrong with the foundations.

People sleep peacefully with restricted knowledge. The Profumo affair proved that disclosure was more disturbing that the original sin which it revealed. But each individual revelation was only a visible part of a much wider setting. To imagine Ward's milieu as typical London life in the 'sixties was to be absurdly provincial.

As Mr Justice Marshall had said: 'One would have thought from what we have all been faced with in the national newspapers that this country has become a sort of sink of iniquity. But you and I know that the even tenor of family life over the overwhelming majority of our population goes quietly and decently on.'

It would, though, be parlous to assume that a society permitted to read only good news would at once be purged and reformed. At least the sinful section of society was egalitarian. Because the class frontiers had been crossed – politically as well as socially – there were signs of defensive actions more intended to resist change than to exorcise decay. The shock created by the knowledge that Dr Ward's world embraced Cliveden was partly because of its imputations of aristocratic weakness.

The defenders of chastity and virtue had to be careful that in putting their case they were not also trying to resurrect class barriers.

Every person and institution which became involved in the affair seemed to become contaminated by it. Now it was the turn of the law. In the backwash of the Ward trial arose the doubts about whether justice had been used as a sledge-hammer to crack a nut. And there had been the spectacle of witnesses able to contradict themselves while on oath without any apparent threat of prosecution for perjury. This questioned the methods used by police to obtain evidence: though there was no proof that corners had been cut, there were suspicions. The police were, in the Ward inquiry, working under circumstances which made the collection of evidence particularly difficult.

While the Ward trial was nearing its end, the Court of Criminal Appeal upheld the appeal of Aloysius Gordon. But the manner in which this was done was disconcerting. The conviction was quashed in nine minutes, but the evidence which had led to the decision was not disclosed. While justice had no doubt been done, it had not been seen to be done. One of the reasons for doing this was certainly the anxiety not to prejudice the trial of Ward. Some of the detailed evidence of the Gordon case might have influenced the Ward jury's view on the reliability of witnesses, either favourably or unfavourably. And if the appeal had been delayed until after the Ward trial the impression would have been given, as Mr Burge had pointed out, of an attempt to help the prosecution's case to hang together.

The Court of Criminal Appeal had no power to order a re-trial: this was not widely realised. A re-trial would have enabled a thorough reappraisal of the merits of the case. But in British law a man may only be tried once for the same offence, and this has much merit. But in the admittedly rare circumstances of cases like that of Gordon, public suspicion could be aroused, even if without justification, if the reversal of a sentence was left unexplained. Perhaps the error which was really exposed by the Ward trial was the belief that nothing could be wrong in the administration of British justice. Because the processes of the law had been evolved over the centuries did not mean that further lessons might not be learned – lessons created by changing conditions and attitudes. To believe otherwise would surely be a dangerous complacency. Certainly the ghost of Stephen Ward would haunt the Old Bailey for some time to come.

19

The Paper Tiger

Two factors, the increasing severity of libel penalties and the exposure of reporting methods by the Vassall Tribunal, contributed fundamentally to the state of mind which the Press found itself in when confronted with the Profumo affair.

The issue was, however, not as clear cut as this made it seem. While the faults of the Press might be manifest, the fact remained that newspapers had become traduced by public opinion. They were themselves to blame for this, but they were nevertheless done injustice by it. Fleet Street thought that the outcome of the Profumo affair had vindicated its reputation: it had not. Intimidated, the newspapers had failed to put to proper use the information they had, information which, in contrast to the Vassall case, was substantial and largely true.

But it was a newspaper which built up no private dossier, and which had no bloodhounds at work, which assumed the most influential rôle in the whole affair: *The Times*. This was largely because of the opinions of its editor, and his determination to express them.

The influence of *The Times* during the period of the affair was by no means as great as it had been in earlier history, at least not in terms of its direct effect on the Executive. Since the Executive emerged as its principal opponent, that is not surprising. Where the paper was influential was in its rôle as a platform for opinion. *The Times* received letters that could have been written to no other paper, it was a unique listening post to the subterranean attitudes of an important minority, and in a country where hidden currents were little understood and sometimes treacherous *The Times* was a rich source for study.

When the readers of *The Times* reacted to the Vassall Tribunal with a vicious hostility to the Press, they provoked a passionate rebuff from its editor. When the world of Mr Profumo was finally bared, the relationship between Sir William Haley and his readers changed. This time, with the editorial in which moral decline was equated with affluence, the reception was on the whole ecstatic. This reaction received far greater prominence than had the earlier, unsympathetic one.

Sir William obviously realised that the first attack on affluence had been too generalised, capable of simplification into the reactionary view that to alleviate poverty was to undermine society and erode morality. Well after the flood of applause which the first leader produced, a second, and more refined, treatise on the strains of affluence was delivered.

It was simple to see why the idea that affluence was to blame should find such support. The readership of *The Times* consisted of many people in a section of society where incomes had either remained static in value or had shrunk, while at the same time a new class was rising in which spending power had increased swiftly. *The Times'* spokesmen represented something of a middle-class citadel. It was surely nonsense, anyway, to imply that standards of behaviour and morality were concomitant with levels of income. It did not need a social historian to prove that some of the tribal customs of the working class were, even if not conducted in such sympathetic surroundings, capable of being as bizarre as the aberrations of the aristocracy.

In its re-definition *The Times* seemed to suggest, still in a far from specific way, that the rot began not in private behaviour but in political attitudes geared to expediency and materialism. The nearest it got to its target was the phrase 'a strand of people who were cheap, clever, opportunistic, and on the make'. In the absence of any exposures in the news columns of *The Times* speculation on the identity of these origins of poison remained wide.

Where *The Times* was on firmer ground was with its warning that public apprehension over the abuse of their freedoms by some newspapers produced the drug in which Executive power grew dangerous – apathy. When an M.P., during the Profumo crisis, said that if it came to a choice between being investigated by the Press or the Secret Police he would choose the Secret Police, he was expressing in extreme form the suicidal self-deception practised by those who imagined that a protected Executive, whatever its secret excesses, was more compatible than a vigilant Press, whatever its shortcomings. For the usurper of freedom, apathy is the greatest agent, and this was apathy or – even worse – a *tolerance* of shrinking liberties.

A reader of *The Times*, Oliver Stewart, provided perhaps the most cogent comment on the people who wished to curb the activities of the newspapers. He wrote to the paper when detailed reporting of the Ward case had caused some alarm. He said: 'Suspicion must be aroused in all who have editorial experience by the new discussions on measures to check the publication in the Press of memoirs of crime and vice. For this is the way freedom filters away.

'People are shocked by something they read. Although circulation figures suggest that they like being shocked, it seems that they feel guilty about it and seek vicarious expiation by trying to prevent others from being shocked. In England shockability is primarily sexual. People who will read calmly and unemotionally about the ultimate obscenity of the hydrogen bomb will rush for restrictive legislation at the mention of prostitution. Yet legislation to prohibit the printed delivery of moral shocks breaks down the structure of justice. . . .

'Past experience suggests that every kind of restriction will eventually be stretched to the limits visualised by Parliament and sometimes beyond them.'

For the popular papers, the Profumo case was an illuminating test of their ability to justify their claim (pleaded most frequently and persuasively by the proprietor of the *Mirror* newspapers, Mr Cecil King) to diminish the restraints, through a relaxation of the libel laws, on the exposure of undetected corruption and crime.

Innuendo is a less discriminating weapon than outright disclosure, and the newspapers had to resort to innuendo when the truth might have proved expensive. But the newspapers were far from confident about their own information. The story which the *News of the World* first took to Admiralty House on February 1 was substantially true. The *News of the World* in fact did what was the next best thing to publishing the story: it took it to the people who should have been able to act on it. The *Sunday Mirror* had at least one piece of evidence which was perhaps worth more than the word of any of the memoir hawkers: the letter from Mr Profumo to Miss Keeler. Having decided that it was 'effusive but not conclusive', the *Mirror* returned it to Mr Profumo! If they had then taken the same attitude as the *News of the World*, and decided that instead of publishing and being damned they could at least communicate privately with the Government, they would probably have had a decisive hand in the outcome: their letter, after all, would have led to discovery of the warning Sir Norman Brook had given Mr Profumo in 1961, which at the time the Prime Minister was not aware of.

If the motive of exposure was the public interest, a private initiative to pass on information and questions to the proper agency was surely more effective than capitulation to libel laws which were so frequently complained of. To establish mutual confidence by such private traffic would not be to surrender the right to publish if justified; it might even strengthen it.

The idea that all newspapers approach unrevealed scandal with a sense of public interest paramount is plainly ludicrous. The lurid, picaresque surroundings of the Profumo case provided a hard, commercial motive for wanting to print the story. The circumstances of the original affair make a poor case on which to build arguments to encourage greater freedom for Press exposure. It was one of the after-effects which most clearly set out the issues involved in watchdog journalism: the Rachman rackets and their ramifications.

First of all, the libel restraint did not apply: Rachman was dead. In fact, when some newspapers first tackled the Rachman story it was significant that when they moved from Rachman himself to his successors they became suddenly coy. While Rachman was still alive the *Daily Mirror* assigned a reporter to investigate him, but when the article was produced it was rejected without even being shown to a lawyer: the libel risk was felt to be too great. Yet here was a real social crime, being practised for years with apparent impunity from either the law, the tax authorities or the newspapers.

The exposure of Rachman, although posthumous, did precisely place the position which the Press can occupy between the law and politics. The law had been impotent, and the few politicians who discovered what was going on came up against a sponge of apathy.

If newspapers had become interested in Rachman at a time when it could be set against no backcloth of sensation and scandal, their reports might well have fallen with a dull thud among a disinterested public. As it happened, the whole machinery of public appetite had been set in motion, the time and the climate were ripe, and reactions were sufficiently violent for some good to be done. This itself reveals some of the questionable precepts which popular journalism applies in deciding where its attentions shall be directed. Its two most mechanical reflexes in this respect are topicality and personalisation. The thirst for topicality rules when a situation, no matter how wretched, somehow seems to have no immediate relevance and should be left to rot. A result of this is the pathetic paper chase which ensues every time one newspaper has the perception to produce an issue of its own making, or of its own discovering, which strikes home with readers unconcerned by the drug of topicality. Then all the other papers join the trail, each desperately seeking an 'angle' of its own to give the impression of proprietary achievement. In doing so the real issues are often obscured, and the facts bent.

To establish the right of newspapers to supplement the law and expose what the law has failed to remedy, it is necessary first to establish a tradition. No such tradition exists in Britain; and pretensions to it have been devalued by performance. The authors of this book have seen this fault at first hand. They initially exposed the Rachman rackets. In doing so they were able to use only a fraction of the material they obtained: because the remainder was uncheckable.

Newspapers which followed them were not so meticulous. Not only did they rely on unsubstantiated information, but they were led by it on to false tracks and therefore drew false or irrelevant conclusions. There was, at first, the tendency also to see this story in personalised terms, building up an ogre of a man instead of revealing an ogre of a system; a dead rogue could not be caught or reformed, but his legacy was there to be dealt with. In the end, happily, this fault was corrected, and in the remarkable time of four weeks the Rachman case had moved from exposure to parliamentary uproar and political action. This was one of the benefits, one of the constructive by-products of the original scandal. A light had been cast on a corner containing misery and exploitation . . . but the misery itself was not news until it fell into bizarre company.

It follows that there is a real need for Britain to have a Press capable of racket-busting. In America the tradition is established, and prosecuted with vigour. It was a newspaper which exposed the monstrous grain swindles of Billie Sol Estes . . . and a local newspaper at that. When was the last time a local newspaper in Britain uncovered corruption? Or isn't there corruption to uncover? One reason for the American success is the encouragement given by the Pulitzer Prize: no award of equal substance exists in Britain. Another is that American editors, not so obsessed with the myopia of topicality and the urge it creates for quick-returns, are prepared to have reporters who take months, even years, to work thoroughly and with scrupulous care to establish not flimsy, generalised cases but incontrovertible evidence.

It is ironic that the papers most inclined towards exposure-journalism (though often into nothing more substantial than some seedy suburban depravities) are the popular ones; the serious papers, which have the reputation for authority, which would make disclosure credible, seldom do it.

Another way in which the Press abrogates its right to public faith is in its pursuit of 'chequebook journalism' – the payment of substantial sums to people on the basis of their notoriety. There was some sign, though, in this affair that as a result of the strengthened Press Council the avarice for sensation was at last being curbed by fear of public reaction. Not enough to commit Christine Keeler to penury; but there were the glimmerings of new restraints.

All through this affair the initial agent of disclosure was rumour, not the newspapers, whose duty, as Sir William Haley had said at such an ironic time, was revelation. Nor, directly, was it achieved by parliamentary means. Rumour, a dark, dangerous and uncontrollable form of communication, was in this case the effective weapon when the others had failed or were slow in publication. The course of the Profumo affair will convert no one to the defence of rumour as a legitimate watchdog: it shows, instead, how dubious and inconstant an ally it is. And it also proves that as other channels of mass communication have evolved, so has the machinery of rumour achieved a new efficiency and potency.

The days when high political scandal could effectively be contained, at the worst, to Mayfair and Bloomsbury cocktail talk are over. (It is ironic that the colourful indiscretions of Lord Palmerston and Lloyd George are freely discussed now without anyone imagining that the political morals of those times were shamefully corrupt, let alone that they were symptoms of a chronically diseased society.) The private lusts of politicians used to be known to their own circles, while the public, neither so cynical nor so well informed as it is today, went mostly in ignorance. But there is now a good deal more exposure to the public: dinner table confidences are apt to flow swiftly down Fleet Street.

Rumour today can be as contagious as the Plague: before even a word of the Profumo affair was published, variations of it, in many cases distorted grotesquely beyond the truth, were known to thousands, if not to the few people who really ought to have known. The first, dormant stage of the rumour began in London Society while the assignations were taking place: the item from the *Queen* magazine, always an *in* publication, shows how far it had gone by mid-1962. But at that time, as it was retailed among the more blasé socialites, it was hazy and insubstantial.

In the second, incubation phase, which began with the pistol shots in December 1962, the story took on more circumstantial form, although many people disregarded it as idle, and malicious, gossip. The Edgecombe case started yielding its 'fall-out'. And the rumour gathered startling variations as it

217

travelled around what is possibly the most lethal gossip shop in the world, the combination of Westminster and Fleet Street. It reached its height, perhaps, with the grotesque tit-bit that no less than nine High Court judges were involved – *are* there even nine?

The only place where the rumour was lethargic in its progress was in its journey to Admiralty House. Mr Macmillan himself said, in the June 17 debate: 'Until my return from an official visit to Rome at the beginning of February I had never heard of Mr Ward.' And speaking of the period when the rumours had first been told to him, and after Mr Profumo's first statements that his acquaintance with Miss Keeler was an entirely innocent one, the Prime Minister revealed some of his attitude towards rumour. He said: 'The situation which then confronted me was that damaging and scurrilous rumours were circulating about a member of the Government which he solemnly and consistently, and on more than one occasion, denied.' He mentioned the Vassall case, and then said: 'Quite apart from any personal considerations, the belief that any individuals innocent of any offence or misdemeanour could be victimised and their careers ended merely on the basis of rumour, which is subsequently shown by the judgment of the courts to be without foundation, would have a profoundly damaging effect upon the whole of political life.'

The Prime Minister in February 1963 was allergic to rumour. He just didn't believe the story. To say that he didn't *want* to believe it is to make an ostrich out of a tiger.

The rumour wasn't nailed in February, it wasn't killed by the lies of March 22 and it wasn't ended by the confession of June 5. Allowed further months in which to multiply, its life-wish had become insatiable. With the arrest of Dr Ward it caught fresh energy and formed virulent new mutations.

In Westminster, in Fleet Street and in the clubs of St James's its elaborations were more grotesque than ever and indiscriminate in their range: other Ministers, the Royal Family and captains of industry were freely named. In the wake of the June 17 debate and the panic of the Tory Party, normally sane and responsible men were prepared to listen to any lurid tale: hadn't gossip they first thought to be wildly exaggerated turned out to be short of the truth? After Lord Denning's inquiry had been established, Lord Poole said in Manchester on June 22: 'It is essential that the large number of rumours surrounding the Profumo scandal should be disposed of as quickly as possible. I never remember a time when so many or so varied a number of rumours were circulating in Fleet Street or Whitehall. These rumours are disgusting in detail and probably disreputable in origin. There are certain curious aspects about them, and certainly most of them are untrue. But rumour and doubt and suspicion are horrible things – where and when possible they should be cleared up.'

There was a far-fetched theory that the rumours had some nihilistic common source. It was more likely that the greatest cause was, as the *Sunday Times* said on June 23: '. . . the simple human failing of taste for scandal, especially that concerning the great or famous – the habit of passing on, at the cocktail party, dinner table or the bar, stories which begin "have you heard . . .?" These rumours, progressing in a trice from hint to certainty, travel so fast and far that the origin – which may have been invention, misunderstanding, ingenious deduction or sheer malice – is soon irretrievably lost.'

The June air was toxic, not only with rumours but with the topical, bawdy jokes that reached from salon to factory floor. The cruel irony was that the Prime Minister's phobia about rumour had been rumour's greatest stimulant: but for the failure to bring out the truth while the rumour was still small enough to be extinguished the subsequent disaster could have been averted. Rumours, unfortunately, are sometimes true.

20

What the Public Thought

IN THE EXCITEMENTS and tensions, the intrigue and
manœuvrings, that permeated Westminster and Fleet Street as
the Profumo affair developed, it was easy to forget what the
British public were really thinking about it. Undoubtedly at
one level they were fascinated; not since the Abdication had a
crisis in the high affairs of state caused so much interest for so
long. But were they really bothered about it in the way newspapers and politicians thought? Was the security issue – on
which the political attack was mounted – taken seriously
enough to become a genuine matter of public concern? Were
the moralising and the shocking *exposés* of Fleet Street actually
read in a spirit of moral questioning and shock? Or was it all
regarded as just one long glorious summer of vicarious excite-
ment, novelettish intrigue and sexual titillation, laced with the
amusement of seeing the hypocrisy and pretensions of the
Establishment exposed? As the dust began to settle, politicians
were coming to believe that the last attitude was predominant.

Opinion in the Labour Party, by the middle of August, was
that the Affair had been a positive *advantage* to the Conservatives. For weeks it had deflected public attention from
serious political issues – or at least from the kind of longer-
term issues on which an election could be fought. The attacks
on Mr Macmillan appeared to have rebounded, and produced
not discredit but widespread public sympathy for him. And
all this came at a time when the Labour Party needed only to
press home their ascendancy on the more permanent aspects
of domestic and foreign policy to make their position unassail-
able. It was ironic that an issue that in June had appeared likely
to topple the Government in the end seemed to have let the
Conservatives off the hook.

Politicians and journalists, of course, do have some means,

besides their instincts, to assess public reactions. Newspapers carefully analyse readers' letters. Often it is the unpublished ones that are most revealing. (For example, one reaction among *Daily Mirror* readers after the Profumo scandal first broke was not shock but pleasure that a working-class girl like Christine should have done so well for herself.) And politicians have the opinion polls.

The general opinion poll trend in favour of the Labour Party had begun, like the Profumo affair, about at the time of Selwyn Lloyd's 'pay pause'. (Until then the Conservatives had held a comfortable lead ever since the 1959 election.) Apart from a few minor fluctuations caused by the brief Liberal revival of early 1962, their fortunes had, according to National Opinion Polls, Gallup* and the *Daily Express* Poll of Public Opinion, been steadily increasing. By February and early March, 1963, Labour's lead was the highest for seventeen years. This was the position on the eve of Profumo's denial to the House of Commons which gave the general public its first glimmerings of the affair. The denial, however, produced no marked effect on the polls. It looked as if it had been accepted at face value, or was thought unimportant. There had, it is true, been an expectation that the Conservative position would brighten in April and May as the economy recovered from the bad winter; it did so, though perhaps not as much as was anticipated. But, so far, there was nothing in the polls that could not be explained by other factors. The only poll result that perhaps revealed some public reaction to the fact that a Government Minister *needed* to reassure the House that he was not having an affair with a model was in answer to a special Gallup question: 'Which party has the best set of leaders?' The answers showed that for the first time in more than a decade, the Tory front bench had lost its lead – each party polled 33 per cent.

The long-term trend in Labour's favour had already been resumed in late May and early June, *before* Mr Profumo's confession. All three of the major polls reported a sharp boom in their popularity at this time. The reasons for the Tory slump,

* National Opinion Polls are commissioned and published by the *Daily Mail*, Gallup Polls by the *Daily Telegraph*.

given by N.O.P., had nothing to do with any anticipation of the Profumo scandal: increased rates, the Enahoro issue, and simply a desire for a change. There was no doubt that, Profumo or not, the Labour Party were in full flood and rising fast.

In the shock that followed Mr Profumo's confession, Gallup recorded the highest Labour lead in the poll's twenty-five-year history – 20½ per cent. If an election had been held immediately, this would have resulted in a majority in the House of 300 seats. Even so, this was only 1½ per cent higher than the very substantial lead before the storm broke. The sharpest reaction was not against the Conservatives as a whole, but against Mr Macmillan personally. Support for him slumped in one month from 41 per cent to 34 per cent. Only once previously had a Prime Minister received a lower rating – Neville Chamberlain, who Gallup-polled 32 per cent in 1940, a month before Churchill took over from him.

This low point in Mr Macmillan's popularity came just after the big debate of June 17. After that his prestige began slowly and erratically to rise. A Gallup question on whether or not Macmillan should retire found 41 per cent believing that he should retire, 30 per cent wanting a General Election, and only 23 per cent in favour of his continuing as Prime Minister. However, fewer people said he should retire than had said so in February.

So far as his party was concerned, the initial shock of the Profumo confession was short-lived. Most of the lost ground had been recovered by the end of June. However, further disclosures – that Philby had been the Burgess-Maclean 'third man', the Rachman property rackets, and the evidence in the magistrates' court on the Ward case – again set the Tory stock falling. A Gallup Poll on July 23, the day after Rachman was debated in the Commons, found that the gap had again widened to 20 per cent. But perhaps the most remarkable thing about all the opinion polls in July was the high proportion of 'Don't Knows': it seemed that the profusion of issues that had developed in the aftermath of Profumo had confused the electorate. There was also an increased tendency for the results of the different opinion polls to disagree with each other. The succession of scandal upon scandal and disclosure upon disclosure were producing fickle political allegiances, and widely differing results were obtained according to the day, and even the time of day the poll was conducted. (The gap between the parties in polls conducted almost simultaneously during the Ward trial was 20 per cent, according to Gallup, and 8 per cent according to N.O.P.)

Then, suddenly, the Ward trial was over, a martyr had died for the cause, the Profumo Affair – for the time being at least – seemed to be over, the Test Ban treaty had been signed, and there was a Great Train Robbery to amuse the public differently. There was an immediate, astonishing recovery of Tory fortunes. The gap had dropped to 13 per cent (Gallup) and 7 per cent (N.O.P.). And whatever the reason for the divergencies, it was clear that Labour's huge lead in the polls before the Profumo affair had begun had been eroded away. Although the August by-election caused by Mr Profumo's resignation showed a thirteen per cent swing against the Government, this was less than might have been expected three months before. And at Stratford, more than anywhere, the Profumo scandal should have bitten deep. Labour M.P.s might well have wondered if it had all been worth it.

So much can be gleaned from the opinion Polls. But it is obviously an incomplete picture of the sort of ways in which public attitudes were formed. At about the time the Profumo affair first broke, an Austrian sociologist, Heinrich Blezinger, who was doing research at King's College, Cambridge, had just begun a series of depth interviews aimed at finding out the ways in which British political beliefs are formed. He decided to take the reaction to the Profumo affair as the basis for his study.

Blezinger's sample was restricted: he decided to confine his study to men, aged between twenty-five and thirty-five, in middle-income groups, mostly in professional, technical, junior executive or white-collar jobs, and mostly living in the Cambridge area. Clearly it would be dangerous to make too wide generalisations from this: but his sample was representative of what politicians regard as one of the key electoral groups – the Orpington-type voter.

These are some of the questions that Blezinger examined:

How important was the Profumo Affair? More than three-quarters of the people interviewed thought it politically only of slight or moderate importance. But there were noticeable differences between the supporters of different political parties. Labour supporters, on the whole, thought it moderately important. Conservatives had a tendency to think it either of no importance at all or very important. Blezinger explains this in terms of the defence mechanisms a person naturally builds up when his own party is under attack. If the defence mechanism is successful, then he thinks it of no importance. But if he cannot rationalise his wish to dismiss it, then he is more likely to go into a detailed analysis of it and worry about it, hence his attachment of high importance to the question. (Blezinger found many other examples among Conservatives of such defence mechanisms. As these built up, the original shock effect on the opinion polls rapidly subsided. The fluctuations of July were because of the difficulty of finding mechanisms to deal with the flow of new information, much of it extraneous and intertwined with sexual implications.)

What was the Profumo Affair about? Blezinger used an oblique question to find how people 'contextualised' the Affair. He simply asked them to list the names of all the people they could remember in connection with the matter. On average, each person produced about ten names. Surprisingly, several times these did not include Mr Profumo himself: the only person mentioned by *everyone* was Christine Keeler.

This was the order of frequency in which names were mentioned: Christine Keeler, Dr Ward, Mr Profumo, Mandy Rice-Davies.Then, equal at about 60 per cent, came Ivanov and Lord Astor. Next, about equal at 30 per cent, came Peter Rachman and Harold Macmillan. After that was a large group mentioned by about 15 to 20 per cent: Mr Wigg, Valerie Hobson, Lucky Gordon, Mr Wilson, the 'five ministers', Lord Denning, Douglas Fairbanks, Jr, Miss Ricardo. Below these came: Vickie Barrett, Mr Griffith-Jones, Mr Eddowes, 'Miss R.', 'Miss X.', Mr Redmayne. On the very fringes of public attention were the royal family, the Duchess of Argyll, Lady Astor, Mrs Rachman, Lord Dilhorne, Mr Grimond, Mr John Hare, and the Archbishop of Canterbury, who made a statement on the matter and gained one mention.

This shows that people were inclined not to see the affair principally in its political context at all. In fact, scarcely half the people interviewed mentioned any Member of Parliament or any administrator, other than Mr Profumo. Nor does it seem as if the security issue was seen as very important. Ivanov, the whole crux of the story, was mentioned only as often as Lord Astor. It was clearly the more exotic elements that people were most aware of – hence the high position of Miss Keeler, Miss Rice-Davies, Lord Astor, and Dr Ward, and the placing of such fringe 'exotic' figures as Douglas Fairbanks, Jr, and Valerie Hobson co-equally with the central political and judicial figures, Mr Wigg, Mr Wilson and Lord Denning.

Blezinger believed that a sample drawn from the whole population would have shown even less political contextualisation than did his sample. This was probably the reason, he says, why the Profumo affair did not strongly affect long-run political allegiances.

Extending this line of analysis on party lines, Blezinger discovered that people with Conservative leanings made stronger connections between the Government and the Affair. Again he interprets this as a defensive attitude: the Conservative supporter felt attacked, and was more eager to know how his party was handling it. On the other hand very few Labour supporters were consciously aware of the attacking rôle of Mr Wigg and his friends. Blezinger had found this 'quasi non-aggressive attitude' a fairly common feature of British political allegiance.

The name analysis also revealed another point: the absence of any mentions of Johnny Edgecombe showed that very few people can have made a conscious connection between the Affair and the incident which brought it to light, despite all the innuendoes that appeared in the Press at the time.

Did people believe Mr Macmillan? About three-quarters of the sample thought that he was telling the truth when he denied having any previous knowledge of the Affair. Interestingly a number of people who had doubts were Conservative supporters, whose allegiance has not been altered and who 'cherish the party, irrespective of minor irregularities'. They took a cynical point of view and were just not bothered by their doubts.

But the trust people had for Macmillan was often only superficial. One person interviewed put it: 'Macmillan chose to be deceived.' Blezinger comments: 'It seems as if quite a lot of people in Britain chose to believe.'

Was Mr Macmillan negligent as head of the Security Services? This, as expected, produced a fairly straightforward party split: most Left-Wing supporters said he was; most Right-Wing supporters said he wasn't. But there was a much greater tendency among Conservatives to put blame on the officials of the Security Services itself. This was interpreted as another example of building a defence mechanism, by finding scapegoats.

Who was the culprit? The principal scapegoat was Mr Profumo. More than half the people interviewed accepted his denial statement as entirely his own responsibility, despite the assistance he had in drafting it. The tendency to localise the blame on Mr Profumo was found to be much stronger among Conservatives than Socialists.

What was the reaction to Profumo's denial? For all but two people interviewed (who each had friends in Fleet Street) the denial was the first they had heard about the matter. With about a quarter of the interviewees the denial did not register at the time; about a half accepted it unquestioningly; the remainder felt somewhat puzzled and suspicious. Both Conservatives and Socialists were among the dubious.

Are the others immoral too? Four-fifths of the people interviewed were prepared to endorse that having mistresses is 'quite current' in high society. But only half of them thought it might be current in Government circles. This showed, says Bletzinger, that there were still signs of reluctance to abandon the idea of the integrity and moral probity in British politics.

Should Mr Macmillan have resigned? About three-quarters of the Conservatives thought he should not, and those who did thought he should not resign over Profumo *only*. Even most of the Labour people thought that Profumo alone was not enough to require his resignation, though almost all thought he should resign for other reasons. This means that although there was a strong wave of opinion against Mr Macmillan it was only in a restricted sense due to the scandal.

What was Profumo's sin? It was asked which aspect people thought more important: the security risk, Profumo's having a mistress, or lying to the House. An overwhelming majority – nearly 80 per cent – thought the lie was the most important, the security aspect was a bad second, and only 8 per cent thought his having a mistress was important.

Blezinger was surprised at this, but there was confirmation from another part of the interview, designed to classify the moral attitudes of his sample. In this he asked them to choose the five of the following attributes they would prefer to have in their friends: tolerance, humour, sociability, reliability, explicitness, honesty, activity, sensitivity, intelligence, fidelity, conscientiousness. More than half the people chose honesty and reliability as the first qualities. After these, humour, tolerance, intelligence and sensitivity were chosen with roughly equal frequency, and the rest could be disregarded.

This revealed that the men in the sample had a very restricted concern for sexual morality, but honesty and reliability were thought basic values for good friendships. And the ethical code they applied in their normal social relationships was extended to their judgment of public figures.

It seems therefore that the sin Mr Profumo was accused before the nation of committing was not of breaking the Seventh Commandment, but the Ninth, 'Thou shalt not bear false witness'. The Seventh was probably relevant only in A. H. Clough's more pragmatic form, in *The Latest Decalogue:*

> Do not adultery commit;
> Advantage rarely comes of it.

DATE DUE

JUN 15 1965 MAY 15 1971			
MAY 30 1971			
GAYLORD			PRINTED IN U.S.A.